FOURTH EDITION

Media Writer's Handbook

A Guide to Common Writing and Editing Problems

George T. Arnold, Ph.D.

W. Page Pitt School of Journalism and Mass Communications
Marshall University

Boston Burr Ridge, IL Dubuque, IA Madison, WI New York
San Francisco St. Louis Bangkok Bogotá Caracas Kuala Lumpur
Lisbon London Madrid Mexico City Milan Montreal New Delhi
Santiago Seoul Singapore Sydney Taipei Toronto

MEDIA WRITER'S HANDBOOK

Published by McGraw-Hill, a business unit of The McGraw-Hill Companies, Inc., 1221 Avenue of the Americas, New York, NY, 10020.

This book is printed on acid-free paper.

2 3 4 5 6 7 8 9 0 DOC/DOC 0 9 8 7 6

ISBN-13: 978-0-07-352606-5
ISBN-10: 0-07-352606-1

Publisher: *Phillip A. Butcher*
Sponsoring Editor: *Phillip A. Butcher*
Senior Marketing Manager: *Leslie Oberhuber*
Editorial Assistant: *Erika Lake*
Senior Project Manager: *Christina Thornton-Villagomez*
Designer: *Marianna Kinigakis*
Cover Designer: *Kristin Hill*
Production Supervisor: *Jason I. Huls*
Media Producer: *Christie Ling*
Composition: *10/12 Times Roman, International Typesetting and Composition*
Printing: *45# New Era Matte Plus, R.R. Donnelley & Sons*

Library of Congress Cataloging-in-Publication Data

Arnold, George T.
Media writer's handbook: a guide to common writing and editing problems / George T. Arnold—4th ed.
p. cm.
Includes bibliographical references and index.
ISBN-13: 978-0-07-352606-5 (alk. paper)
ISBN-10: 0-07-352606-1 (alk. paper)
1. Journalism—Style manuals. 2. Journalism—Authorship. 3. Mass media—Authorship. I. Title.
PN4783.A76 2007
808'.027—dc22

2005043515

www.mhhe.com

To Connie

CONTENTS

PART 3 PUNCTUATING 169

22 Commas 176

23 Semicolons 187

PREFACE

After 10 years and three editions of *Media Writer's Handbook,* students, professors and professional mass communicators have made clear how they use this resource/textbook and what more they want from it.

Students Are Impatient. They want more ways to improve their writing immediately. The fourth edition responds with two new chapters, "The Trouble with 'Only'" and "One Potato, Two Potatoes."

The first explains how the use of "only" sometimes can be insensitive and how putting it in the wrong place can cause a sentence to have an unintended meaning. The second offers simple, easy-to-understand answers about forming plurals and possessives from such difficult word endings as <u>ch</u>, <u>sh</u>, <u>x</u>, <u>sis</u>, <u>ss</u>, <u>zz</u>, <u>y</u>, and <u>o</u>.

The new chapters supplement four others popularly received by all audiences the book reaches. The first two editions featured "25 Ways to Improve Writing Immediately." "Language Lapses," "It's Nobody's Guess," and "Are These Distinctions Worth Making?" were added in the third edition. These six chapters enable students to make a rapid and dramatic difference in both their writing and speaking skills.

Professors Want Better Writing. They need a book that can support a variety of courses. Some want a textbook, supplemented by a workbook and a teacher's manual, to form a complete basic language skills course. Others want a quick-and-easy-to-use resource for their professional writing, editing, and broadcasting courses.

For the first time, the workbook, containing daily lessons and assignments, will cost students nothing. It has been placed on the Web, joining the previously available "Test Yourself" exercises at the end of each related chapter from the textbook.

The Instructor's Manual will be on a compact disk and provided to teachers. It contains answers and explanations for the workbook materials, as well as quizzes and tests that can be graded in part by computer.

Professionals Want Answers Fast. They want a resource they can place on their desks, along with their dictionaries and stylebooks, and use on deadline. They want to be able to find the specific material they need fast, to read it quickly and to understand it instantly.

All of this is made possible by the brief explanations, simple examples, and alphabetical lists found in the five quick reference sections—"Words Frequently Confused," "Words Frequently Misspelled," "Irregular Verbs," "Wordiness and Trite Expressions," and "When to Use a Hyphen, One Word, or Two Words."

Speed and convenience also are enhanced by the comprehensive table of contents and the appendix, as well as by the book's spiral binding which frees both hands for keyboarding at the computer.

Getting Better and Better. A commencement speaker once said to a high school audience, "Don't let your tombstone read: Died at 18, Buried at 80." Learning, he implied, must not conclude with the awarding of a high school diploma or even a Ph.D. degree.

Grammar and punctuation, the tools of a communicator's trade, are explained thoroughly but simply in the 22 chapters placed between the first section offering immediate improvement and the final providing quick reference.

These chapters are filled with detailed explanations, examples and advice on parts of speech, punctuation, sentence functions and structures and syntax. Students may find some comfort in knowing that these chapters stressing fundamentals are not just for them. Professors, professionals and writers of language skills books also need continual review.

Sensitivity in Language. Writing effectively requires not only strong grammar and punctuation skills but also sensitivity. Mass communicators who use language that discriminates against race, religion, ethnicity, age, gender, marital status or physical and mental ability rarely do so from a mean spirit. They are either careless with the language or unaware of what is or is not contemporarily acceptable. The "Sensitivity in Language" chapter provides illuminating examples, insights and explanations.

Building Skills. Fortunately, journalists and other mass communicators can choose to overcome their language skills problems instead of living with a fear of being embarrassed by them. Little, if any, guesswork is involved in using language correctly. Rules cover virtually every writing challenge, and most are easy to understand and to apply. Also encouraging is the fact that each of us already knows a great deal about writing skillfully. All we have to do is build upon that knowledge.

For Use as Needed. The book does not have to be read from beginning to end. Although that approach is recommended for those with fundamental language skills problems, the organization permits "sampling" by writers and broadcasters who use the language well but are nagged by little uncertainties. By design, some sections provide more explanations and examples than many users will need. This arrangement gives everyone an opportunity to work through the book at his or her own pace without feeling either bogged down or inadequately informed.

Acknowledgments. The material has been put together over 35 years. Much comes from a collection of common errors college journalism and mass communications students have made in their writing and editing. Some comes from information gathered from reading, listening to or watching the work of professional mass communicators.

Current and former students, colleagues, and professionals aware of the author's interest have made—and continue to make—valuable contributions and suggestions that have enriched the book. Their help is greatly appreciated, as are the suggestions made by those who reviewed the manuscript or one of the other editions.

Manuscript. Robert Bardeene, University of South Florida at St. Petersburg; Jack Dvorak, Indiana University; George Harmon, Northwestern University; Sherri Hildebrandt, University of Missouri; Bruce Plopper, University of Arkansas; and Jean Ward, University of Minnesota. Special thanks go to two long-time friends, Dr. Deryl Leaming and Dr. Vaughn Rhudy, for reading the final proofs.

First Edition. Martin D. Sommerness, Northern Arizona University; Dr. Betsy Alderman, University of Tennessee at Chattanooga; Dr. Lona Cobb, Bennett College; and four Marshall University colleagues, Dr. Ralph Turner, Dr. Charles Bailey and Professors Janet Dooley and Dwight Jensen.

Second Edition. Rachele Kanigel, San Francisco State University; Robert Bohle, University of North Florida; Keith Terry, University of Nebraska at Kearney; Henry Wefing, Westfield State College; Deborah Menger, University of Texas at San Antonio; and Daniel T. Davis, Michigan State University. Special thanks to Norma Jane Bumgarner of the University of Oklahoma for her extraordinarily thorough review and detailed list of helpful suggestions.

Third Edition. Kevin S. Knight, University of North Carolina-Wilmington; Beth Calhoun Leschper, West Texas A&M University; and Karon Speckman, Truman State University.

To all who have made a contribution of any kind, including supportive family members and friends, please know that your help and your interest are not taken for granted.

The Challenge. As we either develop or refine our language skills, each of us—regardless of whether we are beginners or veteran mass communicators—can take comfort from the fact that no one knows everything about the language. And no one with a love for the language ever stops learning. The challenge is to learn enough to get to the point that we feel confident about our language skills. That's when real progress begins.

George T. Arnold, Ph.D.

IMPROVING IMMEDIATELY

part 1

Introduction

Most professional and student mass communicators enjoy games that test their skills in using words effectively. That explains why their friends and their family members buy them holiday gifts like Scrabble, Scattergories, and Boggle. These devotees of word play undoubtedly are pleased to receive the games, but they dislike reading and learning a long list of rules as much as anyone else. They want to start playing immediately and learn as they go.

Part 1 of this book has six chapters designed with impatient people in mind. The first has 25 quick and easy-to-learn writing tips that can be put to use immediately. That chapter was supplemented in the third edition by three others that present and solve common problems in making distinctions between similar word pairs, in avoiding potentially embarrassing language lapses, and in removing the guesswork from several annoying choices we must make in our everyday writing and broadcasting.

The fourth edition features two new chapters. The first, "The Trouble with 'Only,'" explains how the use of "only" sometimes can be insensitive and how putting it in the wrong place can cause a sentence to have an unintended meaning. The second, "One Potato, Two Potatoes," offers simple, easy-to-understand answers about forming plurals and possessives from such difficult word endings as **ch, sh, x, s, sis, ss, zz, y,** and **o.**

The chapters in Part 2 require some rule reading and review. They cover parts of speech, sentence functions and structures, and syntax. Punctuation follows in Part 3, and Part 4 returns readers to the immediate satisfaction tract, providing quick reference checks for spelling, vocabulary, irregular verbs, wordiness and trite expressions, and words sometimes hyphenated and sometimes used as one or two words.

When used as a reference, the book—or parts of it—can be read in any order and to any extent readers choose. Even when the book is used as a textbook, the parts can be interchanged to suit the needs of teachers and students. The extensive table of contents and the index enable readers to locate quickly whatever they want to check, review or study.

chapter 1 25 Ways to Improve Writing Immediately

Although most language skills problems cannot be solved instantly, journalists and other mass communicators share some common errors that can be corrected quickly. If you want to gain immediate improvement, the opportunity is provided in the following pages. You can put these simple guidelines to work as soon as you read them.

1. Omit *On* before a Day of the Week and before a Month and Date

The preposition ***on*** is rarely needed before a day of the week or a month and date.

(Avoid) City Council will meet at 7 p.m. ***on*** Tuesday.

(Better) City Council will meet at 7 p.m. Tuesday.

— — —

(Avoid) County commissioners will vote ***on*** March 20.

(Better) County commissioners will vote March 20.

2. Avoid *Holding* Meetings/Conferences/Parties/Conventions

Although some mass communicators are not bothered by the use of ***hold, held*** or ***holding*** when reporting about meetings, conferences, parties or conventions, other writers and broadcasters think such use is unnecessary and even silly. A person can ***hold*** another's hand, a fork, a baby or any number of other objects, but how does one ***hold*** a meeting?

(Avoid) City Council will ***hold*** its meeting at 7 p.m. Tuesday.

(Better) City Council will meet at 7 p.m. Tuesday.

— — —

(Avoid) The commission ***held*** its meeting last week.

(Better) The commission met last week.

3. Don't *Invite, Urge* or *Welcome*

In objective news articles, writers and broadcasters should not ***invite, urge*** or ***welcome*** readers and listeners to do anything. To do so is to editorially endorse the activity. (Of course, such remarks may be attributed to sources. Then the endorsement comes from the sources and not from the journalists.)

(Avoid) The public is ***invited.***

(Better) The event is open to the public.

— — —

(Avoid) Volunteers are ***urged*** to give blood between 8 a.m. and 4 p.m. today at the Red Cross Center.

(Better) Volunteers may give blood between 8 a.m. and 4 p.m. today at the Red Cross Center.

(Acceptable) Margaret X. Beatty, director of the Winchester County Red Cross Center, **said she is *urging*** people to give blood because reserves are almost depleted.

— — —

(Avoid) The public is ***welcome*** to attend.

(Better) The event is open to the public.

4. Avoid *Talking Inanimate Objects*

The president's press conference will be postponed one week, ***the White House said*** today.

— — —

Acme University asked the attorney general for a legal opinion.

— — —

The First Johnson National Bank disclosed today that it will lower interest rates by half a percentage point.

Even though they know that the White House, Acme University and the First Johnson National Bank can't talk, journalists commonly attribute remarks to these and other inanimate objects. However, only in uncommon situations is this practice necessary or justifiable.

The first choice is to use the name of a legitimate spokesman or spokeswoman (the White House press secretary or an assistant secretary, an administrator or press officer at the university, or an officer of the bank). In rare instances in which a person cannot be referred to by name, ***spokesman, spokeswoman*** or ***representative*** may be used, although not one of these is a desirable substitute.

(Avoid) ***The First Johnson National Bank*** disclosed today that it will lower interest rates by half a percentage point.

(Better) Interest rates will decrease by half a percentage point at the First Johnson National Bank, ***a company spokesman said*** today.

(Best) Interest rates will decrease by half a percentage point at The First Johnson National Bank, ***according*** to an announcement today by ***Robert J. Straun, company president.***

5. Put the *Name before the Verb* in Attribution

As a rule, use ***Jones said*** in attribution instead of ***said Jones.*** Said Jones is awkward. It's not the way people talk; therefore, it seems unnatural in news stories, broadcasts, advertisements and public relations material.

(Avoid) The bridge will be completed on schedule, ***said Jones.***

(Better) The bridge will be completed on schedule, ***Jones said.***

— — —

However, using ***Jones said*** can be awkward when identifying material is inserted between the two words. In such an instance, putting ***said*** before ***Jones*** may be more desirable, although substituting ***according to Jones*** is a better solution.

(Avoid) The bridge will be completed on schedule, ***Robert T. Jones,*** deputy director of the State Highway Department, **said.**

(Better) The bridge will be completed on schedule, ***said Robert T. Jones,*** deputy director of the State Highway Department.

(Best) The bridge will be completed on schedule, ***according to Robert T. Jones,*** deputy director of the State Highway Department.

6. Be Cautious about Using *According To*

Many journalists avoid using ***according to.*** They consider ***said*** to be shorter and more straightforward. They especially avoid starting a sentence with ***according to*** because it shifts the emphasis to the source instead of to the subject matter.

The best advice may be to use ***according to*** when referring to inanimate objects (The president will veto the bill, ***according to The Washington Post***) and ***said*** when referring to a person (The president will veto the bill, his ***press secretary said***).

An example of how to use ***according to*** when referring to a person may be found above in **Put the *Name before the Verb* in Attribution.**

7. Don't Interchange *Feel, Think* and *Believe*

Feel, think and ***believe*** are not interchangeable.

Use ***feel*** to refer to your sense of touch (The new material ***feels*** soft) and to refer to your health or state of being (I ***feel*** good today, or I ***feel*** uneasy about spending so much money).

— — —

Use ***think*** to express an opinion (The senator said she ***thinks*** the bill will pass).

— — —

Use ***believe*** to refer to a conviction or a principle (The judge said he ***believes*** every citizen has a right to a fair trial).

The delegate said he ***thinks*** **(not *feels*)** his bill will be approved.

The minister said she ***believes*** **(not *thinks* or *feels*)** there is life after death.

The applicant said she ***thinks*** **(not *feels*)** her interview went well, and she ***feels*** good about her chances of getting the job.

8. Don't *Read Minds* or *Make Predictions*

Journalists don't know what their sources are thinking or planning unless their sources tell them. However, journalists sometimes write or broadcast as if they have the power to read minds or make predictions. Avoid this problem by inserting ***he/she said.*** Let your readers or your listeners know the statement came from the source and not from you, the journalist.

(Avoid) Trager ***thinks*** he has enough votes pledged to get his bill passed.

(Better) Trager ***said he thinks*** he has enough votes pledged to get his bill passed.

— — —

(Avoid) McRae ***will announce*** Tuesday that she will seek re-election.

(Better) McRae ***said she will announce*** Tuesday that she will seek re-election.

9. Don't *Give Orders* to Readers/Listeners

Without consciously meaning to, journalists sometimes order their readers and listeners to do one thing or another. By avoiding second-person writing in these instances, journalists can eliminate the problem. (See page, 57–58 for an explanation of second-person writing.)

(Avoid) To apply for a low-interest student loan, ***go*** to the business office before 4 p.m. Friday.

(Better) Applications for low-interest student loans ***may be made*** at the business office until 4 p.m. Friday.

— — —

(Avoid) ***You must bring*** a statement of your annual income and a list of ***your*** dependents when ***you*** apply for the loan.

(Better) ***Applicants are required*** to provide a statement of annual income and a list of dependents when ***they*** apply for the loan.

10. Put Long Titles *after* the Person's Name

Journalists usually capitalize brief titles used directly ***before*** a person's name (***Mayor*** Johnson, ***Coach*** Ridgeway, ***Dr.*** Walker). However, they usually use lowercase letters for titles—brief or long—that ***follow*** a person's name (Ralph B. Hastings, ***associate director of the United Fund Campaign;*** Saul T. Levine, ***president of the Colonial Historical Society***).

Considerable disagreement exists about when and when not to capitalize titles. Because journalists use informal language in their publications and broadcasts, they capitalize less frequently than people who write textbooks, legal documents, master's theses and doctoral dissertations.

One guideline you may find helpful is to use titles ***before*** names ***only*** if you would address those individuals that way if you passed them on the street. You would feel comfortable saying hello to ***Dr.*** **Wong,** ***Coach*** **Menendez** or ***Mayor*** **Wysong.** But you wouldn't even consider addressing someone as ***Professor of Anthropology and Sociology*** **Wong,** ***Head Basketball and Assistant Track Coach*** **Menendez** or ***Mayor of the City of San Francisco*** **Wysong.**

Long titles fit more comfortably ***after*** names where capitalization usually is unnecessary.

11. Make *Quotations* Count

Inexperienced journalists sometimes quote routine information that should be paraphrased. A direct quotation should have an impact on the reader or listener because of its importance, human interest or impressive phrasing.

(Ineffective) "We'll just have to try again next week to get enough votes to pass the bill," Sen. Sandra W. Wiggins said.

(Better) Sen. Sandra W. Wiggins said she and other supporters of the bill will try again next week to gain enough votes to pass it.

— — —

(Ineffective) "The program will begin at 7 p.m. Friday with an address by Sen. R.M. White, and it will wind up Sunday afternoon with the other principal speaker, Walter P. Grassley, president of Unity State University," Beverly J. Robinson, program director, announced.

(Better) The three-day conference will start at 7 p.m. Friday with an address by Sen. R.M. White and will close Sunday afternoon with a speech by Walter P. Grassley, president of Unity State University. (*Attribution is unnecessary if the writer/broadcaster is certain the information is correct.*)

Of course, if reporters can err by quoting information that should be paraphrased, they also can make the opposite mistake—paraphrasing something worth using as a quotation.

(Ineffective) The mayor commended city employees for clearing streets during the three-day snowfall.

(Better) "Our street crews worked courageously and tirelessly during the dangerous snowfall, and they deserve the thanks of every citizen for keeping our roads safe to drive on," the mayor said.

12. *Quickly Identify* the Person Being Quoted

If a quotation continues beyond one sentence, routinely identify the source in the ***first*** sentence. Why make the reader or listener wait to find out who is being quoted? At its best, failing to identify the speaker in the first sentence is an annoying practice; at its worst, it's confusing, especially if more than one person is quoted in the article.

(Avoid) "Our members will strike at midnight unless the company meets our demand for an 8 percent wage increase. We've reduced our offer to the lowest point possible," ***Tarkenton said.***

(Better) "Our members will strike at midnight unless the company meets our demand for an 8 percent wage increase," ***Tarkenton said.*** "We've reduced our offer to the lowest point possible."

Please notice that when attribution is given in the first sentence of a direct quotation, none is needed in the second.

— — —

Another instance in which identification of the person being quoted should be made as quickly as possible is when a paragraph ends with a quotation from one person, and the next paragraph starts with a quotation from another individual. If the second person isn't identified immediately, readers or listeners will think the first person is still being quoted.

(Avoid) "I am thrilled to have been selected for the Pendelson scholarship," ***Hairston said.*** "It's something I've been working for all my life."

"Nothing could be more satisfying. The entire student body of Acme High School is happy about it," ***Principal Randall B. Smithson said.***

(Better) "I am thrilled to have been selected for the Pendelson scholarship," ***Hairston said.*** "It's something I've been working for all my life."

Principal Randall B. Smithson said, "Nothing could be more satisfying. The entire student body at Acme High School is happy about it."

13. *Doctor*—a Title, not a Profession

Avoid writing or broadcasting that a person is a ***doctor.*** Refer instead to that person's profession (physician, minister, dentist, professor, and so forth).

Because most readers and listeners will think of a member of the medical profession when **doctor** is used, clarification is required when the story is about people who have earned doctoral degrees in other disciplines.

Remember that **doctor** is a ***title,*** not a profession. Therefore, avoid using **doctor** generically. Use Dr. Marianne A. Weston, a *neurosurgeon* at Acme General Hospital, or Dr. Martin N. Reynolds, *professor* of journalism, or Dr. Harold C. Pennington, the newly appointed *minister* at Wyoming Presbyterian Church.

14. Don't Presume Readers/Listeners Know the *Background*

Journalists ***should not presume their readers or listeners know the background*** details of a story even if the subject matter has been reported regularly for several days or weeks. Of course, not everything that has been printed or broadcast can be repeated in each additional story, but sufficient background should be provided to present the news in an understandable context.

(Avoid) Despite increased criticism from school administrators, students and some members of the Legislature, the governor said he will not rescind ***Executive Order No. 2.***

(Better) Despite increased criticism from school administrators, students, and some members of the Legislature, the governor said he will not rescind Executive Order No. 2, ***which retains for the state all interest earned on funds allotted to education.***

— — —

(Avoid) P. A. Rodriquez, president of ***CROP,*** said the awards dinner will be March 10.

(Better) P. A. Rodriquez, president of the ***Committee to Recognize Outstanding Pupils,*** said the awards dinner will be March 10.

15. Don't Start First Sentence of Paragraph with a *Coordinating Conjunction*

Your English teachers probably told you that starting a sentence with a coordinating conjunction (and, but, or, for, nor, yet, so) is improper. However, the practice is generally accepted in journalism ***if the sentence is not the first in the***

paragraph. Why? Because both print and broadcast journalists realize their readers and listeners find shorter sentences easier to understand.

16. Don't *Repeat Major Words* in Same Sentence or Headline

One rule that many writers adopt early in their careers is to avoid repeating **major words** in the same sentence or headline. However, repetition of minor words such as articles (a, an, the), prepositions (on, at, in), and some conjunctions (and, or, nor) is necessary.

17. Place Relative Pronoun Immediately *after* Its Antecedent

A **relative pronoun** introduces a dependent clause, further explains or defines its antecedent (the noun it replaces) from the independent clause, and enables the writer to combine two clauses into one effective sentence. The most common relative pronouns are *who, which* and *that.* Others are *whom, what, whose, whoever, whomever, whichever* and *whatever.*

To avoid syntax problems, writers and broadcasters should ***place a relative pronoun immediately after its noun antecedent.*** When that is not possible, special care must be taken to place the relative pronoun where it will promote understanding and not create confusion or give the sentence an unintended meaning. Consider how correct placement is achieved in the following examples:

(Awkward) The ***library*** in McDonald County, ***which*** used to be a barn, also serves as a meeting place for community groups. (The antecedent of ***which*** is ***library***, not ***County.***)

(Better) The McDonald County ***library, which*** used to be a barn, also serves as a meeting place for community groups.

— — —

(Awkward) The ***president*** of the Board of **Trustees,** ***who*** has three years remaining in his term, said today he will resign at the end of the school year. (The antecedent of ***who*** is ***president,*** not **Trustees.**)

(Better) The Board of Trustees ***president, who*** has three years remaining in his term, said today he will resign at the end of the school year. (No apostrophe is needed after **Trustees** because the term is descriptive, not possessive.)

(See pages 74–83 for an explanation of relative pronouns.)

18. Don't Interchange *Which* and *That*

Even experienced writers and broadcasters sometimes have difficulty deciding whether ***which*** or ***that*** is the appropriate relative pronoun to use to introduce a dependent clause. The solution is to determine whether the dependent clause is **essential** or **nonessential** in making the meaning of the independent clause clear.

In other words, can the independent clause stand unchanged in meaning if the dependent clause is removed? Does the dependent clause provide **essential** information, or does it just provide **additional** information?

If the dependent clause is **nonessential,** it is introduced by the relative pronoun ***which,*** and commas are used to set the dependent clause apart from the independent clause. If the dependent clause is **essential,** it is introduced by the relative pronoun ***that,*** and commas are not used to set the dependent clause apart from the independent clause.

The following examples illustrate the use of ***which*** with dependent clauses that are **nonessential** and ***that*** with dependent clauses that are **essential.**

(Nonessential) The reporter covering the circus decided to write a feature story about elephants, ***which*** he found to be fascinating.

The dependent clause, **which he found to be fascinating,** is not needed to make the meaning of the independent clause clear. It just provides additional information. Therefore, ***which*** is used as the relative pronoun to introduce the dependent clause, and a comma is used to set the dependent clause apart from the independent clause.

(Essential) The elephant (***that***) the reporter rode this morning will perform in the matinee.

The dependent clause, **that the reporter rode this morning,** is needed to make the meaning of the independent clause clear. It tells which elephant will perform—the one that the reporter rode. Therefore, ***that*** is used as the relative pronoun to introduce the dependent clause. No commas are used to set the dependent clause apart from the independent clause. ***That*** is placed in parentheses to indicate it does not have to be used. It is understood.

19. Don't Report *Opinions* and *Accusations* as *Facts*

Journalists sometimes inadvertently report opinions or accusations as facts by using careless wording. Such wording may be not only inaccurate but also unfair.

(Avoid) The university's ***inferior*** science program is the main reason Acme State has failed to gain approval to start a medical school, the student body president said today.

(Better) The student body president of Acme State today ***described the university's science program as inferior*** and said it is the main reason approval has not been granted to start a medical school.

or

Acme State University has failed to gain approval to start a medical school because of its ***"inferior science program,"*** the student body president said today.

— — —

(Avoid) The state's ***bad*** labor-management relations will make recruiting industry difficult, a candidate for the State Senate said today.

(Better) A candidate for the State Senate said today that recruiting industry will be difficult because of what ***she described*** as the state's bad labor-management relations.

The problem with these faulty sentences is that they fail to make clear that sources are relating their **opinions** about the quality of the university's science program or the state's labor-management relations. These assessments are not indisputable; they are opinions or accusations and should be presented as such.

20. *Think* before Ending Words with *ize*

If you read in a newspaper or heard during a radio or a television news report that the mayor had been *hospitali**z**ed* ***(confined to a hospital),*** the use of ***ize*** at the end of *hospital* probably would not trouble you. *Hospitali**z**ed* is a word used so frequently that it has become generally accepted. You would doubtlessly be taken aback, however, if you read or heard that after being *hospitali**z**ed* for a week, the mayor was released but would be *hous**iz**ed* ***(confined to his house)*** for a month before he could return to work.

Obviously, no one says or writes *hous**iz**ed.* But the principle is the same. If you can form such ***ize*** words as *hospitali**ze**, institutionali**ze*** and *victimi**ze**,* what is so illogical about saying or writing *hous**ize*** or *schooli**ze?***

You get the point. We injure our language by carelessly attaching ***ize*** to the end of any word we choose. Your school news medium or your mass media company may have guidelines concerning such words. If not, you will have to decide for yourself whether you find acceptable such words as *internali**ze**, externali**ze**, traumati**ze**, actuali**ze**, maximi**ze**, prioriti**ze**, compartmentali**ze**, depersonali**ze*** and *politici**ze**.*

21. *Resist Using* Nouns as Verbs

Some verbs formed from nouns are used so frequently that they have become generally accepted. Examples include *jail**ed**, journey**ed*** and *hous**ed**.* Many argue that turning nouns into verbs is useful and harmless. Others, however, think the practice should be avoided.They have in mind such substitutes as *author**ed*** for *wrote, host**ed*** for *was host for* or *served as host for,* and *impact**ed*** for *affected.*

Mass communicators would be wise to resist using nouns as verbs unless the words have become commonly accepted.

22. *Avoid* Gobbledygook and Words That Are Not Self-Explanatory

Gobbledygook refers to pompous, wordy, needlessly complicated writing or speaking used to impress or to confuse.

> "We facilitated the excavation of the traumatized male child." Translation: "We dug under the collapsed building and saved the scared boy."

A mistake frequently made by beginning journalists and occasionally by professionals is to use **a word or a term not generally known or self-explanatory.**

The error occurs most often when journalists repeat words from news sources who use language generally understood only by their colleagues.

One example related to the medical profession will make the point. A newspaper article in an area where coal mining is a major industry related that a physician was quoted as saying "**pneumoconiosis** is decreasing as an occupational health hazard." What the heck is **"pneumoconiosis"**?

The mass communicator must explain to the reader that **"pneumoconiosis"** means black lung disease. If that report is carried by a newspaper in an area in which residents have little knowledge of coal mining, the reporter must additionally explain that **pneumoconiosis** or **black lung** refers to a disease common among miners who for many years have breathed coal dust into their lungs.

No word or term like **pneumoconiosis** should be used without explanation unless the audience is restricted to those who are sure to be familiar with it.

23. *Maintain* Parallel Construction

Strangers have little difficulty finding their way in cities whose roads are parallel to one another. If they know all avenues run south to north, all streets run east to west, and each road is numbered consecutively, visitors will need only the address of where they want to go.

Likewise, when writing has the balance, rhythm and consistent direction provided by parallel construction, readers should have little difficulty understanding the message. The following examples will illustrate what is meant by parallelism in writing or in speaking:

(Awkward) The retiring editor of the Acme Gazette said she looks forward to travel**ing** more, sleep**ing** later and more frequent **visits** with her grandchildren.

(Improved) The retiring editor of the Acme Gazette said she looks forward to travel**ing** more, sleep**ing** later and visit**ing** her grandchildren more frequently.

— — —

(Awkward) The Flying Eagles used superior runn**ing,** passes and kick**ing** to defeat the Thundering Mustangs in the state championship football game.

(Improved) The Flying Eagles used superior runn**ing,** pass**ing** and kick**ing** to defeat the Thundering Mustangs in the state championship football game.

— — —

(Awkward) The graphic artists **not only** *wanted* to do a good job for their company **but also** to create a unique design.

(Improved) The graphic artists *wanted* **not only** to do a good job for their company **but also** to create a unique design.

— — —

(Awkward) The advertising director left three written instructions for the new employee: (1) You must **answer** the phone. (2) **Checking** expired display advertisements. (3) **To proofread** all classified advertisements ordered since 6 p.m.

(Improved) The advertising director left three written instructions for the new employee: (1) You must **answer** the phone. (2) You must **check** expired display advertisements. (3) You must **proofread** all classified advertisements ordered since 6 p.m.

or

The advertising director left three written instructions for the new employee: **Answer** the phone, **check** expired display advertisements and **proofread** all classified advertisements ordered since 6 p.m.

— — —

Awkward) The professor said he *loves* teaching and *tolerates* grading papers but *hated* attending meetings.

(Improved) The professor said he *loves* teaching and *tolerates* grading papers but *hates* attending meetings.

— — —

(Awkward) *Whether **alert** or when he was **tired,*** Jackson is a good interviewer.

(Improved) *Whether **alert** or **tired,*** Jackson is a good interviewer.

24. *Think* before Splitting Infinitives

The advice about splitting infinitives is similar to the recommendations given previously about starting a sentence with a coordinating conjunction: Do it only when it improves writing and promotes comprehension. Remember that split infinitives rarely are necessary if you are willing to rewrite the sentence.

Before you split an infinitive, try to move the material you are tempted to place between **to** and the **verb.** You can let your ear be your guide, as the following examples illustrate:

(Bad splits) Some people undergo cosmetic surgery ***to forever*** **look** young. (Just place ***forever*** after ***young.***)

The coach tried ***to clearly*** **demonstrate** how **to *properly*** **spike** the volleyball. (Just place ***clearly*** after **demonstrate** and ***properly*** after **volleyball.**)

(OK splits) He wanted **to *radically*** **change** the method used to determine salary levels.

The president tried **to *virtually*** **guarantee** the outcome by offering concessions to individual members of Congress in return for their support.

(***Radically*** and ***Virtually*** would be awkward if placed elsewhere.)

25. Wordiness: Sometimes Never Means *Never*

Saying ***never*** can be risky. An unanticipated exception can prove embarrassing. However, a few of the countless examples of wordiness can be trimmed reasonably safely. Never use **together** after the following words:

assemble	knit
bind	link
blend	merge
bond	mesh
combined	mix
connect	mulch
cooperate	splice
entwined	staple
fused	tangled
gather	tie
huddle	weld
join	

More than 250 of the most common examples of wordiness are listed in Reference 4, Wordiness and Trite Expressions, beginning on page 325.

Are These Distinctions Worth Making?

chapter 2

Who Cares?

If everyone instantly understands what we mean when we say or write ***can*** instead of ***may, persuade*** instead of ***convince,*** and ***each other*** instead of ***one another,*** should we bother making distinctions?

These examples, as well as many other word pairs, are routinely interchanged, not only in casual conversation but also in professional writing and broadcasting. Semanticists, who are concerned about word meanings and changes in meaning, may be willing to accept these interchanges. However, grammarians, who establish and maintain language standards, usually aren't.

The attitude of many students of mass communication is "Who cares?" They consider the conflict to be academic, impractical and unrelated to the "real world." And there are professional mass communicators who agree with them.

It's true—as some students are fond of pointing out—that the fourth or fifth dictionary definition exchanges ***anxious*** for ***eager, since*** for ***because,*** and ***insure*** for ***ensure.*** But should that encourage writers and broadcasters to be casual or careless about word meanings? Should everyone on the newspaper, magazine, broadcast, advertising, or public relations staff be free to determine word meanings?

The fact that stylebooks exist answers the question. Professional mass media managers, as well as the teachers who prepare their employees, establish standards and require a uniformity of style that provide stability and consistency to their publications and broadcasts. That's the practical reason.

Another reason for making careful distinctions is professional pride. After all, who wants to stumble through a career being perceived as a person who is imprecise and risks being misunderstood?

Media managers and teachers can force adherence upon those they supervise. Ultimately, however, individual writers and broadcasters must decide whether the following distinctions are valuable or arbitrary.

20 Examples

1. *Anxious/Eager*

Use **anxious** to indicate concern or worry. Use ***eager*** to show impatient desire.

The city engineer said he is **anxious** (concerned, worried) about tonight's debate on the proposed sewage-treatment plant. However, he said he is ***eager*** (has an impatient desire) to argue his case before opponents of the project. He also said he is ***eager*** for his vacation to begin.

Avoid using the prepositions **to** or **for** after ***anxious.*** When you do that, you usually mean **eager.** ***Anxious*** is more commonly followed by the preposition **about.**

2. *Because/Since*

Use **because** to indicate a cause or a reason. Use ***since*** to refer to time, meaning between then and now.

The sheriff said he will not seek re-election **because** (reason) state law prevents him from succeeding himself.

— — —

The governor said she will not veto the bill **because** (reason) she knows her opponents in the Legislature will override her action.

— — —

Since (time, meaning between then and now) this past Monday's meeting, several members of City Council have expressed their opinions on the road-bond issue.

3. *Disinterested/Uninterested*

Disinterested describes a person who is impartial (unbiased, has not taken sides or made a choice). ***Uninterested*** describes a person who is not interested (bored).

"A jury should be composed of **disinterested** [impartial] individuals," the judge explained to visiting schoolchildren.

— — —

The judge said he is pleased that none of the students appeared to be ***uninterested*** (not interested, bored) during the three-hour court session.

4. *Convince/Persuade*

Convince means to cause someone to believe. ***Persuade*** means to cause someone to do something, to take some action.

In his State-of-the-Union address, the president said he hopes to **convince** (cause people to believe) Americans that Congress should not pass a tax increase.

— — —

He said he also hopes he can ***persuade*** (cause people to act) Americans to express their opposition to a tax increase by contacting their representatives in Congress.

5. *Amount/Number*

Amount is an indefinite quantity (water, flour, sand, grass) that cannot be counted. ***Number*** consists of a quantity of people or things that can be counted.

The ***amount*** of news (a quantity that cannot be counted) published and broadcast each day is amazing.

— — —

The ***number*** of reporters (a quantity that can be counted) covering the convention will not be known for another week, the press officer explained.

6. *Can/May*

Use **can** for ability to. Use ***may*** for permission.

Any eligible student ***may*** (have permission to) enter the mile run in Saturday's track meet, the athletic director said.

— — —

However, he said he doubts any runner **can** (has the ability to) break the record set two years ago.

7. *Ensure/Insure*

Use **ensure** to mean to guarantee or to make certain. Use ***insure*** to mean to make safe from loss or harm.

The best camera equipment available cannot **ensure** (guarantee) good pictures if the photographer lacks skill.

— — —

The publisher ***insured*** (purchased protection to make safe from loss or harm) her company against financially ruinous libel suits.

8. *Farther/Further*

Use **farther** to refer to distance. Use ***further*** to refer to degree or extent.

After completing half of his statewide walking campaign for Congress, the 55-year-old candidate said he couldn't go one mile **farther** (distance) without rest.

— — —

However, he said that at 7 a.m., he would speak ***further*** (degree, extent) with reporters about resuming his trip.

9. *Hanged/Hung*

The present tense of **hang** presents no problem. A person may hang almost anything. The difficulty arises in choosing between the past tense **hanged** (meaning executed) and ***hung*** (meaning placed). The solution is to use ***hanged*** to refer to executions and **hung** for everything else.

The governor refused a last-minute appeal, and the criminal was **hanged** (executed) at 6 a.m.

— — —

The paintings were ***hung*** carefully on the walls of the gallery.

10. *Dragged/Drug*

Use **dragged** as the past tense of **drag** to mean to pull along with considerable effort. As a verb, ***drug*** refers to a medicine or some other chemical substance.

The fullback **dragged** (pulled along) the linebacker 10 yards into the end zone. *Do not use* ***drug*** *to mean to pull along.*

— — —

The physician will ***drug*** (administer a chemical substance) her patient to alleviate his pain. *Please note that* ***drug*** *is more commonly used as a noun: The physician will prescribe a* ***drug*** *to alleviate the patient's pain.*

11. *Fewer/Less*

Use **fewer** for things that can be counted. Use ***less*** for bulk or quantity.

"I have **fewer** than a dozen reporters [individuals who can be counted] to cover a city of 250,000 people," the editor complained to the publisher.

— — —

"We have ***less*** than a month's supply of paper [bulk, quantity] in stock," the pressroom supervisor reported to the publisher.

12. *Lend/Loan*

Perhaps the simplest and easiest way to deal with **lend** and ***loan*** is to use **lend** as a verb and ***loan*** as a noun.

You may **lend** (verb) money to someone, but what that person receives from you is a ***loan*** (noun).

— — —

The Small Business Administration will **lend**/has **lent** (verbs) money to eligible companies at a low interest rate.

— — —

The Water Resources Commission is seeking a $6.5 million ***loan*** (noun) from federal agencies.

13. *Proved/Proven*

The Associated Press Stylebook lists **proved** as a verb and ***proven*** exclusively as an adjective, even though dictionaries allow ***proven*** as an alternative verb for the past-tense **proved.**

The new director's hunches have **proved** (verb) to be true more often than not.

— — —

"When you asked me for a ***proven*** [adjective] method for obtaining the number of votes we needed, I was embarrassed to tell you I didn't know," the aide said.

14. *Each Other/One Another*

Use **each other** when two people, places or things are involved. Use ***one another*** for three or more.

Gov. Mark E. Nicely said he and Lt. Gov. Beverly J. Carson have known **each other** (two of them) for more than 20 years.

— — —

Gov. Mark E. Nicely said he, Lt. Gov. Beverly J. Carson and their seven office staff members have been working with ***one another*** (three or more) for four years.

15. *Among/Between*

Use **between** when two people, places or things are involved. Use ***among*** when the number is three or more.

The general election contest **between** the incumbent and the challenger (two of them) is expected to be close, most political experts agree.

— — —

The winner probably will divide government jobs ***among*** members of the campaign staff (three or more)

— — —

If three or more persons, places or things are considered one pair at a time, **between** may be used instead of ***among.***

Discussions about the proposed teacher pay raise bill are expected in meetings **between** the legislators and committees from the Board of Trustees, university administrators and representatives of the Teachers Union.

16. *Although/While*

Although means despite the fact that. ***While*** means during the time that. Resist the temptation to use ***while*** in place of **although** when the purpose is to show a contrast.

Although (not ***while***) the university president said she wants to obtain a special appropriation from the Legislature, she said she has little hope of getting it. (The meaning is despite the fact that, not during the time that.)

— — —

While (during the time that) they were waiting impatiently, the reporters complained about the governor's habitual tardiness.

17. *Healthful/Healthy*

Healthful refers to something (food, exercise, rest) that promotes good health. ***Healthy*** refers to being in good physical and mental health.

The president jogs because he believes regular exercise is **healthful** (promotes good health).

— — —

Two weeks after being treated for problems with his allergies, the president resumed jogging and said he is feeling **healthy** (in a state of good health).

— — —

Fruit and vegetables are **healthful** (not ***healthy***) foods. Fruit and vegetables are **healthful** (not ***healthy***) for you.

18. *In Behalf Of/On Behalf Of*

In behalf of means for the benefit of. ***On behalf of*** means in place of.

The school's fund-raiser is **in behalf of** (for the benefit of) the band.

— — —

Speaking ***on behalf of*** (in place of) her client, the attorney entered a plea of not guilty.

19. *Who/Whom*

Most people who speak and write in English have no problem deciding when to use **whom** instead of **who.** They gave **whom** the old heave-ho a long time ago. And they gave **whomever** the same treatment.

Whom and **Whomever** are used so infrequently in casual conversation and writing that they sound formal, even pretentious. Banishing them from the language seems a popular resolution.

Nevertheless, both words exist, and like it or not, professional writers must be knowledgeable about when to use them. Choosing not to use them is one thing; not knowing how to use them is a handicap.

Everyone knows the basics: **Who** and **Whoever** are used primarily as *subjects* and ***whom*** and ***whomever*** as *objects.* Hardly any journalist would say or write, "***Whom*** is your favorite person to interview?" or "To **who** do you want the job application sent?"

If all **who/whom** decisions were as simple as these examples, errors would be rare. Unfortunately, there are additional challenges. The following are **who/whom** choices that confound many of us:

1. Give the tickets to **(whoever/whomever)** wants them.

2. The governor gave her assistant a list of names of people **(who/whom)** she plans to appoint to the commission.

3. The city editor is the one **(who/whom)** we were warned would be the least patient with us.

4. The city manager promised to tell us **(who/whom)** his choice is.

5. (Who/Whom) are you voting for in Tuesday's election?

The answer in No. 1 is **whoever,** and that seems weird because we immediately recognize *to* as a preposition that routinely requires an objective case pronoun **(whomever)** as its object. But that reasoning won't work in this example.

Instead of a single word serving as the object, the entire dependent clause **(whoever wants them)** performs that role. The nominative case **whoever** is used because it is the subject of the verb *wants.*

* * *

In No. 2, the answer is the objective case **whom** because it serves as the object of the infinitive, *to appoint.* There is no role for **who** in the sentence. It can't be a subject because it lacks a verb. And if we rearrange the sentence, we can see clearly where **whom** fits (The governor plans to appoint **whom** to the commission?).

* * *

Who is the answer in No. 3 because it serves as the subject of the verb *would be.* The construction of the sentence makes the decision harder because **who** and *would be* are separated by another subject (we) and verb (were warned).

* * *

No. 4 is perhaps the most puzzling of the five examples. The answer is **who** because it follows the nonaction verb *is* and functions as a predicate pronoun. **Whom** cannot be the answer because only action verbs can be followed by objects.

Nonaction verbs often have complements—nouns, pronouns and adjectives—that follow them and provide additional information about the subject (She is *talented.* Jane is my *editor.* It was *he* who wrote the story.). Predicate nouns and pronouns also are interchangeable with the subject (My *editor* is Jane; *he* was it), and that's quite helpful in this example. After all, we wouldn't say or write, **Whom** is the city manager's choice?

* * *

The answer in No. 5 is **whom,** object of the preposition *for.* You, not **who,** is the subject of the verb, *are.* To illustrate the point, put the sentence in the normal subject-verb order: You are voting for **whom** in Tuesday's election?

Of course, we can avoid the **who/whom** question by rewriting sentences 1, 4 and 5 and by leaving **who** and **whom** out of the other two, which make sense without them. But we can't avoid the **who/whom** decision in every instance.

So, when **who/whom** and **whoever/whomever** conflicts cause you to pause at the computer, remember this one generalization that provides the key to the solution: **Who** and **whoever** are nominative case and are used as subjects and as predicate pronouns; **whom** and **whomever** are objective case and function as objects (direct objects, indirect objects and objects of prepositions).

Except for similarities in spelling and pronunciation, **who** and **whom** are as different in function as *I* and *me, we* and *us,* and *they* and *them.*

For additional information on uses of nouns and pronouns in the nominative and objective cases, please see pages 59–61 and 63–65.

20. *Lie/Lay*

Lie and ***lay*** may be the champion of all troublesome word pairs. Most of us have problems with them—and for good reason. They can be very confusing, and the blame can be placed mostly on the word ***lay.*** That confusion can be expressed graphically by displaying each word's principal parts:

(To recline, rest)	**lie**	*lay*	**have/has/had lain**	**lying**
(To place, put)	***lay***	***laid***	***have/has/had laid***	***laying***

Lay is part of each verb, and therein lies the confusion. ***Lay*** is the past principal part of the verb **lie** and the present principal part of the bottom example. Accordingly, it is used in the past tense for the verb **lie** and in the present tense for the verb ***lay.***

Explained briefly, **lie** means *to recline* or *to rest.* It is intransitive, meaning that it is an action verb but it never has an object. ***Lay*** means *to place* or *to put.* It is transitive, meaning that it is an action verb that always has a direct object. Put another way, a person may **lie** down (recline) for a nap, but if the room is cold, he had better ***lay*** (place) another blanket (object) on the bed.

> Mayor Mary L. Ritter said she always **lies** (rests) on her office couch a few minutes to prepare herself mentally for each press conference.

— — —

> She said she ***lay*** (rested) there longer than she intended today and was five minutes late for the conference. *Please note that many people would say or write* **laid** *in this sentence because* **lay** *does not "sound" past tense. However, because* **laid** *means* to place *or* to put, *it won't work because the mayor was not placing or putting anything. She was resting.*

— — —

> The mayor joked that she would have ***lain*** (rested) there all afternoon had she known how tough the reporters' questions were going to be. ***Lain*** *is used to indicate that the mayor was resting.* ***Laid*** *would have meant she was putting or placing something.*

— — —

> "Please **lay** [place] your notes [object] on my desk," the advertising director instructed the copywriter.

— — —

> "I **laid** [placed] them [object] there more than an hour ago," the copywriter replied.
>
> When he was far enough away to be certain the advertising director couldn't hear him, the copywriter said to another employee: "I have **laid** [placed] my notes [object] on that desk at the same time each day for three weeks. You'd think he'd catch on by now."

* * *

One additional significant point requires some explanation. Remember that once a person **lays** (places) an object somewhere, that object then **lies** (rests, reclines, stays) there.

The city architect said the bricks used to construct the new town hall should **lie** (rest, recline, stay) in place for a hundred years or more.

* * *

Test yourself with the following examples:

1. "Now **I lay** me down to sleep" is the first line of a traditional prayer taught to many children. But should the verb be **lie**?
2. **(Lay/Lie)** back in your seat. This is going to be a long trip.
3. The president said worries about the economy **(laid/lay)** heavily on his mind during the first year of his administration.
4. On election nights, tired staff members **(lay/lie)** around the newsroom, saving their energy for when the results start coming in.
5. When the dog jumped at the reporter as she entered the house for her interview, the owner told it to **(lay/lie)** down.
6. That picture of our first news director has **(laid/lain)** on the floor since it fell off the wall three days ago.

7–8. **(Lay/Lie)** your new ad on my desk in the same place your old one **(lay/laid)** before you picked it up yesterday.

9–10. After **(laying/lying)** bricks for six days this week, he'll be **(laying/lying)** in bed for a long time Sunday.

The answers:

1. **Lay** is correct. The children **place** or **put** themselves into bed.
2. **Lie.** The person is **reclining.**
3. **Lay.** The worries were **lying/staying** on his mind.
4. **Lie.** The reporters are **resting.**
5. **Lie.** The owner wants the dog to assume a **reclining** position.
6. **Lain.** The picture is **sitting/lying** on the floor.
7. **Lay.** The person is supposed to **place** the ad on the desk.
8. The answer is **lay,** the past tense of **lie.** The papers were **lying** on the desk.
9. **Laying.** The person was **placing** or **putting** the bricks.
10. **Lying.** The tired worker is **reclining/resting.**

Please see Reference 1, Words Frequently Confused, beginning on page 223, for additional examples.

(You may test yourself on the material in this chapter or section by connecting with the following Web site: www.mhhe.com/arnold.)

Language Lapses

chapter 3

20 Examples That May Cause You to Say "Oops"

No one likes to make mistakes, but language errors are a little easier to live with than languages lapses. Errors often result from ignorance shared by so many others that the result is less than embarrassing. The epidemic misuse of **lie** and **lay** is a primary example. Lapses, however, offer no consolation. They result from brains idling in neutral, not because writers and broadcasters don't know better. And, without failure, they provoke ribbing from colleagues.

Determine whether any of the following examples cause you to say "Oops!"

1. *Try To,* Not *Try And*

A tennis player will **try *to*** win, not **try *and*** win. To write or to broadcast that the player will **try *and*** win is to presume or to predict that he or she will both try and win.

> "We're a 30-point underdog, but we're going to **try *to*** [not **try *and***] win," the coach said.

The same reasoning applies to **be sure *to*/be sure *and*.**

2. Take the *Eye* Out of *Eyewitness*

Eyewitness may sound more dramatic than just plain **witness,** but is there any real difference? Besides, if journalists insist on writing or broadcasting **eye**witness for a person who sees something, why should they discriminate against the other senses? How about **ear**witness for people who hear something but don't see it, or **nose**witness for those who smell something but neither see nor hear it?

3. *Want,* Not *Wish*

When reporters write or broadcast that some organization or club is available to people who **wish** to join, they probably are overestimating the desire the potential recruits have for membership. **Want** is usually the more appropriate word.

"Students who **want** [not **wish**] to join may apply in person before April 15," the club president said.

4. *Feel Bad,* Not *Feel Badly*

Don't be surprised to hear many well-educated people say, " I feel **bad*ly*** about forgetting our appointment," or "I feel **bad*ly*** about the death of your uncle." **Bad,** not **bad*ly*** is the correct word in these examples. To use **bad*ly*** after the word **feel** gives the impression that the speaker has an inferior sense of feel.

Remember that **bad** is usually an adjective and **badly** is usually an adverb.

"I feel **bad** [not **bad*ly***] about missing the deadline," the reporter told his editor. (**Bad** is an adjective modifying the pronoun ***I.***)

— — —

The soccer player performed **bad*ly*** (not **bad**) after he injured his leg. (**Bad*ly*** is an adverb modifying the verb **performed.** It tells how the player performed.)

5. *When,* Not *After*

Both print and broadcast journalists sometimes mistakenly use **after** instead of **when** in spot news stories about accidents. If a victim is injured, the journalist should write or broadcast that Luther N. Craycraft was injured **when** he was hit by a car at the corner of Fifth Avenue and 10th Street ***(not <u>after</u> being struck by a car)***. To report that the person was injured **after** the accident is to imply that he wasn't injured by the car that hit him but by something else that happened subsequently.

6. *Former Student,* Not *Former Graduate*

The person who placed a sign of welcome in front of city hall meant well. "Welcome **former** Acme High School **graduates,**" the message read. What was meant, of course, was "Welcome Acme High School **graduates**" or "Welcome Acme High School **alumni.**" A person's student status changes eventually, but a graduate remains a graduate forever.

7. Where Else Would *Time Out* Be?

Radio and television sportscasters routinely inform their listeners and viewers that there is time out **on the field** or time out **on the court.** Where else would it be? In the dressing room? In the parking lot? The same lapse occurs when the journalists say a player has 15 points **in the game** or gained six yards **on the play.**

8. Avoid Saying *Those Interested*

When writing or broadcasting information about something that people may apply for, avoid using **those interested.** Who else would apply other than those who are interested? Just give the information necessary for applying or participating.

9. *Past* and *Future* Usually Are Obvious

Guard against using **past** and **future** when they are so obvious they need not be stated. For example:

Her **past/previous/prior** job experience includes . . .

His **past** history indicates . . .

Her **future** plans are . . .

"We'll save this for **future** reference . . ."

10. All Mobs Are *Angry;* All Beatings Are *Brutal*

Because there is no such thing as a pleasant mob or a gentle beating, journalists consider **angry** mob and **brutal** beating redundant. For writers who insist that the addition of **angry** and **brutal** is more descriptive and sounds worse than **mob** and **beating** alone, editors and news directors suggest they save those terms for their short stories and novels. The same advice applies to **dangerous** weapon and **sad** tragedy.

11. All Babies Are *Little;* All Babies Are *New*

Some babies are bigger or smaller than others, but all are little compared with adults. Likewise, some babies are older than others, but all of them are young. Therefore, writing or broadcasting that someone had a **little** baby or a **new** baby is unnecessary even if she had another the previous year. How about saying she had **another** baby instead of a **new** one?

12. *Gift,* Not *Free Gift; Free,* Not *Free of Charge*

Gifts are obviously free; otherwise, they would not be gifts. And if something is free, obviously there is no charge.

13. The "Case" *of* Compound Objects

People who would be embarrassed to say, "My editor told ***I*** to trim my story" or "The photographer asked ***she*** to ignore the camera" frequently make that pronoun case error when a verb or a preposition has two or more objects joined by ***and.***

The same people don't even flinch when they say, "My editor told ***John*** and ***I*** to trim our stories," or "The photographer asked ***she*** and her ***husband*** to ignore the camera."

This pronoun case trap sometimes snares even well-educated and experienced journalists. It can be avoided by giving attention to two points related to personal pronouns.

First, objects of verbs and objects of prepositions must come from the objective case pronouns me, him, her, us, them and never from the nominative case pronouns I, he, she, we, they. Second, the error can be avoided by saying or writing each of the objects separately (told ***John***/told **me**—not told ***I***); asked her ***husband***/asked ***her***—not asked ***she***).

This pronoun case problem fortunately does not affect nouns. We get a merciful break with nouns because they are spelled and pronounced the same in both the nominative and the objective cases. ***Johnson,*** for example, remains the same whether it is used as a nominative case subject (***Johnson*** won the award) or as an objective case object of a preposition (The award was given to ***Johnson.***) See pages 147–148 for additional explanation and examples.

14. Drop *Old* before Adage, Cliché, Tradition, Habit and Maxim

If an expression, a rule or a custom could become an **adage,** a **cliché,** a **tradition,** a **habit** or a **maxim** overnight, distinguishing between the old and the new might be necessary. However, because considerable time is involved in their development, to use the adjective ***old*** before them is as unnecessary as saying someone has given birth to a ***new*** baby.

15. *Can't Help,* Not *Can't Help But*

Use *can't help. Can't help but* is a double negative.

The mayor said, "I **can't help thinking** [not **can't help *but* think**] the council members were wrong when they reduced our budget."

16. *Center ON,* Not *Center AROUND*

On and **around** are not interchangeable in these two sets of words. Something may **center *on*** but never ***around.***

"The legislative debate will **center *on*** [not ***around***] tax reform," Sen. Maxine C. Perkowski said.

17. *O* Is a Letter; *Zero* Is a Number

Sometimes when speakers provide a telephone or a license number or a college course number, they pronounce **zero** as **O** (a letter).

The witness said the license number of the suspect's car is "four, seven, one, three, zero [not **O,** the letter]."

18. Just Because You're Repeating Doesn't Mean You Have to Use Past Tense

When an event has concluded or an opinion has been expressed, past-tense verbs clearly are in order: The team narrowly **lost** the game. The senator said she **did** not vote because she **was** ill.

However, journalists sometimes use the past tense inappropriately when the expression or the situation is **ongoing** and requires a **present**-tense verb. The following examples illustrate the point.

> After the game, the coach said the defeat ***was*** the worst in the school's history. (The defeat still **IS** the worst, isn't it?)

— — —

> The mayor said she ***hoped*** the city will end the year with a surplus. (She still **Hopes** so, doesn't she?)

19. You're Not *Nauseous* Unless You're Sickening

Nauseated means feeling sick or disgusted. **Nauseous** and mean causing sickness or disgust.

> "I ate so much food at last night's awards dinner that I felt **nauseated** [sick] all morning," the governor said.

— — —

> The candidate's behavior at the political rally was **nauseating** (disgusting).

Do not write or say that someone is **nauseous** unless you mean that the person is sickening or disgusting. If you mean the person is sick, say **nauseated.**

20. Is Something *Funny* or Is It *Strange?*

Funny refers to something that causes laughter or amusement. **Strange** refers to something odd or unusual. Journalists should be careful about interchanging the two. For example, journalists would not want to report that just before his stroke, the mayor said he was feeling **funny.**

Language lapses are funny only to those who catch them—not to those who commit them.

(You may test yourself on the material in this chapter or section by connecting with the following Web site: www.mhhe.com/arnold.)

chapter 4

It's Nobody's Guess

Rules Eliminate Guesswork

Pick your favorite sport—one that you watch regularly on television—and chances are you have an extensive knowledge of the rules. Watch an athletic contest with which you are unfamiliar—perhaps one that is indigenous to a small region of the world—and you will have little understanding of what is happening.

Learning rules is a prerequisite to effective participation or watching, even though the latter is unquestionably more enjoyable. Understanding the rules eliminates guessing.

Veteran media copy editors and experienced writing teachers can recite lists of errors they see all too often. Fifteen are presented in this chapter, along with explanations and examples that remove the guesswork.

15 Examples

1. *One Word or Two?*

"I don't write editorials ***anymore,***" the editor in chief said. "I just can't spare the time to write ***any more*** of them."

* * *

"***Anyone*** who studies can make a good grade on the test," the professor advised. "***Any one*** of you is capable of making the highest grade."

* * *

"You may submit your proposal ***anytime*** next week," the advertising director said. "I don't have ***any time*** this week to look at it."

* * *

"You may write the feature article ***any way*** you want," the editor said. However, the next day when she informed the writer that she no longer wanted the article, the writer said he didn't want to do it ***anyway.***

* * *

"Our department store has ***everyday*** low prices," the advertising manager claimed. "We definitely have the lowest prices ***every day***."

In these examples, ***anymore, anyone, anytime, anyway*** and ***everyday*** are used correctly as one word and as two words. But how do we decide whether to pick one word or two with such frequently used examples as these five, as well as ***anybody,*** **everyone,** ***everybody*** and ***sometimes?*** The answer, of course, is rules.

As a single word, ***anymore*** means any longer. As two words, ***any more*** means any additional.

"I can't play the leading role ***anymore*** [meaning any longer], but I can still enjoy doing character parts," the veteran actor said.

— — —

The news director wants to know if ***any more*** (meaning any additional) video is available on the fire.

* * *

Because the same rule applies equally to ***anyone, anybody, everyone*** and ***everybody,*** one explanation will cover all of them. As a single word, each refers to a group but not to any specific person. As two words, the reference is to an individual person or body.

Anyone (no particular person) may try out for the Community Players' next production, the director said.

— — —

The police chief said ***any one*** (emphasis on the individual) of the three people questioned could be the suspect sought by the FBI.

— — —

The mayor said she would speak to ***anybody*** (no person in particular) about any issue at any time.

— — —

"***Any body*** [individual corpse] found in the rubble of the building destroyed by the earthquake must be removed quickly and taken to the morgue," the coroner said.

In addition to this rule, pronunciation also helps determine whether to use one word or two. Notice that when two words are used, the emphasis goes on the second word.

* * *

Anytime means *whenever* as one word and refers to *an amount of time* as two words.

"We have deadlines," the city editor complained. "Reporters can't just turn in their stories ***anytime*** [*meaning whenever*] *they* feel like it."

* * *

"***Any time*** [meaning an amount of time] you can spare to work on the special edition will be appreciated."

* * *

Anyway and ***any way*** are determined as follows: Use one word when the meaning is *regardless* and two words when the meaning is *method, choice,* or *direction.*

"Even if I had enough money, I couldn't go to the concert ***anyway*** [regardless] because I have to study," the student complained.

— — —

The senator said he is determined to get re-elected ***any*** fair ***way*** (method) he can.

— — —

"***Any way*** [choice] you want to write the article is all right with me," the editor said.

— — —

"***Any way*** [direction] you travel, the trip will take about four hours," the guide explained.

* * *

Everyday as a single word is an *adjective* and refers to days in general without emphasizing any specific day. When ***every day*** is used as two words, ***every*** is used as an *adjective* modifying ***day,*** a *noun.* Also helpful is remembering that if ***each*** can be substituted for ***every, every day*** will be used as two words.

Acme Department Store has ***everyday*** (an adjective referring to no day in particular) low prices. (Substituting ***each*** for ***every*** makes no sense in this example, so one word is used.)

— — —

Acme Department Store has the lowest prices ***every day*** (the adjective ***every*** modifies the noun ***day***). (Substituting ***each*** for ***every*** makes sense, so two words are used.)

* * *

Sometime as one word means at some unspecified time. As two words, ***some time*** means an unspecified *quantity* of time.

The Pulitzer Prize winner said she hopes to progress from writing features to writing novels ***sometime*** (an unspecified time) before she retires.

— — —

However, she said she will have to spend ***some time*** (an unspecified *quantity* of time) preparing herself financially before she can try her luck as a fiction writer.

2. *One of* Those Who *Are/The Only One* Who *Is*

Relative pronouns—the most common of which are **who, which** and **that**—can be either singular or plural when they serve as subjects. But how is the writer or speaker to know? The pronouns are spelled and pronounced the same in the singular and in the plural.

The solution, of course, is to locate the antecedent (the noun that the pronoun replaces), determine whether it is singular or plural, and use a verb of the same number. The decision is easy when the pronoun immediately follows its antecedent:

The advertising **director,** ***who*** *is* retiring next month, has been an employee of the company for 40 years. (**Director** is the noun antecedent of the pronoun ***who.*** The noun is singular; therefore, the pronoun substitute is singular and takes the singular verb *is*. Had the noun antecedent been plural, the verb following ***who*** also would have been plural.)

The difficulty arises when there is more than one potential antecedent, and they are a mixture of singular and plural. Which antecedent controls whether the relative pronoun will require a singular or a plural verb? Consider the following sentences:

Ralston is *one* of the *editors* **who** is/are patient with interns. (*Ralston, one,* and *editors* are potential controlling antecedents. However, several editors are patient, so that rules out *Ralston* and *one* as controlling antecedents. And because editors is plural, **who** is plural and takes the plural verb **are.** *One of* provides the key to the answer because these words always precede a plural.)

— — —

Ralston is the only *one* of the *editors* **who** is/are patient with interns. (In this example, only *one* of the editors is patient, so that rules out *editors* as the antecedent. And because *one* is singular, **who** is singular and takes the singular verb **is.** *The only one* provides the key to the answer because these words tell us that both the antecedent and the relative pronoun will be singular.)

3. *None* as a Singular/*None* as a Plural

The indefinite pronoun **none** can be either singular or plural depending on its **antecedent,** the noun or the pronoun to which **none** refers. When **none** is used to mean ***not one,*** it is singular; when used to mean ***not any,*** it is plural. When the potential for singular-plural confusion is great, the solution may be to avoid using **none.** Use **not one** for singular and **not any** for plural.

The first step in deciding whether to use **none** as a singular or as a plural is to determine what there is none of (money? crops? outfielders? citizens? fruit?). After locating the antecedent, the writer can decide quickly whether to use a singular or a plural verb.

If the antecedent means a *quantity* or an *amount* (such as liquid, cement, flour, sand, patriotism), the verb should be singular because no one would expect a reader or a listener to consider each particle or element separately.

> **None** of the *flour* (the singular noun to which **none** refers) *is* (singular verb) worth saving.

— — —

If the writer intends **none** to mean *several* or *a number that can be counted* (such as journalists, leaders, oceans, desks), the verb should be plural.

> **None** of the *leaders* (the plural noun to which **none** refers) *are* (plural verb) available to meet with members of the press.

— — —

> The rules for **none** also apply to its fellow indefinite pronouns **any, some, such, most** and **all.**

4. *Either/Or* as a Singular; *Either/Or* as a Plural

Everyone knows that when *and* is used to join two singular subjects, a plural verb is required: **Farley** *and* **Jenkins** *are* our graphic artists. Of course, the same is true when one of the subjects is singular and the other is plural: **Farley** *and* her **assistants** *are* designing our next edition.

However, when compound subjects are preceded by the correlative conjunctions **either/or** or **neither/nor,** more decision-making is required. When both subjects are singular, the verb is singular (**Either** a parking *building* **or** a parking *lot is* to be funded); when both subjects are plural, the verb is plural (**Either** two parking *buildings* **or** three parking *lots are* to be built). The problem comes when one of the subjects is singular and the other is plural. How do we know whether to use a singular or a plural verb?

The rule requires the verb to agree with its nearer subject:

> **Either** a parking *building* **or** three parking *lots are* to be funded. (The subject nearer the verb is plural [lots]; therefore, the verb [are] must be plural.)

— — —

Either three parking *lots* **or** a parking **building** *is* to be funded. (The subject nearer the verb is singular [building]; therefore, the verb [is] must be singular.)

However, the rule fails to consider the effect on the reader or the listener when the singular subject is listed after the plural one. *Either three parking lots or a parking building is to be funded* "reads" awkwardly and "sounds" strange. The solution: When one subject is singular and the other is plural, place the plural one last and follow it with a plural verb.

5. *Other* or *Else* in Comparisons

When we compare persons, places or things with other persons, places or things from the same grouping or class (such as newspapers with other newspapers, photographers with other photographers, or advertisements with other advertisements), we need to insert either **other** or **else** to make the comparisons clear.

The basketball team's center said he is **taller than anyone** in his family. (That's impossible. The center is a member of his family, and he certainly is not taller than himself. Therefore, the sentence should include ***else*** after **anyone** to remove him from the other family members with whom he is being compared.)

— — —

"Last night's broadcast was **worse than any** I've ever heard." (Last night's broadcast cannot be worse than itself; therefore, ***other*** needs to be inserted between **any** and **I've** to remove last night's broadcast from the others with which it is being compared.)

Of course, we can eliminate the entire problem by writing that the team's center is the **tallest** person in his family and that last night's broadcast was the **worst** ever heard.

6. Commas between Adjectives

When several words are used to modify the same noun or pronoun, the writer must decide whether to place commas between them. If the adjectives are *coordinate,* they modify the noun or the pronoun equally and commas go between them. If they are not coordinate, no commas are used.

Two simple tests will tell the writer whether commas are needed. If the coordinating conjunction ***and*** makes sense between the adjectives, commas are needed. If the adjectives can be interchanged without harming the meaning of the sentence, commas are needed.

The **cool summer** breeze provided relief to players at the football training camp. (**Cool** and **summer** are not coordinate adjectives. Neither test works on them. **And** makes no sense inserted between them, and neither does interchanging them.)

— — —

The new reporter's **spelling, punctuation** and **grammar** skills are highly developed, the city editor said. (**Spelling, punctuation** and **grammar** are coordinate adjectives. **And** makes sense between them, and they can be interchanged without harming the meaning of the sentence.)

7. Apostrophes Showing Joint and Separate Ownership

Add an **'s** only to the last noun to indicate joint ownership.

Ed and Wilma***'s*** Coffee Shoppe will open Jan. 10.

The winning entry is Ed and Wilma***'s.***

— — —

Add an **'s** to each noun to indicate separate ownership.

Wilma***'s*** and Ed***'s*** spouses are physicians.

Some of the diplomas on the office wall are Wilma***'s,*** and some are Ed***'s.***

8. No Colon Needed

Let Your Ear Be Your Guide. A colon is not needed after a verb used to introduce a list or a series unless a pause is clearly necessary.

No colon is needed after the verb in the following sentence because no pause is needed:

The five winners **are** Kesha V. Snow, Wade C. Canterbury, Livingston P. Stone, Travis D. Willis and Nikki A. Forrester.

— — —

A colon is needed after the verb in the following sentence because a pause is clearly intended before the list:

The following states **were represented:** Alaska, Florida, New Mexico, Missouri, Vermont and West Virginia.

9. Comma or Semicolon?

Words such as *however, therefore, nevertheless, consequently, subsequently, moreover* and *furthermore* create a punctuation problem for many writers. They are preceded sometimes by a semicolon, sometimes by a comma and sometimes by no punctuation.

As **conjunctive adverbs,** these words join two complete sentences and are preceded by a semicolon and followed by a comma:

The candidate's plane was delayed in Oklahoma; **therefore,** his speech had to be postponed. (**Therefore** joins two complete sentences.)

— — —

As **parenthetical adverbs,** these words are usually preceded and followed by commas:

> "I can tell you, **however,** that the election will be won by my party," the governor said. (As a parenthetical adverb, **however,** is used for emphasis or to make the transition smoother. It does not join two complete sentences, and that is why the first comma is used instead of a semicolon.)

— — —

Although commas are generally in order before and after parenthetical adverbs, some grammarians suggest that commas are unnecessary if no pause is needed or intended:

> The poll results were so disappointing that the candidate **consequently** withdrew from the election.

For a detailed explanation of the use of semicolons and commas with **conjunctive adverbs** and **parenthetical adverbs,** please refer to pages 136–138.

10. Commas and Dependent Clauses

Read virtually any mass communications publication, and you will notice quickly that the combination of commas and clauses leads to considerable confusion. **Nonessential** dependent clauses should be set off by commas from the rest of the sentence; **essential** dependent clauses are not set off by commas.

A nonessential dependent clause provides information that adds to but does not affect the meaning of the independent clause. Nonessential clauses may be omitted without harming the meaning of the independent clause. Conversely, essential dependent clauses affect the meaning of the independent clause and cannot be omitted. Therefore, no commas are used to set off essential clauses.

The way to determine whether a dependent clause is essential is to read the sentence with the clause included and then to read the sentence with the clause omitted. If the meaning of the independent clause is unchanged by the omission, the dependent clause is nonessential and must be set off with commas. If the meaning of the independent clause is changed by the omission, the dependent clause is essential and no commas are used.

> News reporters, ***most of whom are notorious for their skepticism,*** question whatever they doubt. (The meaning of the independent clause—News reporters question whatever they doubt—is unaffected by the omission of the **nonessential** dependent clause.)

— — —

> Club members **who arrive before 6 p.m.** will be admitted free. (The meaning of the independent clause—Club members will be admitted free—is affected by the omission of the **essential** dependent clause. Only the club members who arrive before 6 p.m. will be admitted free.)

11. Choosing between *It's* and *Its* and *Who's* and *Whose*

The solution is simple. **It's** and **who's** are contractions for **it is** and **who is.** ***Its*** and ***whose*** (without the apostrophe) are possessive pronouns. When confused about which to use, just say **it is** or **who is** at the point where the word is to be placed in the sentence. Your ear will provide the answer.

> **"It's [contraction for it is]** a good news story," the editor said, "but *its* **[possessive pronoun]** potential for disrupting the election is troubling."

— — —

> **"Who's [contraction for who is]** responsible for missing the assignment and ***whose*** **[possessive pronoun]** job is likely to be lost as a result?"

— — —

> **It is** and **who is** make no sense when substituted for the possessive pronouns ***its*** and ***whose***

12. When (and When Not) to Use *self* and *selves*

Pronouns ending in **self** in the singular and ***selves*** in the plural are used in only two circumstances (see pages 69–71 for numerous examples). These pronouns are classified as ***intensive*** when they are used for emphasis and ***reflexive*** when they come after the verb and refer to the subject. Please remember that words ending in **self** and **selves** must have a clearly established antecedent, a noun or a pronoun to which they refer.

Intensive

"If you can't do it, I will finish the article **myself,**" the angry city editor said. (The antecedent of **myself** is the pronoun **I.**)

— — —

> The editors ***themselves*** are to blame for setting such severe deadlines, the reporters claimed. (The antecedent of ***themselves*** is the noun **editors.**)

— — —

> **Myself** and ***themselves*** are not needed for the sentences to make sense. They are used only for emphasis.

Reflexive

> "When I slipped on the stadium steps, I hurt ***myself,"*** the reporter said. (The antecedent of **myself** is the pronoun **I.**)

— — —

The graphic artists brought honor to **themselves** and to their company when they won first prize in the regional competition. (The antecedent of **themselves** is the noun **graphic artists.**)

Reflexive pronouns must be used. The sentences would make no sense without them.

When Not to Use self and selves

Belinda and **myself** will share responsibility for the projects. (***I*** is the correct choice for the subject of the sentence. There is no antecedent for **myself.**)

— — —

"That decision will be made by the advertising director or **myself** at the appropriate time," the graphic arts director said. (***Me*** is the correct choice for an object that does not refer to the subject. There is no antecedent for **myself.**)

— — —

"We're just fine, thank you for asking. How are **yourselves**? (***You*** is the correct choice. There is no antecedent for ***yourselves.***)

13. When to Use *Were* or *Was* after If

The subjunctive mood (see pages 106–108) has always been tricky. It requires us to use the plural **were** after a singular subject to express a wish (I wish I ***were*** a wealthy network news anchor) or a condition contrary to fact (If the **center** on our basketball team ***were*** taller, he would be a better rebounder).

That's not too hard to understand. We recognize that a wish does not represent the truth, and we know that saying *if I were smarter,* if *she were more patient, if my boss were more flexible* does not represent reality.

The difficulty is choosing between **was** and ***were*** when they are preceded by **if. If** is a conditional word. It represents a supposition or an uncertain possibility, regardless of whether it is followed by **was** or ***were***.

Here's the solution. If you are expressing a wish or something that definitely is not true, use **were**:

If he **were** taller, he could wear his brother's clothes. (He is not taller.)

— — —

If Jane **were** more patient, people would like her better (She is not more patient.)

— — —

If I **were** you, I would finish earning that college degree. (I'm not you.)

If you are using a clause that starts with **if** and you are expressing something that could be true, use ***was:***

"If the police chief ***was*** wrong, I did not know it," the reporter explained to her editor. (The police chief could have been wrong. That could be true.)

— — —

"If I ***was*** impatient, I beg your pardon," the advertising client said. (The advertising client could have been impatient. That could be true.)

— — —

"If the defendant ***was*** not guilty, then the jury made a big mistake," the prosecutor said. (The defendant could be innocent. That could be true.)

14. When (and When Not) to Use *Of* after *All, Both, and Off*

Using ***of*** after **all, both,** and **off** does no great harm. It is just sometimes untidy and wordy. A few examples should eliminate any doubt about when and when not to include ***of***.

The best guideline is to trust your ear. Say or write the phrase with and without **of:**

(Wordy but not awkward)	Juan asked **all of** the editors for advice.
(Better)	Juan asked **all** the editors for advice.

— — —

(All right but wordy)	**Both** ***of*** them are members of Congress.
(Clearly awkward)	**Both** them are members of Congress.
(Best)	**Both** are members of Congress.

— — —

(Wordy)	The referee pulled the tackler **off** ***of*** the quarterback.
(Better)	The referee pulled the tackler **off** the quarterback.

— — —

Omitting ***of*** before a **pronoun** is awkward and sounds bad to the ear **(both** ***us*** want to succeed, **all** ***them*** hope for advancement, **all** ***ours*** are stored in the closet).

Omitting ***of*** before a **noun** is not awkward and sounds all right to the ear (**both** ***photographers*** are award-winners, **all** ***students*** must pass the final examination). Of course, **both** ***of*** the photographers and **all** ***of*** the students sound all right, too. They are just wordy

* * *

Of is rarely needed after **off**.

The computer fell **off** (***not off of***) the table.

"Please get **off** ***[not off of]*** my back," the frustrated council member told the mayor.

That program is being taken **off** (***not off*** **of**) the schedule.

One of the exceptions might be the following:

"I do not want fingerprints on the photograph," the editor warned. "Please take your hand **off** ***of*** it." (**Off** ***of*** sounds better than just **off** it, but please don't touch it sounds even better.)

15. When to follow *Than* with *I or Me, He* or *Him, She* or *Her, We* or *Us, They* or *Them*

Most of us have to pause when choosing between these pairs of pronouns at the end of a sentence in which a comparison is being made. Do we say or write that Samantha Pinkston is a better writer **than I** or **than me**? Let's work our way to the correct answer by considering three points.

1. Nominative case pronouns (including **I, he, she, we** and **they**) function as subjects in these comparisons. Objective case pronouns (including ***me, him, her, us*** and ***them***) serve as objects. Therefore, if we want a subject to follow **than,** we choose from the nominative case pronouns; if we want an object to follow **than**, we choose from the objective case pronouns.
2. The confusion comes from the words we omit. If we put those words back in, our choice is simpler: Samantha Pinkston writes better **than *I* write**. We would never hesitate in choosing between **I write** and ***me write.***
3. Some people think that ending a sentence with **than I/he/she/we/they** sounds stuffy, formal or pretentious because in casual conversation most people say ***than me/him/her/us/them.*** If you don't want to risk sounding stuffy, put the verb back in and you won't.

* * *

Let's consider these three points in determining which pronoun case to use in each of the following examples:

"We are upset with the public relations director because he gave better assignments to the new employees **than we/*us.*"**

(The answer is ***us***. With the omitted words restored, the complete sentence is "We are upset with the public relations director because he gave better assignments to the new employees than he gave to us." The objective case ***us*** is needed because it serves as the object of the preposition to.)

— — —

"I should earn my college degree sooner than my sister because I am one year older **<u>than</u>** **<u>she</u>**/***<u>her</u>***."

(The answer is **<u>she</u>**. The complete sentence is "I should earn my college degree sooner than my sister because I am one year older <u>than she is</u>. The nominative case **<u>she</u>** serves as the subject of the verb is.)

* * *

If the words omitted cause the sentence to sound too ambiguous, restore the missing words. Reducing wordiness is a worthwhile goal, but not if it causes miscommunication. Consider the following example:

Our professor gave my fellow students more credit for their work on the project **<u>than I</u>**/***<u>me</u>*.**

(Either **<u>I</u>** or ***<u>me</u>*** could be correct. **<u>Than I</u>** means the professor gave the other students more credit than I did. ***<u>Than me</u>*** means the professor gave the other students more credit than he gave me. To make the meaning clear, restore the missing words.)

(You may test yourself on the material in this chapter or section by connecting with the following Web site: www.mhhe.com/arnold.)

THE TROUBLE WITH "ONLY" chapter 5

How the Use of *Only* Can Be Insensitive

The use of **only** presents potential problems for the unwary. First, it can be insensitive if used in connection with death, serious injury or other significant loss. Second, it can give an unintended meaning to a sentence if placed where it does not belong.

The following are examples of the first problem.

Only four American soldiers died during the three-day battle.

— — —

Twenty cars collided in the chain-reaction wreck during thick fog early today, but **only** one person was seriously injured.

— — —

All 10 mountain climbers rescued Thursday suffered frostbite, but **only** one had to have part of a foot amputated, according to hospital reports.

In one respect, the use of **only** seems justified. More deaths, injuries and amputations would be expected under such circumstances. However, few editors or other media managers would permit employees to use **only** in these examples. The word is far too insensitive to the families of those affected, as well as to other readers, listeners and viewers who surely would be offended.

Furthermore, **only** is unnecessary. Leaving it out harms neither dramatic impact nor comprehension. Rewrite the sentences as follows:

Four American soldiers died during the three-day battle.

— — —

Twenty cars collided early today in a chain-reaction wreck during thick fog, and one person was seriously injured.

or

One person suffered serious injury early today when 20 cars collided in a chain-reaction wreck in thick fog.

— — —

All 10 mountain climbers rescued Thursday suffered frostbite, and one had to have part of a foot amputated.

In a situation in which the number of deaths, serious injuries or other significant loss is so extraordinarily low that it requires mention, use the words of a news source.

"We're fortunate that more people were not injured in that 20-car pile-up," Sgt. R.S. Martinez of the Milton County Police Department said. "If drivers had not been traveling slowly, we could have had a disaster."

— — —

"Considering the extreme weather conditions, it's a miracle that we were able to rescue any of those mountain climbers," Capt. Bernis M. Johnston of the State Park Service said. "I'm amazed that more of them didn't suffer severe frostbite."

How the Incorrect Placement of *Only* Can Cause Misunderstanding

The second problem is a little harder to solve because writers and broadcasters can misplace **only** in a sentence without realizing what they have done. Observe how moving **only** gives a different meaning to the following sentence: The mayor said that he made one major error in his failed re-election bid.

The mayor said that he made **only** one major error in his failed re-election bid. (This means he made only one mistake.)

— — —

The mayor said **only** that he made one major error in his failed re-election bid. (This means he said only one thing.)

— — —

Only the mayor said he made one major error in his failed re-election bid. (This means the mayor was the only person to say he made a major error.)

The Erroneous Use of *One of the Only*

A third troublemaker is the increasing misuse of the phrase **one of the only.** It is used erroneously as follows:

Hairston is **one of the only** professional receivers to catch more than 100 passes in a single season.

— — —

She is **one of the only** officers of the company to serve as president for more than 25 years.

— — —

He is **one of the only** writers to win both a National Author's Award and a J.A. Sutherland Medal.

A person may be ***the only* one**, but he or she cannot be ***one of the* only.** The former is always restricted to one person, place, thing or group; the latter always refers to more than one.

The solution is to change **one of the only** to **one of only 10,** or whatever the specific number is. If the number is unknown, **one of only a few** should suffice. Please note that **only** is used just for emphasis. The phrases also could be written as **one of 10** or **one of a few.**

The three erroneous examples can be rewritten as follows:

Hairston is **one of only 10** professional receivers to catch more than 100 passes in a single season.

Hairston is **one of 10** professional receivers to catch more than 100 passes in a single season.

— — —

She is **one of only a few** officers of the company to serve as president for more than 25 years.

She is **one of a few** officers of the company to serve as president for more than 25 years.

— — —

He is **one of only a few** writers to win both a National Author's Award and a J.A. Sutherland Medal.

He is **one of a few** writers to win both a National Author's Award and a J.A. Sutherland Medal.

How to Avoid Problems in Using *Only*

To avoid problems in using **only,** writers and broadcasters should take care to place it directly before the word that represents whoever or whatever is the lone or the sole one.

"I need **only** one internship to complete requirements for graduation," the student said.

— — —

"We want a deadline extension of **only** two days," the photographer told her editor.

— — —

The thieves reportedly took **only** $5, $10 and $20 bills in the robbery at the First National Bank.

Obviously, **only** should arouse warnings of danger whenever writers and broadcasters are tempted to use it. And that's a good thing. **Only** deserves that much caution.

(You may test yourself on the material in this chapter or section by connecting with the following Web site: www.mhhe.com/arnold.)

ONE POTATO, TWO POTATOES

chapter 6

Forming Plurals and Possessives from Words Ending in ch, sh, x, s, sis, ss, zz, y, and o

Forming plurals from singular words is usually easy, as we all know. We just add an **s**: girl to girl**s**, tree to tree**s**, school to school**s**, and dog to dog**s**.

Likewise, forming possessives from singular words requires just an **apostrophe** and an **s**: boy to boy**'s**, Smith to Smith**'s**, team to team**'s**, and writer to writer**'s**.

Making plural possessives takes two easy steps. We make a singular word plural by adding an **s** and place an **apostrophe** after the **s** to make it possessive: girl**s'**, writer**s'**, and dog**s'**.

If forming plurals and possessives were this simple for all words, each of us would have mastered the entire process in elementary school. Unfortunately, like so many other aspects of the English language, there are troublesome exceptions. Included among them are words that end in **ch**, **sh**, **x**, **s**, **sis**, **ss**, **zz**, **y**, and **o**.

The good news is that rules exist for making plurals with these words endings. The bad news is that even the rules for these exceptions sometimes have exceptions.

Frustrating? Yes.

Unconquerable? No.

Worth the time and effort? Yes, especially if you are or want to be a professional writer.

Forming Challenging Plurals

Add *es* to Form Plurals from Words Ending in *ch*, *sh*, *x*, *s*, *ss*, and *zz*

Words ending in *ch*		Words ending in *sh*
batch**es**	hitch**es**	accomplish**es**
bleach**es**	itch**es**	blush**es**
botch**es**	nich**es**	brush**es**
catch**es**	notch**es**	crush**es**
ditch**es**	peach**es**	distinguish**es**

glitch**es**	pitch**es**	gush**es**
reach**es**	switch**es**	push**es**
rich**es**	twitch**es**	rush**es**
snitch**es**	watch**es**	shush**es**
stretch**es**	witch**es**	slush**es**

Words ending in *x*

box**es**
fax**es**
hoax**es**
prefix**es**
tax**es**
wax**es**

Words ending in *s*

bus**es**
caucus**es**
census**es**
genius**es**
plus**es**
thesaurus**es**

Words ending in *ss*

address**es**	glass**es**
boss**es**	harass**es**
business**es**	hiss**es**
compress**es**	loss**es**
cross**es**	mass**es**
dress**es**	miss**es**
embarrass**es**	pass**es**
fuss**es**	suppress**es**

Words ending in *zz*

buzz**es**
fizz**es**
razz**es**
quizz**es** (double the **z**)

Change the Singular sis *Ending to* ses *for the Plural*

analy**sis**	analy**ses**
cri**sis**	cri**ses**
diagno**sis**	diagno**ses**
hypno**sis**	hypno**ses**
progno**sis**	progno**ses**
synop**sis**	synop**ses**

If y *is Preceded by a Vowel, Just Add an* s

all**e**y*s*	pl**o**y*s*
attorn**e**y*s*	Mond**a**y*s* (and all other days of the week)
bu**o**y*s*	r**a**y*s*
b**o**y*s*	rel**a**y*s*
j**o**y*s*	t**o**y*s*
nowad**a**y*s*	yesterd**a**y*s*
parl**a**y*s*	

If Proper Nouns End in y, *Just Add an* s

Barry	I know three **Barry**s.
Farley	There are six **Farley**s in our neighborhood.
Hundley	The **Hundley**s all become lawyers.
Mary	The class list includes three **Mary**s.

If y *is Preceded by a Consonant, Drop the* y *and Add* ies

apolo***gies***	dictiona***ries***
balco***nies***	dormito***ries***
catego***ries***	ju***ries***
colo***nies***	laborato***ries***
courte***sies***	sto***ries***

Add s *or* es *to Form Plurals From Words Ending in* o

Most Words Ending in o Follow the Traditional Rule of Adding Just an s

cell**o** to cello**s**
crescend**o** to crescendo**s**
pian**o** to piano**s**
radi**o** to radio**s**
rati**o** to ratio**s**
studi**o** to studio**s**
zer**o** to zero**s**
zo**o** to zoo**s**

Some Words Ending in o Add es to Form a Plural

ech**o** to echo**es**
her**o** to hero**es**
mosquit**o** to mosquito**es**
potat**o** to potato**es**
tomat**o** to tomato**es**
vet**o** to veto**es**

Dictionaries List Some Others with Both Endings

carg**o** to cargo**s**/cargo**es**
placeb**o** to placebo**s**/placebo**es**
lass**o** to lasso**s**/lasso**es**
mement**o** to memento**s**/memento**es**
tornad**o** to tornado**s**/tornado**es**

How much help do we get from the examples with **"os"** or **"oes"** endings? Certainly not enough to make us feel confident that we know how to form all the plurals from words ending in **o.** However, just knowing that not all end in just s is valuable. That will send us to our traditional and electronic dictionaries and stylebooks to check those words that we have not committed to memory.

Forming Challenging Possessives

Proper Nouns that End in s

Singular*	**Singular possessive**
Charles	Charles' or Charles**'s**
Chris	Chris' or Chris**'s**
Bess	Bess' or Bess**'s**
Hayes	Hayes' or Hayes**'s**
Jones	Jones' or Jones**'s**
Lucas	Lucas' or Lucas**'s**
Roberts	Roberts' or Roberts**'s**
Williams	Williams' or Williams**'s**
Willis	Willis' or Willis**'s**

Plural	**Plural possessive**
Hayes**es**	the Hayes**es'** house
Jones**es**	the Jones**es'** children
Lucas**es**	the Lucas**es'** computer
Roberts**es**	the Roberts**es'** annual picnic
Williams**es**	the Williams**es'** college fund
Willis**es**	the Willis**es'** new car

*Journalists following the Associated Press style use only **s'.** For formal English, use **s's.**

Common Nouns with a Variety of Endings

Grammarians once frowned upon the use of an apostrophe to show possession for inanimate objects. They did so so for at least two reasons. For one, they insisted that inanimate objects like trees and buildings cannot possess anything (the tree's branches, the building's ledge). For another, they preferred rewriting the possessive to avoid using an apostrophe (the branches of the tree, the ledge of the building).

However, the advice now is to trust your ear. If "the university's president" and "the city's oldest building" sound all right, use them. If "the president of the university" and "the oldest building in the city" sound better, use them.

To avoid violating style, check your school's or your company's stylebook. If an apostrophe is permitted, follow the same possessive form as you would for people.

With an apostrophe	**Without an apostrophe**
the building**'s** ledge	the ledge of the building
the buildings' ledges	the ledges of the buildings

the tree**'s** trunk the tree**s'** trunks	the trunk of the tree the trunks of the trees
the dress**'**/dress**'s** neckline the dress**es'** necklines	the neckline of the dress the necklines of the dresses
the box**'s** border the box**es'** borders	the border of the box the borders of the boxes
the tomato**'s** shape the tomato**es'** shapes	the shape of the tomato the shapes of the tomatoes
the zoo**'s** animals the zoo**s'** animals	the animals in the zoo the animals in the zoos
the balcony**'s** design the balcon**ies'** designs	the design of the balcony the designs of the balconies

Something Fun (At Least by Grammarians' Standards)

The following just beg to be corrected by grammarians—and everyone else who has gone through the drudgery involved in language study:

1. A yard sign proclaiming that "The Johnson'**s**" live there instead of "The Johnson**s.**" *("Johnson'**s**" refers to one person who possesses something.)*
2. A name on a mailbox informing the mail carrier that the container belongs to "the Barkl**ies**" instead of **"**the Barkle**ys."** *(Proper nouns that end in **y** just add an **s** to form a plural.)*
3. An engraved stone that identifies the occupants of the house as "The Jones**"** instead of "The Jones**es."** *("The Jones" refers to one person.)*
4. A classified advertisement that informs potential employees that recruiters from "20 compan**y's**" will be present instead of "20 compan**ies.**" ("*Compan**y's*** refers to one company that owns something.)
5. A speaker at any function who warns of "impending cris**ises"** instead of "cri**ses.**" *(Words that end in **sis** change to **ses** for the plural.)*

Be aware, of course, that not everyone who makes these errors will appreciate having them pointed out. Be tactful. A superior attitude or a condescending manner will not be rewarded. Pestering, however, is permissible.

(You may test yourself on the material in this chapter or section by connecting with the following Web site: www.mhhe.com/arnold.)

Building Sentences

part 2

Introduction

The eight parts of speech are the building blocks of the English language. Each has clearly defined individual roles to play, but they combine to form phrases and clauses that enable us to communicate in ways ranging from the very simple to the most complex.

Perhaps the best way to gain a confident attitude about using parts of speech correctly and effectively is to consider them as a cohesive group instead of as isolated parts. In the 12 chapters that follow, we will examine each part of speech individually but with the goal of connecting one with the other as we progress. They are all brought together in the final Part 2 chapter, "Sentences and Syntax."

After spending years acquiring language skills, college students, professional mass communicators and teachers may have difficulty summoning enthusiasm for re-examining nouns, pronouns, verbs, adjectives, adverbs, prepositions, conjunctions and interjections. Reviewing parts of speech probably has about as much appeal as sitting through an old movie they didn't like much the first time.

However, watching as an adult a movie seen previously as a child or as a teenager can have some surprising and worthwhile effects. The experience each of us has gained in the intervening period can make us more sympathetic to the characters' plight. Maturity can provide insights, perspective and understanding not yet developed during the first viewing.

The same can be true for a fresh study of language skills and common writing and editing problems when they haven't been concentrated on for a while. Because we have become more aware of our communications deficiencies and the problems they cause us, we will have more incentive and willingness to learn.

The presentation of parts of speech is comprehensive for those with fundamental language needs. However, the organization also allows faster movement for those whose needs range from a good review to a little brushing up.

chapter 7

NOUNS

Functions

As a rule, words do not function as ***a*** part of speech; they may function as several. The part of speech is determined by how a word is used in a sentence. For example, we all know that **Australia** is a **proper noun** because it is the name of a country. But we can make **Australia** and other proper nouns function as **adjectives** by using them in the possessive case (One of **Australia's** major exports is wool). Similarly, **occurred** is a past tense verb, but we can make a **noun** out of it by using it as the subject of a sentence (**Occurred** is a frequently misspelled word). In addition, **whose** can be a **pronoun** (**Whose** is this?) or an **adjective** (**Whose** newspaper is this?).

Remember, the way a word functions in relation to other words in a sentence is much more important than any part-of-speech label it may usually wear. We should keep this in mind as we study nouns, pronouns, verbs, adjectives, adverbs, prepositions, conjunctions and interjections. For each part of speech, we'll review what it is, what it does, what its relationship is to other words or groups of words in sentences and how it is often misused.

Perhaps the best place to start a study of nouns is to recall the lessons our elementary school teachers taught us. They told us that **nouns** are the words we use to identify **people** (such as ***editors, public relations directors, advertisers, friends*** and ***neighbors***), **places** (such as the ***newsroom, city hall,*** the ***football stadium*** and ***New York***), and **things** (such as ***computers, television cameras, magazines*** and ***dreams***).

If we could stop with this simple definition, nouns would cause no problems. People, places and things are easy to identify. However, nouns have other qualities that we sometimes find confusing and consequently misuse. As we consider the following points, identify those that cause you difficulty.

Nouns May Be Concrete *or* Abstract

This one is easy. College students and professional mass communicators have few or no problems with it, but let's review it briefly just to make certain.

If a noun has a **visible form** (as do a ***pencil,*** a ***notebook*** and a ***microphone***), it is **concrete.** If a noun **lacks a visible form** (as do ***love, friendship*** and ***democracy***), it is **abstract.**

Nouns May Be Proper *or* Common

This one is a little more difficult. We all know that **proper nouns** are capitalized because they refer to specific people, places or things and that **common nouns** are not capitalized and refer to any one of a group of people, places or things. We have no problem differentiating between proper and common nouns when considering **people** such as ***Sally L. Cunningham*** and ***citizens,*** **places** such as ***Cleveland*** and the ***baseball field,*** and **things** such as the ***Washington Monument*** and ***coffee cups.*** We do have difficulty choosing between proper and common nouns when referring to people by their titles.

Journalists usually capitalize brief titles used directly **before** a person's name (**Captain** Wingate, **President** Treadway and **Senator** Menendez), but we usually use lowercase letters for titles—brief or long—when they **follow** a person's name (LaDonna J. Barbour, **senior vice president** for marketing; Josh R. Ridgeville, **manager** of social services; and Chris C. Eplin, **executive director** of the Fairmont Advertising Agency).

You will recall from Chapter 1 (page 6) that journalists capitalize less frequently than writers in some other fields. They also place titles **before** names only if they would feel comfortable addressing the person that way on the street. Mass communicators would feel comfortable calling someone **Senator** Menendez but uncomfortable addressing the person as **Junior Republican Senator from Iowa** Menendez.

When in doubt about whether to capitalize a title or whether to place the title before or after the person's name, consult *The Associated Press Stylebook* or your school's or company's guidelines. If your question is not addressed in the stylebook, follow the advice in the previous paragraphs.

Nouns Have Gender (Masculine, Feminine, Neuter, Common)

Some languages apply masculine or feminine gender to virtually everything whether it is animate or inanimate. Fortunately, gender in the English language is easily determined. **Males,** both human and animal, are **masculine gender; females** are **feminine gender; inanimate objects** (such as *film, tests* and *money*) are **neuter gender;** and nouns that can refer to males or females or include **both males and females** (such as *students, photographers, graphic artists* and *professors*) are **common gender.**

Nouns May Be Singular *or* Plural *(a Quality Called* Number*)*

If you can count to two, you should be able to distinguish **singular** ***(one)*** from **plural** ***(two or more).*** Right? Regrettably, it's wrong. Dealing with **number** can be puzzling and tricky.

Number is complicated by **collective nouns** that describe more than one person, place or thing but act as a unit and therefore take **singular** verbs ***(team, group, flock);*** by words that appear **plural in form** but are **singular in meaning** ***(mathematics, mumps, news);*** and even by some **compound subjects joined by the conjunction** ***and*** that take **singular verbs** if they are dealt with **individually** (***each desk*** **and**

***every drawer was* searched**) or if they **jointly constitute one thing (*vinegar and oil is* a salad dressing).**

However, most of the time, determining whether a noun is singular or plural is as easy as counting to two. If you are considering **one** person *(Mayor Javier),* **one** place *(a courtroom)* or **one** thing *(a book),* the noun is **singular.** If you are considering **two or more** *(mayors, courtrooms, books),* the noun is **plural.**

Nouns alter their form when they change from singular to plural, usually by adding ***s, es*** or ***ies*** to the singular. One bo*y* becomes two or more bo***ys;*** one Jone*s* becomes two or more Jones***es;*** and one countr*y* becomes two or more countr***ies.*** Of course, some nouns develop from singular to plural by making more drastic changes in spelling (chil*d* to chil***dren,*** f*oo*t to f***ee***t, and m***ous***e to m***ic***e).

Another significant point is that nouns used as subjects determine what the number of the verb will be. If the **subject is singular,** the **verb will be singular** (The **mayor** *is* in his office). If the **subject is plural,** the **verb will be plural** (The **mayors** ***are*** attending the conference).

* * *

If the discussion ended at this point, singulars and plurals would present no problem except for spelling changes that require no more effort on the part of the writer than looking into a stylebook or a dictionary. The troublemakers are the collective nouns mentioned earlier. They require more explanation and study.

The **collective noun** sometimes confuses even the experienced writer or broadcaster. Words such as ***team, group, jury*** and ***flock*** usually are **singular** even though they comprise more than one person, place or thing. A team, regardless of how many members it has, is just one team. The same goes for a group, a jury or a flock. The team (group, jury, flock) functions as one unit; therefore, it is considered singular most of the time. The ***team*** *is* playing *its* 15th game. The ***jury*** *is* composed of eight women and four men. The ***flock*** of sheep *is* grazing on the hillside.

The problem is that **collective nouns also can be plural** at times. A journalist can write or broadcast that the **faculty *is*** meeting at 4 p.m. Friday. **Faculty** in this example is used as a collective singular, meaning that the faculty as a whole is meeting. A journalist also can write or broadcast that **faculty *are*** in their offices meeting with students. **Faculty** in this example is used as a plural because the individual teachers are functioning apart from one another.

The singular-plural problem can be overcome easily by using exclusively as singulars such collective words as ***faculty, team, group*** and ***jury.*** When a plural is wanted, **faculty** can become ***professors, teachers*** or faculty ***members.*** **Jury** can become ***jurors*** or ***members*** of the jury, and so forth.

* * *

This final reminder about collective nouns may be unnecessary, but it could eliminate a potentially confusing situation you might encounter. If you communicate with someone from England, do not be surprised when he or she uses a plural verb with family, team, Parliament or other words Americans consider collective singulars. We say my **family *is*** visiting; they say my **family *are*** visiting. We refer to a collective unit; they refer to individuals. This is just one of several peculiar differences in the way Americans and English use their "common" language.

Some words that end in ***s*** and therefore appear plural are used collectively with **singular** verbs: The **news** on the front page ***was*** (not ***were***) rather boring in today's paper. **Physics *is*** (not ***are***) a difficult subject for most students. Although **mumps *is*** (not ***are***) a common disease among children, it is potentially dangerous. Fifty **dollars *is*** (not ***are***) too much to pay for a roll of film.

* * *

Singular-plural confusion also is common for compound subjects joined by ***and*** but taking a singular verb. After all, this is atypical; most compound subjects take plural verbs. The **singular verb** is used if each subject is considered individually: **Each desk** and **every drawer** ***was*** (not ***were***) searched.

A **singular verb** also is used when **either/or** or **neither/nor** precedes two singular subjects: ***Neither* the president *nor* the vice president *was*** (not ***were***) available for comment.

Even if **one subject is plural** and **the other is singular,** use the **singular verb** if the last subject is singular: ***Either* two playgrounds *or* a swimming pool *is*** to be built with the surplus funds, the mayor said. However, because this construction sounds awkward even though it is grammatically correct, you would be better off **always placing the plural noun last** and using a plural verb: ***Either* a swimming pool *or* two playgrounds *are*** to be built with the surplus funds, the mayor said.

* * *

Several other factors also influence whether noun subjects take plural or singular verbs. For additional information, see indefinite pronouns on pages 72–73, subject-verb agreement on pages 124–126, and "none as a singular, none as a plural" on page 34.

Nouns Also Have a Quality Called *Person*

Person refers to the one speaking (**first** *person*), the one spoken to (**second** *person*), and the person, place, or thing spoken or written about (**third** *person*). **Nouns** are used almost exclusively in the **third person.** Journalists write or broadcast that City Council **members** passed an ordinance, or that **sidewalks** will be repaired, or that **Henry P. Carlton** and **Margaret E. Rush** were elected to office. All of the examples in the previous sentence are ***third-person*** nouns—persons, places or things being written or spoken about.

Nouns of direct address, which print journalists rarely use, are ***second person*** because they are used to address people directly, usually to get their attention or to make them feel that they are being involved personally. Broadcast journalists sometimes say, "**Picnickers,** you'd better pack an umbrella in your basket today because the probability of rain is 80 percent." In this example, **picnickers** is the noun being addressed directly, making it second person.

If you need a few more examples to understand fully what a noun of direct address is, consider the following:

"**Mr. Mayor,** do you think you'll have the funds to open all city swimming pools this year?"

— — —

"I've been told, **Mary,** that you are the best photographer on the staff."

— — —

"**LeRon,** I am going to make you the news director of our station in Las Vegas."

— — —

"**Friends,** you are the reason I decided to move my advertising headquarters to the city where I was born."

The only way for a noun to be used in the ***first person*** is when a father, for example, says to his child: "**Dad** wants you to take a nap." Except in this circumstance in which an individual refers to himself by the name his children call him, substitute pronouns for nouns to shift to the first or second person. Use the pronoun **I** instead of your own name to express yourself in the first person (**I** want you to run the campaign). When talking or writing directly to an individual, use the pronoun **you** instead of the person's name (I want **you** to run the campaign).

Journalists quote sources directly in the first person ("**I** will veto the bill," the president said). But they do not use the first person without quoting unless they are directly involved in the story themselves. Any time journalists write or broadcast the words **I, we, me, us, our** or **ours** without putting them in quotation marks, they are referring to themselves. Print journalists avoid inserting themselves into the story unless they are a part of the event (such as accompanying a mountain-climbing team or giving a first-person account of what it is like to go down a bobsled course). Broadcast journalists sometimes permit themselves to use first-person involvement in otherwise objective reports ("**We're** in for a six-inch snowfall today").

Nouns Are Classified or Grouped by *Case:* *Nominative, Objective* and *Possessive*

Case is deceptively important and is the source of a variety of embarrassing problems for the unaware. However, pronouns, not nouns, are the major troublemakers. We get a merciful break with nouns. **Nouns** are **spelled and pronounced** the same in both the nominative and the objective cases. Most pronouns change their spelling from one case to another. Nouns change their form only in the possessive, and even then they could hardly be confusing because **possessive case nouns always have an apostrophe** before or after an ***s*** at the end of each word.

To be classified as possessive case, a noun must change its form. To show possession, a noun must add an apostrophe (John*'s,* girl*'s,* boy*s',* journalist*s',* men*'s,* child***'s***, children***'s*** and so forth). Where the apostrophe is positioned in relation to the *s* depends on whether the noun is singular (John*'s*) or plural (girl*s'*) and the spelling used to form the plural (editor*s',* women*'s*). For more detailed information on how nouns are used in the possessive case, please turn to the section on apostrophes on pages 205–208.

* * *

Case classifies nouns according to the function each performs in a sentence. To be classified as **nominative case** (also called **subjective case**), a noun will function as one of the following:

1. A subject.

The **governor** will arrive at 7 p.m.

2. An appositive to another nominative case noun.

Albert A. Swanson, **president** of Acme University, will resign effective July 1.

An **appositive** is a noun or a pronoun that follows another noun or pronoun and explains or identifies it. The appositive, which has no case of its own but assumes the case of the noun or pronoun it follows, may be a single word or contain additional modifying words.

In this example, **president** is a noun functioning as an appositive to **Albert A. Swanson.** The appositive further identifies Swanson by providing his title/occupation. Because Swanson is the subject and subjects are always in the nominative case, the appositive **(president)** also is in the nominative case.

3. A predicate noun.

LaDonna R. Pender is my **editor.**

A **predicate noun** follows a **nonaction verb** and renames (identifies, provides additional information about) the **subject.** In other words, the subject and the predicate noun are either the same person, the same place or the same thing.

In this example, **editor** is a **predicate noun** renaming the **subject. Editor** and **Pender** are the same person, and because of this direct relationship, the predicate noun takes the same case as the subject.

4. A noun of direct address.

"**Mr. Mayor,** are you pledging to eliminate the city income tax?"

In this example, the mayor is being addressed directly by a journalist asking a question. **Mr. Mayor** is the noun of direct address. The subject **you** is in the nominative case; therefore, the noun of direct address is also in nominative case.

* * *

To be classified as **objective case,** a noun will function as one of the following:

1. A direct object.

The heavyweight champion knocked out his **opponent.**

A **direct object** is a noun or a pronoun that follows an **action verb,** "answers" the question **whom** or **what,** and **receives the action** transmitted from the subject through the verb.

In this example, **opponent** is an **objective case** noun serving as a **direct object.** It "answers" the question **whom** after the verb (**knocked**) and receives the action transmitted from the subject (**champion**).

2. An indirect object.

The heavyweight champion gave his favorite **charity** $1 million.

Keep three things in mind when you are dealing with an **indirect object:**

a. An indirect object comes only in a sentence that already contains a direct object.

b. The indirect object positions itself between the action verb and the direct object.

c. Direct objects are used alone much more frequently than they are with indirect objects.

As noted in the previous example, we ask the questions **whom** or **what** after an **action verb** to determine whether the sentence contains a **direct object.** After finding that the sentence has a direct object, ask **to whom** or **to what** or **for whom** or **for what** to determine if an **indirect object** also is present.

In this example, **charity** is an objective case noun serving as an **indirect object.** It "answers" the question **to what** after the action verb (**gave**). The **direct object** is **$1 million,** which "answers" the question **what.**

Be careful not to confuse an **indirect object** with an **object of a preposition.** If we changed our example to *The heavyweight champion gave $1 million to his favorite charity,* we no longer would have an indirect object. **Charity** would become the **object of the preposition *to*.** Another reason **charity** cannot be an indirect object in this sentence is that it comes ***after*** the direct object. Indirect objects always come ***before*** direct objects.

3. The object of a preposition.

The governor read his State-of-the-State speech to the **legislators.**

The **object of a preposition** is a noun or a pronoun that follows a preposition (*to the* **game,** *up the* **tree,** *around the* **building,** *in front of the speaker's* **platform,** etc.). For additional explanations and examples, please refer to the section on prepositions on pages 144–150.

In this example, **legislators** serves as the object of the preposition ***to*** and tells to whom the governor read his speech.

4. An appositive to an objective case noun.

The governor handed a copy of his speech to Sen. Yvonne S. Minnix, **president** of the Senate.

You will recall from our explanation of nominative case nouns that **appositives** have no case. They assume the case of the noun or pronoun they follow. In this example, **Minnix** is an **objective case** noun serving as the **object of the preposition** ***to.*** **President** is a noun serving as an **appositive** to Minnix, and because Minnix is in the **objective case, president** is as well.

5. An objective complement.

The president called his negotiator a **genius.**

An **objective complement** follows an object and provides additional information about it. In this example, **genius** is an objective complement that provides additional information about the direct object **(negotiator).**

Gerunds and Infinitives as Nouns

Gerunds always function as nouns, and infinitives sometimes do. Members of the verbal family, gerunds and infinitives are more complicated than regular nouns because they often come in phrases.

Relaxing is not easy for a student taking a test in statistics.

The gerund **relaxing** functions as a noun and serves as the **subject** of the sentence.

— — —

Journalism historians love ***reading*** **old newspapers.**

The gerund phrase ***reading*** **old newspapers** performs the noun function of **direct object.**

— — —

To build **confidence** is reason enough to study grammar.

The infinitive phrase ***to build*** **confidence** performs the noun function of **subject** of the sentence.

— — —

The public relations executive wanted ***to purchase*** **two smaller firms.**

The infinitive phrase ***to purchase*** **two smaller firms** performs the noun function of **direct object.**

See pages 108–110 for additional information on how gerunds and infinitives can serve as nouns in the nominative and objective cases.

(You may test yourself on the material in this chapter or section by connecting with the following Web site: www.mhhe.com/arnold.)

chapter 8

PRONOUNS

Functions

If you have a good understanding of nouns and their functions, working with pronouns will be easier. Pronouns substitute for nouns; therefore, they can be used in the same ways. Like nouns, pronouns have gender, number, person and case. In addition, pronouns are classified into eight distinct functions:

1. personal
2. demonstrative
3. reciprocal
4. interrogative
5. reflexive
6. intensive
7. indefinite
8. relative

Pronouns are more difficult to master than nouns because they change their form (spelling) not only from singular to plural (***I*** to ***we***) but also from **nominative** ***(I, we, they)*** to **objective** ***(me, us, them)*** to **possessive** ***(mine, ours, theirs).*** Consequently, pronouns cannot be used interchangeably as nouns can be in the nominative and objective cases. You will recall from Chapter 7 that nouns are spelled and pronounced the same regardless of whether they are used in the nominative case (The **president** is seeking a second term) or in the objective case (The people elected the **president**). Notice how differently pronouns are used in the **nominative** case (**He** is seeking a second term) and the **objective** case (The people elected **him**).

We need to be familiar with each type of pronoun, to be knowledgeable of common examples from each group and to be aware of the many ways pronouns are used in sentences.

Personal Pronouns

Personal pronouns are of the utmost importance because they **substitute directly for nouns.** Without personal pronouns, we would have to use the name of a source in every reference to the person. Imagine the awkwardness in saying, "The **governor** will meet with the **governor's** advisory council when the **governor** returns from the **governor's** meeting with legislative leaders."

The best way to study personal pronouns is to reconstruct the organizational chart our elementary school teachers introduced us to years ago. If you still have not committed that chart to memory, do so or you may muddle through the remainder of your professional career making fundamental errors such as **between *he*** and ***I,* told *she*** and ***Helen,* this** is ***me,* without *him* knowing,** and so forth.

Nominative Case

Singular	**Plural**
first person—I	we
second person—you	you
third person—he, she, it	they

Objective Case

Singular	**Plural**
first person—me	us
second person—you	you
third person—him, her, it	them

Possessive Case

Singular	**Plural**
first person—my, mine	our, ours
second person—your, yours	your, yours
third person—his, her, hers, its	their, theirs

To review how each of these pronouns may be used in sentences, please refer to the explanations given for nouns on pages 59–61. Like nouns, personal pronouns may be used as subjects, appositives, direct objects, objects of prepositions and so forth.

Keep in mind that third-person singular personal pronouns in the nominative case use a different verb form (spelling). **I *go*** in the first person and **you *go*** in the second person changes to **he/she/it *goes*** in the third-person singular. Likewise, **I *have*** in the first person and **you *have*** in the second person changes to **he/she/it *has*** in the third-person singular.

* * *

Another significant point to remember is that **predicate pronouns** are selected from the **nominative case,** not the objective case. Like the predicate noun discussed in Chapter 7, the predicate pronoun follows a nonaction verb and renames (identifies, provides additional information about) the subject. In other words, a predicate pronoun and the subject are the same person, the same place or the same thing. Analyze the following examples:

It was **he (not *him*)** who gave me the writing assignment.

He is a **nominative case** predicate pronoun that comes after the nonaction verb **was** and renames the subject **it.** The subject and the predicate pronoun are the same person. If you are still confused, try this test: Substitute the subject and the predicate pronoun for each other. Obviously, you would not say, "**Him** was **it.**"

— — —

It was **they (not *them*)** who stood in line for 18 hours to purchase concert tickets.

They is a **nominative case** predicate pronoun that comes after the nonaction verb **was** and renames the subject **it.** The subject **it** and the predicate pronoun **they** are the same people. You would not say, "**Them** were **it.**"

— — —

"If I were **she [not *her*],** I would learn to use a computer."

She is a **nominative case** predicate pronoun that comes after the nonaction verb **were** and renames the subject **I.** The subject **I** and the predicate pronoun **she** are the same person. You would not say, "If **her** were **I.**"

(You are aware, of course, that in informal speech and writing, people commonly use the objective case pronouns—**me, him, her, us, them**—as predicate pronouns. Check your stylebooks to determine what is acceptable at your school or media company.)

* * *

When pronouns function as **objects of prepositions,** as **direct objects** or as **indirect objects,** they are selected from the **objective case,** not the nominative case.

Responsibility for the special edition will be shared between you and **me (not *I*).**

The **objective case *me*** serves with **you** as the compound **object of the preposition *between. I*** cannot be used as the object because ***I*** is a nominative case pronoun and objects of prepositions are always in the objective case.

— — —

"That's a medical decision," the judge said. "That's between **him [not *he*]** and his physician."

The **objective case *him*** must be used as the **object of the preposition *between.*** **He** is a nominative case pronoun.

— — —

"Between you and **me [not *I*],** I don't think your team stands a chance of winning the game Saturday."

The **objective case *me*** must be used as the **object of the preposition *between. I*** is a nominative case pronoun.

— — —

"I warned **her [not *she*]** and her friends that they would be fined if they did not move their cars," the police officer explained.

Her is the direct object of the action verb ***warned*** and answers the question **whom.** Direct objects are always in the objective case. **Her** is **objective** case; **she** is **nominative** case.

— — —

"The force of the crash knocked my passenger and **me [not *I*]** through the front window of the car."

Me is the direct object of the action verb ***knocked*** and answers the question **whom.** Direct objects are always in the objective case. **Me** is **objective** case; **I** is **nominative** case.

* * *

Like several other types of pronouns, **some possessive case personal pronouns** also can be used as ***adjectives.***

This is **my/our *(adjective)*** typewriter.

This is **her/his *(adjective)*** desk.

This is **its *(adjective)*** purpose.

Your *(adjective)* work is satisfactory.

Their *(adjective)* deadline has been changed.

Demonstrative Pronouns

Perhaps no other pronoun is as easy to understand as the demonstrative. There are only four of them (**this** and **that** in the **singular,** and ***these*** and ***those*** in the ***plural***). We use them to **point out and identify.**

At the beginning of any study of demonstrative pronouns, an obvious question to ask is why do we need two singular and two plural examples? **Proximity** is the answer. The singular **this** and the plural **these** are used to identify and point out people, places and things **nearby: This** is my favorite newspaper. **These** are my award-winning articles. The singular ***that*** and the plural ***those*** are used to identify and point out people, places and things more ***distant: That*** is where my office is located. ***Those*** are the lamps I'll place on the desk.

We can conclude our study of demonstrative pronouns by considering two other factors. These pronouns also can **serve as adjectives** when they modify nouns or pronouns. And when they are used as adjectives, we have to be careful not to use a **singular** demonstrative word to modify a **plural** noun or pronoun and vice versa:

This (pronoun serving as a *subject*) is my favorite advertisement.

***This* (*adjective modifying the* subject)** advertisement is my favorite.

— — —

That (pronoun serving as a *subject*) is our best typesetting machine.

***That* (*adjective modifying the* subject)** typesetting machine is our best.

— — —

These (pronoun serving as a *subject*) are our story assignments.

***These* (*adjective modifying the* subject)** story assignments are ours.

— — —

Those (pronoun serving as a *subject*) are the news director's orders.

***Those* (*adjective modifying the* subject)** orders came from the news director.

These/Those kinds ***(not kind)*** of public relations campaigns usually are profitable.

> **These** and **those** are ***plural;*** therefore, they must modify only ***plural*** nouns and pronouns.

— — —

This/That criterion ***(not criteria)*** was set by the publisher.

> **This** and **that** are ***singular;*** therefore, they must modify only ***singular*** nouns and pronouns.

Reciprocal Pronouns

Each other and **one another** are the only pronouns classified as ***reciprocal,*** meaning that they express mutual action, effect or relationship. Because our experience teaches us that many people use these terms interchangeably, we may ask **why we need both.** If we accept the notion that they are interchangeable, we don't need both. However, we will find both useful if we use them traditionally; that is, we use **each other** to refer to ***two*** people, places or things and **one another** to refer to ***three or more.***

What do we mean by reciprocal, or mutual action, effect or relationship? Consider how people, places and things are mutually affected in the following examples:

The **two** boxers landed punches simultaneously and hurt **each other.**

Each boxer ***struck*** a hurtful blow and in turn **each** ***was hurt*** by the other fighter.

— — —

Members of the championship football team congratulated **one another.**

We use **one another** because a football team consists of far more than two people. **All** the members ***were congratulating*** the others and **all** ***were being congratulated*** themselves.

— — —

The **mayor** and the **governor** will help **each other** during the campaign.

Each ***will give*** help and **each** ***will receive*** help.

— — —

The **five members** of the investigative reporting team will work with **one another** on the story.

Each reporter will benefit from what **he** or **she** ***gives*** and what **he** or **she** ***receives.***

* * *

Sometimes deciding whether to use **each other** or **one another** is not as simple as determining whether the number is restricted to two or refers to three or more. If the number is unknown or is infinite, either **each other** or **one another** may be appropriate. The three examples that follow should prove helpful:

- During a religious ceremony, the minister, priest or rabbi may instruct members of the congregation to offer **each other/*one another*** a greeting. Either term could be appropriate because if the greeting is a handshake, that usually will involve only **two people *(each other)*** at a time. However, because each person undoubtedly will shake the hand of **more than just one other individual,** ***one another*** also would be appropriate.

— — —

- A presidential candidate could say, "As Americans, we must do all we can to help **each other/*one another*** protect freedom." The candidate could mean that we are to help individually or collectively.

— — —

- The Senate president says she wants members of the Education Committee to meet with representatives from both the American Federation of Teachers and the National Education Association. She could say, "We are going to meet with **each other,**" or "We are going to meet with **one another.**" If the Senate committee is to meet with each of the other groups **one at a time,** ***each other*** would be appropriate. **If all three groups** are to meet simultaneously, ***one another*** would be the proper term.

Interrogative Pronouns

Interrogative pronouns ask questions. There is nothing especially tricky about them; you just need to be aware of when they are being used as **adjectives** instead of as **pronouns.** Remember that an interrogative pronoun is not always the subject of the sentence even though it commonly occupies the position usually reserved for subjects.

Who, whom, whose, which and **what** are interrogative pronouns. Because asking questions in English results in inverting normal sentence order ***(subject—verb—object)*** the interrogative pronoun (or the interrogative adjective) usually appears first.

Who is your favorite broadcast journalist?

The normal sentence order would be **Your favorite broadcast journalist is *who?*** But that's not the way we ask questions in our language. However, the subject is **journalist** regardless of which of the two sentence structures we use. In both the normal and the inverted structures, **who** serves as the **predicate pronoun.**

— — —

Whom are you talking about?

Whom serves as the **object** of the preposition ***about.*** **You** is the **subject.**

— — —

Whom are you interviewing this morning?

Whom serves as the **object** of the verb ***are interviewing.*** **You** is the **subject.**

— — —

Whose are these notes?

Whose serves as the ***predicate pronoun.*** **Notes** is the **subject** and ***are*** is the nonaction verb. Remember that predicate complements—predicate **nouns,** predicate **pronouns** and predicate **adjectives**—follow nonaction verbs but never come after action verbs.

— — —

Which do you prefer?

Which serves as the ***object*** of the action verb ***do prefer.*** **You** is the **subject.**

— — —

What is your name?

What is the ***predicate pronoun.*** **Name** is the **subject** and ***is*** is the nonaction verb. Remember that predicate nouns and predicate pronouns not only follow nonaction verbs but also "rename" the subject. In this example, **what** and **name** are the same thing.

* * *

In the following sentences, ***interrogative pronouns*** serve as **subjects:**

Who is there?

What's happening?

Which is correct?

* * *

Observe how some of these ***interrogative pronouns*** can be turned into ***interrogative adjectives*** by making them modifiers:

Whose notes are these?

Which method do you prefer?

What brand of ink are you using?

In each of the three examples, the boldfaced words are used as adjectives instead of as pronouns. How do you know? They modify nouns, and the only part of speech that can modify a noun is an adjective. **Whose** modifies ***notes,*** **which** modifies ***method,*** and **what** modifies ***brand.***

* * *

Indirect Questions. All of the examples of interrogative pronouns and adjectives raise questions **directly.** However, pronouns also may raise questions i**ndirectly,** as the following example demonstrates:

The editor said she does not know **what** she did with your notes.

The **direct question** would be **What did she do with your notes?**

(See "How Not to Use Question Marks" on page 174.)

Reflexive and Intensive Pronouns

Reflexive and ***intensive pronouns*** end in **self** in the **singular** and ***selves*** in the ***plural.*** Using them correctly is not difficult if you will remember the following:

Pronouns ending in **self** or **selves** must have a clearly established **antecedent** (the noun or the pronoun to which **self** or **selves** refers).

(Unclear) "Maureen and **myself** will produce the play."

Myself lacks an antecedent. Who is **myself?** "Maureen and **I** will produce the play."

(Clear) The **actor** hurt ***himself*** when he fell off the stage.

Actor is clearly the antecedent of **himself.** Do not use as subjects pronouns ending in **self** or **selves.**

— — —

(Unclear) "I'm feeling fine. How's **yourself?"**

Yourself lacks an antecedent. Who is **yourself?** "I'm feeling fine. How are **you?"**

(Clear) "The advertising **director** talks to **herself** when she is worried."

Director is clearly the antecedent of **herself.**

— — —

(Unclear) "When you are finished with the assignment, give your photographs to the city editor or **myself.**"

Myself lacks an antecedent. Who is **myself?** "When you are finished with the assignment, give your photographs to the city editor or **me.**

(Clear) "**She** did it **herself.**"

She is clearly the antecedent of **herself.**

The **singular "self" pronouns** are **herself, himself, itself, myself** and **yourself.** The ***plural "selves" pronouns*** are ***themselves, yourselves*** and ***ourselves.*** DO NOT use any of the following erroneous combinations: ***his*self, *their*self, *our*self** and ***their*selves.** In other words, **his** and **their** may not serve as prefixes for reflexive and intensive pronouns. Please also remember that ***self* must follow a *singular* prefix *(him, her, my, it)*** and ***selves*** **must follow a *plural* prefix *(our, them).* Your** may be followed by ***self*** or ***selves.***

* * *

Reflexive pronouns come after the verb and refer to the subject. They serve as either the direct object or the predicate complement.

The **reporter** hurt **himself** when he dropped the camera on his foot.

The reflexive pronoun **himself** comes after the verb but refers to the subject. **Reporter** and **himself** are the same person. **Himself** serves as the ***direct object*** of the action verb ***hurt*** and answers the question ***whom.***

— — —

The copy desk **editor** promised **herself** that she would never again make a simple grammatical error in a 72-point headline.

The reflexive pronoun **herself** comes after the verb but refers to the subject. **Herself** and **editor** are the same person. **Herself** serves as the ***direct object*** of the action verb ***promised*** and answers the question ***whom.***

— — —

After watching the actor flub his lines all morning, the director concluded his star **performer** was just not **himself** that day.

The reflexive pronoun **himself** comes after the verb ***was*** and refers to the subject **performer. Himself** and **performer** are the same person. **Himself** serves as the ***predicate complement*** following the nonaction verb ***was.***

* * *

Intensive pronouns are used for **emphasis.** In the sentences illustrating intensive pronouns, you will notice that their only purpose is to add emphasis. Otherwise, they could be dropped from the sentences. Notice also that intensive pronouns may come anywhere in the sentence (unlike reflexive pronouns that come only after verbs).

The **players themselves** vowed to avenge last year's humiliating loss to their intrastate rival.

What purpose would using **themselves** in the sentence have if not for emphasis?

— — —

The magistrate said **he** would direct his campaign **himself.**

Again, there is no reason to use **himself** other than to add emphasis.

Keep in mind this important point concerning reflexive and intensive pronouns: Before you use one, ask yourself who or what the "self" is. **If there is not a clearly established antecedent, do not use a self pronoun.**

Indefinite Pronouns

Indefinite pronouns, which also can serve as adjectives, are what their name implies. They are **vague** and refer to things generally rather than specifically. For example, rather than stating that 10 students earned all A's, an indefinite pronoun would indicate that a **few, several** or **some** earned all A's. Instead of stating that an advertisement will be published in 300 newspapers, an indefinite pronoun would indicate that the advertisement would be published in **many** newspapers.

Specific references are better than general ones. However, there are times when specifics are unknown. That's when we reach into our supply of indefinite pronouns. Take a look at some that are used most frequently:

Singular	**Plural**	**Singular or Plural**
another	few	all
anybody	many	any
anyone	ones	none
anything	several	some
each	others	most
either		such
everybody		
everyone		
everything		
much		
neither		
nobody		
no one		
other		
somebody		
someone		
something		

* * *

Mass communicators should use great care to select the indefinite pronoun that most precisely expresses their thought. There are significant differences to be considered in selecting from **few, some, most, many** and **several.** To publish or broadcast the statement that ***some*** citizens failed to vote because they were apathetic undoubtedly would be true in any election. But to charge that ***most*** citizens failed to vote because they were apathetic would be a challengeable statement if not supported by facts.

Because journalists cannot maintain credibility with readers and listeners by making gross generalizations, writers and broadcasters must rely on indefinite pronouns to qualify their statements. The decision is not always easy, but those familiar with the functions of indefinite pronouns are better prepared to make an acceptable choice.

* * *

You can help yourselves use these pronouns more effectively by conquering problems with number (singulars and plurals) and determining whether you are using these indefinite words as pronouns or as adjectives.

In the columns listed previously, the most commonly used indefinite pronouns are grouped according to those that are singular, those that are plural and those that may be either singular or plural. To determine whether the indefinite pronoun is singular or plural, remember that if **all** (or **any, none, some, most,** or **such**) is considered an **uncountable quantity** or a **lump sum,** it is singular; if the meaning of **all** is **several** or if it is a **countable number,** it is plural. The antecedent of each indefinite pronoun provides the answer. But don't be surprised when the antecedent reverses its customary position and follows the pronoun instead of preceding it.

All of the ***workers*** **are** exhausted.

The indefinite pronoun **all** is the ***subject.*** **Workers,** the ***object*** of the preposition ***of,*** is the countable quantity that **all** refers to; therefore, **all** is considered plural and takes the plural verb are.

— — —

All of the ***water*** **was** contaminated by the oil spill.

The indefinite pronoun **all** is the ***subject.*** **Water,** the ***object*** of the preposition ***of,*** is not a countable quantity but is referred to in lump sum by **all;** therefore, **all** is considered singular—one quantity—and takes the singular verb ***was.***

— — —

Some of the antique ***typewriters*** are still in working order.

The indefinite pronoun **some** is the ***subject.*** **Typewriters,** the ***object*** of the preposition ***of,*** is the countable quantity that **some** refers to; therefore, **some** is considered plural and takes the plural verb ***are.***

— — —

Some of the ***ink*** **is** still wet.

The indefinite pronoun **some** is the ***subject.*** **Ink,** the ***object*** of the preposition ***of,*** is not a countable quantity but is referred to in lump sum by **some;** therefore, **ink** is considered singular—one quantity—and takes the singular verb ***is.***

* * *

In determining whether an indefinite word is an adjective or a pronoun, just remember that the function of a word in a sentence determines its part of speech. You cannot say that **few, many, several, each** and **some** are pronouns and never give the words another thought. These words are used frequently as adjectives. Consider the following examples (and if necessary, refer to the section under nouns on pages 59–61 to review the ways in which nouns and pronouns may be used in sentences).

Few ***(pronoun subject)*** of us will win a Pulitzer Prize for our work in journalism and mass communications.

Few ***(adjective modifying the following noun)*** journalists will earn a Pulitzer Prize.

— — —

Most journalists hope to win **several** ***(adjective modifying the following noun)*** awards.

Most journalists hope to win **several** ***(pronoun serving as the object of the infinitive to win).***

— — —

The public relations director gave **each** ***(pronoun used as an indirect object)*** of us a raise.

The public relations director gave **each** ***(adjective modifying the following noun)*** employee a raise.

Relative Pronouns

Make yourself comfortable. Discussing ***relative pronouns*** takes both time and energy, and even experienced mass communicators who conscientiously study rules of grammar can have trouble with them. Grammar and punctuation problems resulting from their use are so commonplace that mistakes involving relative pronouns can be found every day in many news publications and broadcasts.

Before you attempt to study relative pronouns further, be sure you understand the functions pronouns perform in the nominative and objective cases (see pages 59–61) and the purposes of and differences between independent and dependent clauses (see pages 153–155 and 179–180).

Ten pages are devoted in this section to the relative pronoun. That alone tells you these pronouns have many features that require detailed explanation. Another reason is the attempt to provide a bulk of reference material that will make available a reasonably uncomplicated example for virtually every common way a relative pronoun may be used.

* * *

The elements we need to be knowledgeable about to understand these pronouns thoroughly are:

- Their **purpose.** Why do they exist, and what are they designed to do?

— — —

- How to **recognize them.** What are the relative pronouns? Commit them to memory.

— — —

- How to **attach them to their antecedent** in the independent clause. What word in the independent clause does the relative pronoun in the dependent clause take the place of?

— — —

- The **placement** in the sentence of the relative pronoun in relation to its antecedent. Most syntax problems result from incorrect placement.

— — —

- How to recognize when some relative pronouns (especially the pronoun *that*) are **understood rather than written or spoken.**

— — —

- How to figure out what **function** (subject, object, predicate complement) **the relative pronoun has in its own dependent clause.**

— — —

- How to determine what **relationship** the relative pronoun (and the remainder of the dependent clause) has **to the antecedent in the independent clause.**

If you can put all of these together, you can master relative pronouns. The detailed examples and explanations that follow should enable you to reach that goal.

Purpose

A relative pronoun **introduces a dependent clause,** further **explains or defines its antecedent** in the independent clause, and **enables the writer to mold two clauses into one effective sentence.**

Consider how these purposes are fulfilled in the following example:

The article, ***which*** **was a last-minute substitute for another story,** won a statewide award.

> The relative pronoun **which** serves as the **subject** of the verb ***was*** and introduces the dependent clause **which was a last-minute substitute for another story.** The **antecedent** of **which** is ***article,*** **subject** of the independent clause **The article won a statewide award.**

The purpose of the dependent clause is to provide additional information about the antecedent, ***article,*** giving the reader or listener a little piece of interesting information about how an award-winning story almost failed to be published or broadcast.

In this example, the dependent clause is considered **nonessential** (also called **nonrestrictive**) because it simply provides additional information and is not needed to make the meaning of the independent clause clear. A **nonessential** dependent clause is set apart from the independent clause with commas. Commas are not used when the dependent clause is **essential** to make the meaning of the independent clause clear—as in the next example. See pages 9–10 and 179–180 for additional examples and explanations of essential and nonessential dependent clauses.

— — —

Blankenship is the editor **who hired me.**

The relative pronoun **who** serves as the **subject** of the verb ***hired*** and introduces the dependent clause **who hired me.** The **antecedent** of **who** is *editor,* **predicate noun** of the independent clause **Blankenship is the editor.** The dependent clause provides information needed to make the meaning of the independent clause clear. The purpose of the sentence is not just to point out that Blankenship is **an** editor but to explain that Blankenship is **the** editor who did the hiring. Therefore, the dependent clause is **essential** and is not set apart from the independent clause with a comma.

Words Used as Relative Pronouns

The most common relative pronouns are **who, which** and **that.** Others are **whom, what, whose, whoever, whomever, whichever** and **whatever.**

We have just analyzed an example using **which** and another using **who.** Consider how the other relative pronouns are used in the following examples:

Basketball is the sport **(that) I most enjoy covering.**

The relative pronoun **that** serves as a **connective** and introduces the dependent clause **that I most enjoy covering.** The **antecedent** of **that** is *sport,* **predicate noun** in the independent clause **Basketball is the sport.** The dependent clause provides **essential** information that defines what is meant by the use of the word **sport.**

The purpose of the independent clause is not to make the point that basketball is **a** sport but to show that basketball is **the** sport the reporter most enjoys covering. Because the dependent clause is needed to make the meaning of the independent clause clear, no comma is used to set the two clauses apart.

The relative pronoun **that** is placed in parentheses in this example to indicate that it does not have to be written or broadcast. It is understood.

— — —

The angry source demanded to know **what the reporter wanted.**

The relative pronoun **what** serves as the **object** of the verb ***wanted*** and introduces the dependent clause **what the reporter wanted.** When used as a relative pronoun, **what** does not have an expressed **antecedent;** however, the entire dependent clause serves as the **object** of the infinitive **to know** from the independent clause. As the object of the infinitive, the dependent clause is **essential** to make the meaning of the independent clause clear. Therefore, no comma is used to set the two clauses apart.

— — —

Give the advertising account to **whoever is available.**

The relative pronoun **whoever** serves as the **subject** of the verb ***is*** and introduces the dependent clause **whoever is available.** The entire dependent clause serves as the **object** of the preposition **to** from the independent clause. As the object of the preposition, the dependent clause is **essential** to make the meaning of the independent clause clear. Therefore, no comma is used to set the two clauses apart.

— — —

The vice president for public relations will be pleased with **whomever you hire.**

The relative pronoun **whomever** serves as the **object** of the verb ***hire*** and introduces the dependent clause **whomever you hire.** The entire dependent clause serves as the **object** of the preposition **with** from the independent clause. As the object of the preposition, the dependent clause is **essential** to make the meaning of the independent clause clear. Therefore, no comma is used to set the two clauses apart.

— — —

The company president will purchase either another newspaper or a television station, **whichever becomes available first.**

The relative pronoun **whichever** serves as the **subject** of the verb ***becomes*** and introduces the dependent clause **whichever becomes available first.** The **antecedents** of **whichever** are **newspaper** and **station,** compound **direct objects** of the verb **will purchase** from the independent clause. The dependent clause is **nonessential.** It simply provides additional information about the antecedents and is not needed to make the meaning of the independent clause clear. Therefore, a comma is required between **station** and **whichever** to set the two clauses apart.

— — —

"I'll do **whatever you wish,**" the mayor said.

The relative pronoun **whatever** serves as the **object** of the verb ***wish*** and introduces the dependent clause **whatever you wish.** The entire dependent clause serves as the **object** of the verb **will do** from the independent clause. As the object of the verb, the dependent clause is **essential** to make the meaning of the independent clause clear. Therefore, no comma is required to set the two clauses apart.

— — —

I don't know **whose it is.**

The relative pronoun **whose** serves as the **predicate pronoun** in the dependent clause **whose it is.** The entire dependent clause serves as the **object** of the verb ***do know*** from the independent clause **I don't know.** As the **object** of the verb ***do know,*** the dependent clause is **essential** to make the independent clause clear. Therefore, no comma is used to set the two clauses apart.

Antecedents of Relative Pronouns

Who, whom, whoever and **whomever** are used to refer to people (and to animals if the animals are referred to by their pet names).

The **mayor, *who*** was a police officer before he entered politics, is serving his second term.

The relative pronoun ***who*** refers to **mayor,** a **person.**

— — —

The president of Acme Kennel Association predicted that his dog, **Brandy, *whom*** he has been training for two years, will win first place in next month's show.

The relative pronoun ***whom*** refers to **Brandy,** the **pet name** of an animal.

— — —

The editor in chief checked the resumes of the 15 job **applicants** and told the city editor to hire ***whoever*** is best qualified.

The relative pronoun ***whoever*** refers to **applicants, people.**

— — —

The editor in chief said she would be pleased with ***whomever*** the city editor hires.

The relative pronoun ***whomever*** refers to the **people** seeking the job.

— — —

Remember that **who** and **whoever** are used exclusively in the nominative case for subjects, predicate pronouns and appositives to nominative case nouns. **Whom** and **whomever** are used exclusively in the objective case for direct objects, indirect objects, objects of prepositions, and appositives to objective case nouns.

* * *

Which and **whichever** are used (usually in nonessential dependent clauses) to refer to animals, to inanimate objects and to people referred to by collective nouns (such as class, team, jury, etc.).

The reporter covering the circus decided to write a feature story on **elephants, which** he found to be fascinating.

The relative pronoun ***which*** refers to **elephants, animals.**

— — —

The **computer, which** costs more than $1 million, is needed by the business office.

The relative pronoun ***which*** refers to **computer,** an **inanimate** object.

— — —

The **team, *which*** won seven consecutive games, earned a bid to the playoffs.

The relative pronoun ***which*** refers to **team,** a collective noun that refers to **people** as a group.

— — —

The offices of the public relations agency will be furnished with either an Acme or an Ajax communications **system, whichever** is least expensive, the vice president for finance announced.

The relative pronoun ***whichever*** refers to **system,** an **inanimate** object.

* * *

That is used (usually in essential dependent clauses) to refer to animals, to inanimate objects and sometimes to people.

The **elephant *(that)*** the television reporter was allowed to ride will perform in the show this afternoon.

The relative pronoun ***that*** refers to **elephant,** an **animal.** Note that the relative pronoun is placed in parentheses to indicate that it does not have to be written or spoken. It is understood.

— — —

The **cameras *(that)*** the chief photographer ordered should arrive Monday.

The relative pronoun ***that*** refers to **cameras, inanimate** objects. Note that the relative pronoun is placed in parentheses to indicate that it is understood and does not need to be stated.

— — —

She is the **editor *that*** assigned the story.

The relative pronoun ***that*** refers to **editor,** a **person.** Note that although **that** is used correctly, the relative pronoun **who** is used more frequently to refer to people.

Placement of the Relative Pronoun

As a rule, a relative pronoun should be placed **immediately after its antecedent.** When that is not possible, the writer or broadcaster must take special care to place the relative pronoun where it will promote understanding and not create confusion or give the sentence an unintended meaning.

Consider the placement of the relative pronouns in relation to their antecedents in the following examples:

(Awkward) The police **station** in Fargo County, ***which*** is a converted gymnasium, also serves as a meeting place for community groups.

The antecedent of the relative pronoun ***which*** is **station,** not **county.**

(Improved) The police **station,** ***(which is)*** a converted gymnasium in Fargo County, also serves as a meeting place for community groups.

Now the relative pronoun ***which*** directly follows its antecedent, **station,** and eliminates the confusion. **Which is** is placed in parentheses to indicate that the words do not need to be written or broadcast. They are understood.

— — —

(Awkward) The tax **bill** discussed for eight days by members of the Senate Finance Committee, ***which*** would raise $40 million in its first year, passed by two votes.

The antecedent ***of which*** is ***bill,*** not ***Committee.***

(Improved) The tax **bill,** ***which*** would raise $40 million in its first year, passed by two votes after being discussed for eight days by members of the Senate Finance Committee.

Relative Pronouns Understood Instead of Stated

Both print and broadcast journalists try to eliminate superfluous words whenever they can without causing confusion or misunderstanding. In several examples used previously in this section on pronouns, some words have been placed in parentheses to indicate they need not be written or broadcast because they are understood to be present.

Consider the relative pronouns placed in parentheses in the following examples to indicate they don't need to be written or broadcast:

The political convention, ***(which is)*** scheduled for April 10–17, is expected to attract 1,200 delegates.

— — —

The mayor, ***(who was)*** elected to his first term two decades ago, said he will seek a sixth term this year.

— — —

Writing political advertisements is the assignment ***(that)*** Shanda E. Marcum said she enjoys the most.

— — —

The governor gave his public relations staff a list of names of people *(whom)* he planned to appoint to the commission.

To determine whether the relative pronouns need to be written or broadcast, read the sentence with the words included and again with the words omitted. If the sentence makes sense without the relative pronoun, leave it out.

Function of the Relative Pronoun within Its Own Dependent Clause

Within the dependent clause it introduces, a relative pronoun serves as either the **subject, object** or **predicate pronoun.**

Consider the function of the relative pronoun in each of the following examples:

(Subject) The golfer ***who*** **wins the playoff** will earn $120,000.

The relative pronoun ***who*** serves as the **subject** of the verb **wins** in the boldfaced dependent clause.

— — —

(Object) Select ***whichever*** **you prefer** as the lead story for tonight's telecast, the news director instructed.

The relative pronoun ***whichever*** serves as the **object** of the verb **prefer** in the boldfaced dependent clause. Do not be confused by the inverted order of the object, verb and subject in the dependent clause. The **subject** is ***you,*** the **verb** is ***prefer*** and the **object** is ***whichever.***

— — —

(Predicate pronoun) The governor told reporters at the press conference to identify themselves when they asked questions. "I don't know ***who*** **you are,**" he said.

The relative pronoun ***who*** is the **predicate pronoun** in the boldfaced dependent clause. The **subject** is ***you*** and the **verb** is ***are.***

— — —

(Subject) The football coach instructed the quarterback to pass the ball to ***whoever*** **breaks away from the defenders.**

The relative pronoun ***whoever*** serves as the **subject** of the verb **breaks** in the boldfaced dependent clause.

(Predicate pronoun) The reporter will broadcast the verdict as soon as the judge announces ***what*** **it is.**

The relative pronoun ***what*** serves as the **predicate pronoun** in the boldfaced dependent clause. The **subject** is ***it*** and the **verb** is ***is.***

Relationship of the Relative Pronoun and the Remainder of the Dependent Clause to the Antecedent in the Independent Clause

In the preceding section, we considered the function of the relative pronoun within its own clause. Now we'll examine the relationship the relative pronoun and the remainder of the dependent clause have with the antecedent in the independent clause.

The golfer ***who*** **wins the playoff** will earn $120,000.

The dependent clause is ***who wins the playoff.*** **Golfer,** the **subject** of the independent clause, is the **antecedent** of **who,** the relative pronoun that introduces the dependent clause. The entire dependent clause is used as an **adjective** to explain the noun subject, **golfer,** from the independent clause. The dependent clause must function as an adjective because only an adjective can modify a noun subject.

— — —

Select ***whichever*** **you prefer.**

The dependent clause is ***whichever you prefer,*** and the entire dependent clause serves as the **direct object** of the verb **select** from the independent clause. Remember that a direct object follows an action verb and answers the questions **whom** or **what. Select** is the action verb of the understood subject **you,** and asking **what** after **select** reveals the direct object, ***whichever you prefer.***

— — —

The football coach instructed the quarterback to pass the ball to ***whoever*** **breaks away from the defenders.**

The dependent clause is ***whoever breaks away from the defenders,*** and the entire dependent clause serves as the **object** of the preposition **to** in the independent clause.

— — —

A feature story is ***whatever*** **you decide to make it.**

The dependent clause is ***whatever you decide to make it*** and serves as the **predicate pronoun** of the independent clause. Remember that a predicate pronoun follows a nonaction verb and renames the subject, providing additional information about it. **Story,** the **subject** of the independent clause, and **whatever,** the **predicate pronoun,** are the same thing.

— — —

The halfback enjoyed passing ***whoever*** **was in his way.**

The dependent clause is ***whoever was in his way*** and serves as the **object** of the gerund **passing.** Remember that a **gerund,** as a verb form, can express action and pass that action on to an **object.** By asking the questions **what** or **whom** after the action word **passing,** we get **whoever** as the **object.**

— — —

Praising **whoever** ***was in sight,*** the editor carried the reporting award into the newsroom for all to see.

The dependent clause is ***whoever was in sight*** and serves as the **object** of the participle **praising** for the same reason cited in the previous example.

— — —

The editor in chief wants the personnel director to hire ***whoever*** **is best qualified for the job.**

The dependent clause is ***whoever is best qualified for the job*** and serves as the **object** of the infinitive **to hire.** An **infinitive,** as a verb form, may express an action and pass that action on to another word. By asking **what** or **whom** after the action word **hire,** we get **whoever** as the **object.**

To review verbals—participles, gerunds and infinitives—see pages 108–113.

(You may test yourself on the material in this chapter or section by connecting with the following Web site: www.mhhe.com/arnold.)

chapter 9

NOUN–PRONOUN AGREEMENT

Let's discuss this issue as simply as possible.

Pronouns take the place of nouns. After using the name of the mayor, we then may use **he/she, him/her** or **his/hers** instead of repeating the person's name or title. After writing or broadcasting that 15 mayors are meeting in Atlanta, we may substitute **they** or **them** or **their** instead of repeating the noun ***mayors.***

1. Making Antecedents Clear

The noun that the pronoun replaces is called the ***antecedent,*** meaning that the noun ***(mayor)*** is used first and then the pronoun **(he/she)** is substituted on the next reference. Virtually all of the problems writers have in using pronouns develop because the pronouns they select conflict with their noun antecedents in either **person, number** or **gender.** Let's examine these types of errors and some solutions for correcting them.

(Clear) The **sheriff** said ***he*** will seek re-election.

Sheriff is clearly the **noun antecedent** of the pronoun ***he.***

(Clear) The **senator** said **she** will vote for the tax increase. ***She*** said ***her*** vote probably will not make ***her*** constituents happy.

Senator clearly is the **noun antecedent** for the pronouns ***she*** and ***her.***

— — —

(Misleading) The **mayor** will share the award with the **president** of the County Commission. ***He*** described the honor as "uniquely satisfying."

We have a **noun-pronoun agreement problem.** Does the pronoun ***he*** refer to the ***mayor*** or to the ***president?***

(Clear) The **mayor,** who will share the award with the president of the County Commission, described the honor as "uniquely satisfying."

As **subject** of the verb **described,** ***mayor***—not ***president***—clearly is the person who made the statement.

— — —

(Misleading) The **news director** instructed the **reporter** to trim ***his*** story by 30 seconds.

Is the **reporter** supposed to trim his own story or the **news director's**?

(Clear) Because the reporter's ***story*** was too long, the news director instructed him to trim ***it*** by 30 seconds.

The noun ***story*** clearly is the **antecedent** for the pronoun ***it.*** Therefore, there is no doubt that the story is the reporter's, not the news director's.

— — —

(Misleading) The **art director** discussed the picture with the **photographer,** and ***she*** seemed happy about it.

Who was happy—the **art director** or the **photographer?**

(Clear) The **art director** seemed happy as ***she*** discussed the photograph with the photographer.

Art director clearly is the **noun antecedent** of the pronoun ***she;*** therefore, there is no doubt that the art director is the one who seemed happy.

2. Repeating the Noun for Clarity

Because every **noun antecedent** should be **unmistakably apparent,** mass communicators sometimes need to **repeat the noun** instead of replacing it with a pronoun.

(Misleading) **Journalists** from 25 states were invited to San Francisco in September for a special seminar on common **errors** committed by investigative **reporters.** ***They*** are expected to increase significantly unless immediate action is taken, the journalists were told.

The pronoun ***they*** lacks a clear **noun antecedent.** Are the **journalists,** the **errors** or the investigative **reporters** expected to increase significantly unless immediate action is taken?

(Clear) Journalists from 25 states were invited to San Francisco in September for a special press conference on common **errors** committed by investigative reporters. The **errors** are expected to increase significantly unless immediate action is taken, the journalists were told.

By repeating the noun **errors,** the writer can make the meaning clear.

— — —

(Misleading) Members of the Senate Finance Committee debated the proposed tax increase for three hours without reaching a decision. **This** will make meeting their deadline difficult.

The noun antecedent for the pronoun **This** is unclear.

(Clear) **Members** of the Senate Finance Committee debated the proposed tax increase for three hours without reaching a decision. ***Their lack of agreement*** will make meeting their deadline difficult.

By using **Their lack of agreement** instead of the pronoun ***this,*** the writer is able to make the meaning clear.

— — —

(Misleading) The Senate president said **it** is important that committee members understand the need to reach a decision quickly.

The **pronoun *it*** lacks a **noun antecedent.**

(Clear) The Senate president said committee members need to understand the importance of reaching a decision quickly.

The lesson: Do not use the **pronoun *it*** unless you have established a clear **noun antecedent.**

3. Solving Problems with Indefinite Pronouns

Some **indefinite pronouns *(everyone, everybody, anyone, anybody, each, every,*** etc.) raise **gender** problems writers and broadcasters should avoid. The use of a **masculine pronoun** to replace a noun or a pronoun of **common gender** is not well received by people concerned about language they consider sexist.

(Avoid) Each **reporter** is to complete ***his*** assignment before the 11 p.m. deadline.

Reporter is a **common gender noun** because a reporter can be a male or a female. **Reporter** also is singular and requires a singular pronoun replacement. Traditionally, the masculine gender ***his*** is used, but that tradition is unacceptable to many people and can be avoided easily.

(Incorrect) Each **reporter** is to complete ***their*** assignment before the 11 p.m. deadline.

By using ***their,*** we have avoided a **gender** problem but have created a **number** conflict. **Reporter** is singular and must have a singular pronoun replacement.

(Solution) **Reporters** are to complete ***their*** assignments before the 11 p.m. deadline.

By using the plural noun **reporters** as the antecedent, and the plural pronoun ***their*** as its replacement, we have eliminated both the gender and number problems from the previous examples.

— — —

Sometimes the **antecedent** of a pronoun is ***another pronoun.***

Twenty-two **women** tried out for the tennis team. ***Each*** did ***her*** best to win a position.

The **antecedent** of the pronoun ***her*** is the pronoun ***each.*** The **antecedent** of the pronoun ***each*** is the noun **women** from the first sentence.

4. Using Plural Forms with Singular Meanings

Nouns that have a ***plural form*** (spelling) but are ***singular in meaning*** require a **singular pronoun substitute.**

Physics is a difficult subject, and ***it*** appeals primarily to students who enjoy studying science.

Physics is only one subject even though it has a plural spelling; therefore, it requires the singular pronoun substitute ***it.***

The same rule applies to similar words such as ***measles, news, economics, mathematics,*** and so forth.

— — —

Use a **plural pronoun** when the **noun *antecedents*** (two or more) are joined by the conjunction *and.*

The **prosecutor *and*** the **attorney** for the defense are making ***their*** final statements to the jury today.

The **pronoun replacement** refers to more than one noun antecedent. Therefore, the plural ***their*** must be used.

— — —

The judge's ruling will affect the way the **mayor, members** of the City Council ***and*** the **chief** of police use ***their*** expense accounts.

In this sentence, the **pronoun replacement** refers to more than one noun antecedent. Therefore, the pronoun replacement—***their***—must be plural.

5. Simplifying the Use of Either/Or and Neither/Nor

The **pronoun** can be either ***singular*** or ***plural*** when it is substituted for noun antecedents joined by **either/or** and ***neither/nor.*** The choice between using a singular or a plural pronoun is simple if the writer or broadcaster will remember three rules (which also apply to subject–verb agreement, pages 121–122):

1. If the **noun antecedents** (two or more) are **singular,** the pronoun that substitutes for them will be **singular.**

   Either the **city editor *or*** his **assistant** will have to change ***his*** vacation schedule so both will not be absent at the same time.

2. If the **noun antecedents** (two or more) are **plural,** the pronoun that substitutes for them will be **plural.**

   Neither the **reporters *nor*** the **editors** will have ***their*** pay reduced even though the newspaper lost money last year, the publisher said.

3. If **one (or more)** of the **noun antecedents** is **singular** and ***one* (or more)** is plural, the pronoun substituted for them will take its number from **the closer antecedent.** If the closer antecedent is singular, the pronoun substitute will be singular; if the closer antecedent is plural, the pronoun substitute will be plural. However, the writer or broadcaster would be wise to use the plural antecedent last because a plural substitute "sounds" much better. Note how the first example that follows "sounds" much better than the second one.

   Neither the **vice president *nor*** the **graphic artists** lost ***their*** jobs.

   The **plural antecedent,** graphic ***artists,* is closer** to the pronoun substitute; therefore, the pronoun should be **plural.**

   — — —

   Neither the **graphic artists *nor*** the **vice president** lost ***his*** job.

   The **singular antecedent, *vice president,* is closer;** therefore, the pronoun should be **singular.** Please note, however, that even though this last sentence is structurally correct, it "sounds" awkward. The solution: **When one of the antecedents is plural and one is singular, use the plural antecedent last.** Then you will need to use a plural pronoun, and the sentence will read more smoothly because of its plural "sound."

6. Agreeing in Person, Number and Gender

Pronouns must **agree** with their **antecedent nouns** in ***person, number*** and ***gender.***

Photographers must keep ***your*** equipment in the designated area, the judge warned.

Photographers is **third person** and **your** is **second person.** The **third-person** pronoun ***their*** must be used instead of ***your.***

— — —

Acme Shoe Store is having **their** clearance sale today.

Acme Shoe Store is **singular;** therefore, the **singular** pronoun substitute ***its***—not ***their***—must be used.

— — —

Every **member** of the debate team must have ***his*** luggage packed by the 3 p.m. departure time.

Member is a **common gender** noun and ***his*** is **masculine gender.** Presuming that the team includes both males and females, you may solve the gender problem by making a **plural of both the subject and its pronoun replacement: *Members*** of the debate team must have ***their*** luggage packed by the 3 p.m. departure time.

(You may test yourself on the material in this chapter or section by connecting with the following Web site: www.mhhe.com/arnold.)

chapter 10 VERBS AND VERBALS

Functions

Verbs are the most important, the most powerful and the most complicated part of speech. Understanding them thoroughly is essential to effective communication because they offer no compromise. If we don't master them, they will hinder us all our working lives.

Verbs are important because they control the subject's action and the receiver's reaction to the message. "My employer **praised** me" requires a vastly different action by the subject and provokes a radically different reaction from the receiver than "My employer **fired** me." The same is true for "I **love** you" and "I **loathe** you."

Even nonaction words have power. "You **were** my first choice for the promotion" and "You **are** my first choice for the promotion" will cause different responses from the person hoping for advancement.

Sometimes verbs show their power through modifiers:

The president's speech **was (verb)** ***effective (predicate adjective).***

The president's speech **was (verb)** ***boring (predicate adjective).***

The soloist **performed (verb)** ***well (adverb).***

The soloist **performed (verb)** ***badly (adverb).***

* * *

Verbs are complicated because they have so many forms and functions. Analyzing verbs and their relationships to subjects and other words in sentences is no easy task. Let's organize ourselves with the following system:

1. Locate the verb. **Where is it** in the sentence?
2. Find out whether the **form** (spelling) of the verb is regular or irregular.
3. Decide whether the verb expresses **action** or shows a state of being or a condition **(no action).** We will consider explanations and examples of transitive, intransitive and linking verbs.

4. Consider the question of **voice.** Is the subject the "doer" of the action, the receiver of the action, or is there no action expressed through the verb?
5. Confront the issue of **"person."** Remember that nouns and pronouns must agree with the verb about who is speaking, being spoken to or being spoken about.
6. Determine the proper **tense** to provide a time reference.
7. Ascertain what the **mood** is. Is the sentence making a statement, asking a question, giving an order or making a wish?
8. Check for subject–verb agreement. Compare the subjects(s) with the verb(s) and determine their number (whether both are **singular** or **plural**).

Because these elements are difficult to determine simultaneously by glancing at the verb, let's consider them one by one.

Locate the Verb

Except in sentences that ask questions or begin with explanatory material, the normal sentence order is subject-verb-object/complement. Therefore, the verb usually can be found between the subject and the object or complement:

The **photographer took** the **picture.**
(subject) (verb) (object)

— — —

Take the **photograph** again, please.
(verb) ***(object)*** (The unexpressed subject is **you.**)

— — —

The **photograph is fantastic!**
(subject) (verb) (complement)

— — —

Go!
(verb) (The unexpressed subject is **you.** No **object** or **complement** is needed to complete the meaning of the verb.)

* * *

There are four types of sentences: **declarative, imperative, exclamatory** and **interrogative.** The first three usually follow the normal sentence order. The first example above makes a statement (declarative), the second makes a request (imperative), and the last two express strong feelings or emotions (exclamatory).

The fourth type of sentence (interrogative) asks a question, and to ask a questions in English, the normal subject-verb-object/complement order is rearranged by placing all or part of the verb first:

Is the **editor** present?
(verb)(subject)

— — —

Are you going to tonight's meeting?
(verb)(subject)(verb)

Is the Spelling Regular or Irregular?

The form or spelling of verbs is either regular or irregular. If the spelling is regular, the verb adds ***d*** or ***ed*** in both its past principal part and its past participial principal part. The troublemakers are the irregular verbs. Unlike regular verbs, irregular ones follow no pattern and must be memorized. To the uninformed, irregular verbs constantly cause problems.

All verbs have three principal parts: present, past and past participle. The present principal part is the root form of the word (talk, look, hope, etc.). Regular verbs form their past principal part by adding ***d*** to words that end in ***e*** (hope**d,** prove**d,** score**d**), or by adding ***ed*** to the present principal part of words that do not end in ***e*** (talk**ed,** look**ed,** want**ed**). The past participial principal part is formed by placing have, has or had before the past principal part (**have** talk**ed, has** look**ed, had** hope**d**). Irregular verbs make minor (r**u**n, r**a**n, have/has/had r**u**n) or drastic (**go, went,** have/has/had **gone**) changes in forming their principal parts.

If that explanation isn't enough, consider the following:

Principal Parts

Regular Verbs

Present	**Past**	**Past Participle**
jump	jumped	have/has/had jumped
help	helped	have/has/had helped
score	scored	have/has/had scored
hope	hoped	have/has/had hoped

Irregular Verbs

go	went	have/has/had gone
run	ran	have/has/had run
swim	swam	have/has/had swum
swing	swung	have/has/had swung
take	took	have/has/had taken

People who don't know enough about how principal parts are formed can make embarrassing mistakes when selecting tenses because tenses are formed from the principal parts. Fortunately, college students and professional communicators rarely make such fundamental errors as "I seen," "she has took" or "we throwed." Unfortunately, they are not exempt from such common errors as "could have went," "shouldn't have drank" and "could have swam."

Keep the principal parts in mind. We will return to them when we consider tenses. See Reference 3 on pages 321–324 for an extensive list of irregular verbs.

Does the Verb Show Action?

Determining whether the sentence has an action or a nonaction verb is critically important. Action verbs project movement and excitement; nonaction verbs explain a state of being or a condition and are followed frequently by complements. Being skillful in the use of each type is vitally important to journalists, advertising copywriters, public relations practitioners and fiction writers. Consider these examples:

Action Verbs

Flood water **ravaged** the small community of Perrytown.

— — —

She **ran** the distance in record time.

— — —

Thoughts of vengeance **race** through his mind whenever he thinks of his cousin's murder.

These examples can "perk up" readers or listeners by requiring them to be more alert and responsive. Sportscasters and mystery writers don't want passive listeners or readers. When broadcasters and writers use action verbs, especially the present participle (is ravag**ing,** is runn**ing,** is rac**ing**), they hope their listeners and readers will get excited.

Nonaction Verbs

The scenery **is** lovely.

— — —

She **was** my favorite writer.

— — —

They **were** at home throughout the day.

These messages provide useful information but are devoid of movement and excitement. They're quiet and calming and can be received passively by readers or listeners. However, if used too frequently, nonaction verbs quickly bore readers and listeners.

Transitive Verbs

Action verbs that pass the action of the subject to a receiver are classified as ***transitive.*** **Action verbs** whose message is complete without the need to pass the action to a receiver are classified as ***intransitive.*** **Nonaction verbs** followed by a complement (either a predicate noun, a predicate pronoun or a predicate adjective) are classified as ***linking.*** And **nonaction verbs** not followed by complements are classified as ***intransitive.***

Transitive verbs don't make sense without a receiver (direct object) for the action of the verb. To say that "I hit" or that "I enjoy" fails to answer the questions **whom** or **what** was hit or enjoyed. "I unintentionally **hit** my ***friend***" explains ***who*** was hit. "I **enjoy** ***writing***" explains ***what*** is enjoyed.

To determine whether a verb is transitive, follow these three steps:

- Locate the verb and determine if it shows action. In most cases, that's easy. Only a few words (explained later under linking verbs) can be either action or nonaction verbs.

— — —

- Ask the questions ***whom*** or ***what*** after the action verb. If you get an "answer," you should have a direct object (which is always either a noun or a pronoun). Only transitive verbs have direct objects.

— — —

- Figure out if the subject is the "doer" of the action or the receiver. (We will consider this further under **voice.** However, we should point out that only transitive verbs have voice.)

Analyze these examples of transitive verbs:

The archer's *arrow* **hit** the ***target.***

The active voice subject *arrow* is the "doer" of the action. The verb **hit** shows action. The direct object ***target*** answers the question **what** and receives the action.

— — —

The *reporter* **was given** a ***Pulitzer Prize*** by the selection committee.

The passive voice subject *reporter* is the receiver of the action.

Indirect Objects

Although **direct** objects are used frequently, they are only occasionally accompanied by **indirect** objects. To determine whether a sentence has an indirect object, keep in mind the following:

- The sentence **must** have a direct object.

— — —

- After you have found the direct object by asking **whom** or **what** after an action verb, then ask ***to whom*** or ***to what*** or ***for whom*** or ***for what.*** If you get an "answer," you probably have an indirect object (which is always either a noun or a pronoun).

— — —

- The indirect object **always** comes between the action verb and the direct object.

— — —

Analyze these sentences containing indirect objects:

The *editor* **gave** ***me*** an important **assignment.**

Assignment is the **direct object** answering the question **what** after the action verb **gave.** ***Me*** is the **indirect object** answering the question **to whom.**

— — —

Do your ***parents*** a **favor.**

Favor is the **direct object** answering the question **what** after the action verb **do.** ***Parents*** is the **indirect object** answering the question **for whom.**

If you want to move the indirect object out of its position between the action verb and its direct object, you must change the indirect object into a prepositional phrase.

The editor gave an important assignment **to me.**

Do a favor **for your parents.**

Both **to me** and **for your parents** are prepositional phrases. **Me** and **parents** serve as objects of prepositions, not as indirect objects. Note that **me** and **parents** do not come **between** the verb and the direct object as indirect objects would.

Intransitive Verbs

Intransitive verbs include both action and nonaction words. What makes them different from transitive verbs is the absence of direct objects. They don't need objects; they make sense without the need to pass their action along to another word in the sentence. What makes intransitive verbs different from linking verbs is the absence of complements (predicate nouns, predicate pronouns and predicate adjectives). Intransitive verbs make sense without the help of complements to complete their meaning.

Analyze these sentences containing intransitive verbs:

Band members **played** enthusiastically.

The action verb **played** is intransitive because it neither has nor needs an object to receive the action. It makes sense without an object. Do not be tricked into thinking **enthusiastically** is an object. It is an **adverb** answering the question **how** or **in what manner,** and it modifies the verb.

— — —

The frustrated news director **screamed.**

The action verb **screamed** has no object. Its meaning is complete without one.

— — —

The photographer **was** in the right place at the right time.

The nonaction verb **was** has no complement. Its meaning is clear without one. Don't be tricked into thinking that **in the right place** and **at the right time** are predicate complements. Both are **prepositional phrases serving as adverbs** answering the questions **where** and **when.** They modify the verb and explain the location of the subject.

— — —

Behind by 50 points, the players **were** without hope.

The reasoning is the same as in the previous example. The nonaction verb **were** neither has nor needs a predicate complement to make its meaning clear. **Without hope** is a prepositional phrase explaining the condition of the players.

Linking Verbs

Linking verbs are intransitive, have no voice and do not express action. They link predicate complements (predicate nouns, predicate pronouns and predicate adjectives) with the subject of the sentence. Predicate nouns and predicate pronouns rename and further describe the subject. Predicate adjectives describe or limit the subject.

The only thing that makes predicate adjectives different from attributive or appositive adjectives is that they come **after a nonaction verb.** Attributive adjectives come **before the noun or the pronoun** they modify and appositive adjectives come **immediately after the noun or pronoun** they modify. Attributive, appositive and predicate adjectives are discussed on page 130.

Commonly used linking verbs are sensory verbs like *taste* and *feel,* and any of the forms of the verb *to be.*

Johnson *is* the leading candidate.

Is is a nonaction verb linking the predicate noun **candidate** with the subject **Johnson.** The predicate noun complements the subject by telling more about it. Notice that the subject and the predicate noun are interchangeable: **Johnson** is the leading candidate; the leading **candidate** is **Johnson.**

— — —

Who left the meeting early? **It *was* she.**

Was is a nonaction verb linking the predicate pronoun **she** with the subject **it.** The predicate pronoun serves the same function as the predicate noun in the previous example. The predicate pronoun also is interchangeable with the subject: **It** was **she; she** was **it.**

— — —

Most professional basketball **players *are* tall.**

Are is a nonaction verb linking the predicate adjective **tall** with the subject **players.** The predicate adjective describes the subject. The only thing that makes it different from any other adjective is that it comes **after the verb** and "crosses back over it" to modify the subject.

* * *

Don't be fooled by words that can serve as action verbs in one circumstance and as nonaction verbs in another. You can't always tell whether they are transitive or linking by looking at them. You have to consider their meaning, and you do that by examining the words on each side of them.

These confusing words include **appear, feel, get, grow, hear, look, smell** and **taste.**

Analyze the following examples:

I always **feel** the ***material*** before buying a sweater.

Feel is an *action verb.* The subject, **I,** always physically feels the material before buying the sweater. The action of the subject is passed along through the verb to the **direct object, *material;*** therefore, **feel** is a **transitive verb.**

— — —

I feel *weak.*

In this case, **feel** is a nonaction verb linking the predicate adjective ***weak*** with the subject **I. Feel** represents a state of being or a condition. Therefore, **feel** is a **linking verb.**

— — —

The editor **looks** everywhere for new ideas.

Looks is an *action verb.* The editor is physically looking. The verb needs neither objects nor complements to make its meaning clear; therefore, **looks** is a **"complete" intransitive verb.**

— — —

The front page **looks *great.***

In this case, **looks** is a *nonaction verb.* It refers to the condition of the front page rather than implying that the inanimate newspaper page is capable of seeing. ***Great*** is a **predicate adjective** describing the subject; therefore, **looks** is a **linking verb.**

— — —

Smell the perking ***coffee.***

Smell is an *action verb* requiring the subject to sniff. ***Coffee*** is the **direct object** answering the question **what** after the verb; therefore, the verb is **transitive.**

— — —

"This stale coffee **smells** terrible," she complained.

Smells is a *nonaction verb* describing a state of being or a condition. Unlike the previous example, no one is performing a physical function such as sniffing. The verb joins the predicate adjective, **terrible,** with the subject, **coffee;** therefore the verb is **linking.**

* * *

Sometimes a linking verb followed by a predicate adjective is confused with a passive voice verb. A quick judgment could cause that mistake. Remember that a predicate adjective **describes** the subject; a passive voice verb **affects** or **influences** the subject. By looking closely, you can avoid the error. Consider the following examples:

The detectives ***were confused*** by the conflicting evidence.

Were confused is a *passive voice verb.* **By the conflicting evidence** is a prepositional phrase serving as an adverb. It modifies the verb and explains why the detectives were confused.

— — —

The detectives ***were confused.***

Were is a *linking verb.* It joins the predicate adjective ***confused*** with the subject **detectives.** The predicate adjective describes the state of being or the condition of the detectives.

What makes ***confused*** appear to be a verb is the fact that it often is one. **Confus*e*** is the present principal part, **confus*ed*** is the past principal part, and **have/has/had confus*ed*** is the past participial principal part. However, in this example, ***confused*** is functioning as a **participle,** a verb form always used as an adjective.

For ***confused*** to be a verb in this example, the sentence would have to contain information explaining what confused the detectives. In the absence of such information, ***confused*** can function only as an adjective to describe the detectives' state of mind.

— — —

The detectives **were *enlightened*** by a piece of additional evidence.

The detectives **were *enlightened.***

In the first example, ***were enlightened*** is a *passive voice verb.* The two prepositional phrases, **by a piece** and **of additional evidence,** explain how the detectives came to be enlightened.

In the second example, ***enlightened*** is a participle serving as a **predicate adjective.** The verb **were** links the predicate adjective with the subject. ***Enlightened*** explains that the detectives are free from ignorance, prejudice and superstition. In the first example, the verb combines with the prepositional phrases to explain how the detectives were freed from their ignorance.

* * *

Remember that linking verbs require predicate adjectives, **not adverbs.** Consider the following examples:

Because she has a headache, the graphic artist **feels *bad.***

Bad is an *adjective* describing the subject **artist. *Badly*** cannot be used because it is an *adverb.* Remember, we are trying to describe the subject's condition, not her ability to physically feel something.

— — —

The losing boxer **looks *terrible.***

Apply the same reasoning used in the previous example. ***Terrible*** is an *adjective* describing the subject, **boxer.** Boxer is a noun and nouns can be modified only by adjectives; therefore, the *adverb* ***terribly*** would be incorrect.

(See additional examples on pages 138–139 in the chapter on adverbs.)

Voice (Active and Passive)

Recall from our previous explanations that transitive verbs are action words that pass the action to an object. All transitive verbs have voice. If the subject is the "doer" of the action, we have active voice; if the subject is the receiver of the action, we have passive voice. To explain verbs and the element of voice, let's review two of the examples we used previously:

The archer's *arrow* **hit** the *target.*

The active voice subject *arrow* is the **"doer"** of the action. The verb **hit** shows action. The direct object ***target*** answers the question **what** and receives the action. Because the subject is the "doer" of the action, we have **active voice.**

— — —

The *reporter* **was given a *Pulitzer Prize*** by the selection committee.

The subject, **reporter,** is the **receiver** of the action; therefore, we have **passive voice.** The passive voice is formed by using the appropriate form of the verb **be** with the past participle of the main verb. Remember that if the main verb is in the *ing* form (was giv*ing*), it cannot be passive voice because the subject will be the "doer" of the action.

To determine the issue of **voice,** consider this simple guideline. Active voice is present if the subject is the **doer** of the action. Passive voice is present if the subject is the **receiver** of the action. Some handbooks, like this one, attribute voice only to transitive verbs. Others identify all verbs as active unless they meet the criteria for passive voice: a transitive verb acting on its subject and made up of the past participle and a form of the verb *to be.*

Passive voice is useful when you do not know or you want to conceal the subject (Orders were posted on the bulletin board), or when you want to name the object of the action before the doer (Three world records were broken by the Americans on the first day of the Winter Olympics).

Passive voice also is used extensively in scientific writing, especially in describing research projects, to emphasize what is being done and to avoid saying "I" or "we" repeatedly throughout the paper (Treatment was found to be effective in 95 percent of the cases).

Most of the time, the features that the cumbersome and wordy passive voice offers are not needed; therefore, good writers give preference to active voice.

Person (First, Second and Third)

Subjects and verbs have to agree not only in number (both must be either singular or plural) but also in **person *(first person, second person and third person).*** First person refers to the person communicating the message either in written or spoken form. Second person refers to the person receiving the written or spoken message. Third person refers to the person, place or thing being written or spoken about.

I and **we** are **first-person** personal pronouns used as subjects:

I (the **singular** speaker/writer) ***am*** hoping to become a journalist.

We (the **plural** speakers/writers) ***are*** hoping to become journalists.

— — —

You is the **second-person** personal pronoun used as a subject regardless of whether the subject is singular or plural:

You (the **singular** person being spoken/written to) ***are*** a finalist for the job.

You (the **plural** people being spoken/written to) ***are*** finalists for the job.

— — —

He, she, it and **they** are **third-person** personal pronouns used as subjects:

He/she/it (the **singular** person, place or thing being spoken/written about) ***is*** not available.

They (the **plural** people, places or things being spoken/written about) ***are*** not available.

* * *

Keep in mind that third-person singular personal pronouns in the nominative case use a verb form (spelling) different from that used by singular nominative case pronouns in the first and second persons. Because nouns are almost always used in the third person, they also share with pronouns the spelling of the verb in the third person. The following examples will illustrate the point:

(First person)	I **want.**
(Second person)	You **want.**
(Third person)	He/She/It **wants.**
(First person)	I **go.**
(Second person)	You **go.**
(Third person)	He/She/It **goes.**
(First person)	I **carry.**
(Second person)	You **carry.**
(Third person)	He/She/It **carr*ies*.**
(First person)	I **have.**
(Second person)	You **have.**
(Third person)	He/She/It **has.**
(Third person nouns)	Jones **wants.**
	The team **goes.**
	The horse **carr*ies*.**
	The library **has.**

Remember that pronouns and their noun antecedents also must agree in number and person. An explanation of noun–pronoun agreement is presented on pages 84–89.

Tense

Tense tells readers and listeners the time to which the verb refers. That seems easy to understand. After all, how many times can there be? We have a past tense for things that already have happened, a present tense for things going on now and a future tense for things to come.

At this point in our study, however, we know how misleading an apparently simple concept can be. For example, the present tense is not limited to current happenings, and each of the three perfect tenses can refer to at least two things that have a time relationship with each other. Furthermore, each simple tense and every perfect tense has a progressive form ending in ***ing*** to provide motion.

The goal for mass communicators is to know how to form each of the tenses and when to use them. With our study of principal parts of verbs freshly in mind, let's take a step-by-step approach toward that goal.

Present Tense

- It refers to something happening **now.** We use the present principal part of the verb to form the present tense: The editor **understands** our problem.

— — —

- It refers to something that happens **continually:** The editor **always understands** our problems.

— — —

- It refers to something **commonly accepted:** Hard work and dedicated study **lead** to good grades in school and success on the job.

— — —

- Headline writers and others use the present tense to refer to the **classical** or **historical** present: Rutledge **wins** close race for county clerk.

Past Tense

It is simple to understand because it refers to things that have been **completed.** We use the past principal part of the verb for past tense: The editor **understood** our problem. Our late editor **always understood** our problems.

Future Tense

It refers to things **to come.** We form the future tense by placing **will** or **shall** in front of the present principal part of the verb (the same principal part we use for present tense): The editor **will assign** most of your stories. I **shall remember** your kindness forever.

Mass communicators prefer the informal **will** over the more formal **shall** even though they are aware that **shall** is recommended for first person **(I, we)** and **will** for second and third persons **(you, he, she, it, they).**

Present Perfect

The present perfect tense is formed by placing **has** (in the third-person singular) or **have** (in all other instances) before the past participial principal part of the verb. This tense refers to **something** that **already** has been **completed** but **still affects the present:** The leader **has finished** the first three miles. *(Three miles have been completed, but the leader is still running.)*

Past Perfect

The past perfect tense is formed by placing **had** before the past participial principal part of the verb. This tense refers to two things that have concluded and shows **which was over first and which second:** The winner **had completed** the race long **before** her major opponent. *(Both runners have completed the race, but one finished before the other.)*

Future Perfect

The future perfect tense is formed by placing **shall have** or **will have** before the past participial principal part of the verb. This tense refers to two things that will occur before a specified time and shows **which will occur first and which second:** By the time you earn your college degree four years from now, your father **will have retired** from the advertising business. *(The father will retire before his son or daughter finishes college.)*

* * *

Each of the simple and perfect tenses also has a progressive form that places an ***ing*** ending on the present principal part of the verb and expresses motion. It is used frequently in the simple tenses and occasionally in the perfect tenses. While keeping in mind both the principal parts of verbs and the six tenses we have just discussed, study the following uses of the progressive form.

Present Progressive

The present progressive is formed by placing the appropriate form of the verb **be** (**am, are** or **is**) before the present principal part of the verb with an ***ing*** ending. The present progressive shows **continuous action** and is used more often than simple present tense to show that something is happening now: I **am hoping** for a good grade. They **are studying** for their examinations. He **is applying** to graduate school.

The simple present tense would have expressed these thoughts as follows: I **hope** for a good grade. They **study** for their examinations. He **applies** to graduate school. Clearly, the present progressive form is a better choice.

The *present perfect progressive* is expressed as follows: I **have been hoping** for a good grade since the class began three months ago. He **has been applying** to graduate school all summer.

Past Progressive

The past progressive is formed by placing the appropriate form of the verb **be** (**was** or **were**) before the present principal part of the verb with an ***ing*** ending. The past progressive shows **continuous action from the past:** I **was hoping** for a good grade, and I got it. He **was applying** to graduate school because he couldn't get a job.

The *past perfect progressive* is expressed as follows: I **had been hoping** for a good grade, but I didn't get it. He **had been applying** to graduate schools for half a year before he was accepted.

Future Progressive

The future progressive is formed by placing **shall be** or **will be** before the present principal part of the verb with an ***ing*** ending. The future progressive shows **continuous action for the future:** I assure you that I **shall be** (formal)/**will be** (informal) **working** as hard as I can to make good grades. He **will be applying** to graduate school next month because he is getting discouraged with his job search.

The *future perfect progressive* is expressed as follows: By the time they hire the new employee, they **will have been reviewing and interviewing** applicants for three months. By next September, he **will have been working** here five years.

Be Careful with Tense Shifts

Probably as much as any other group, comedians make tense shifting errors while trying to make their stories current. For example, during a 10-minute presentation, a 45-year-old comedian said: "That reminds me of something that **happened** (past tense) to me when I was a kid. **I'm** (present tense) in the fourth grade, and the teacher **catches** (present tense) me **pestering** (present tense) Becky Ann Perry. . . ."

Comedians may get by with such awkward tense shifts, but mass communicators cannot. However they, too, can shift tenses in the same sentence, but they must do it logically. Consider the following examples:

(Avoid) The defense attorney **said** (past tense) his client deserves mercy, but the prosecutor **says** (present tense) the defendant should be executed.

(Better) Use either **said** or **says** twice, but do not use one of each. Journalists prefer **said** over **says** in most circumstances.

— — —

(Avoid) The prosecutor **said** (past tense) he **believed** (past tense) the death penalty is justified.

(Better) Change **believed** to **believes** (present tense). To use **believed** indicates incorrectly that the prosecutor has had a change of mind.

— — —

(Avoid) When the alarm **sounded** (past tense), the firefighters **hurry** (present tense) to their truck.

(Better) Either make both present tense **(sounds, hurry)** or past tense **(sounded, hurried).**

— — —

(Avoid) The group **meets** (present tense) at 5 p.m. Thursday.

(Better) The group **will meet** (future tense) at 5 p.m. Thursday.

— — —

(Avoid) The group **is meeting** (present progressive) at 5 p.m. Thursday.

(Better) The group **will meet** (future tense) at 5 p.m. Thursday.

Mood

Mood helps readers and listeners interpret the purpose of the sentence. Is the writer or the broadcaster presenting a fact? a question? a request? a command? a condition contrary to fact? a possibility? a desirability? The three moods—indicative, imperative and subjunctive—provide the means for making the interpretation.

Indicative

The indicative mood is used for statements and questions. A statement ends with a period, and a question that requires a response ends with a question mark. This mood is used far more often than the other two combined, for what writers and broadcasters do most is make statements and ask questions.

(Statement) Everyone's copy needs to be edited.

(Question) Does everyone's copy need to be edited?

Imperative

The imperative mood expresses a request or a command. The subject is ***you,*** which is usually understood but not written. The end punctuation may be either a period or an exclamation mark, depending on the degree of emotion being expressed by the writer or the speaker.

(Request) Please complete this story before the deadline.

(Command) Meet your deadline or you'll be fired!

* * *

Also note that when a speaker or a writer puts a request or a command in the form of a question to be polite, the mood is still imperative. **Do not end the sentence with a question mark.** The speaker or the writer is still making a request or a command. The person receiving the request or command is not being asked if he or she wants to comply.

(Request) "Shall we gather in the adjoining room for refreshments."

(Command) Will you please hold still while I'm shaving your neck!

* * *

When a request or a command is preceded or followed by a person's name, the understood but usually not expressed subject is still ***you,*** not the person's name. The person's name is a noun of direct address.

Jacob, please write the lead editorial for Thursday's newspaper.

Please write the lead editorial for Thursday's newspaper, **Jacob.**

Jacob is the noun of direct address, and the unexpressed ***you*** is the subject.

Subjunctive

The primary functions of the subjunctive mood are to express a wish or to make a statement contrary to fact. This mood is far more difficult than the other two, primarily because it does some strange things with basic rules of grammar. Fortunately for people who have trouble with it, the subjunctive mood is used far less frequently than it once was.

In most subjunctives, we use the plural form of the verb, even when the subject is singular (for example, *were* instead of *was*). Use the subjunctive in the following ways:

1. **To express a wish** (use the plural verb *were* even when the subject is singular).

   I wish I **were** the editor.

   — — —

   Humphreys wishes he **were** 2,000 miles away from the graphics laboratory.

   — — —

   The president of the advertising agency said she wishes I **were** available for an interview.

2. **To express a condition contrary to fact** (especially, but not limited to, clauses that begin with *if*).

   If I were you, I'd apply for the job as director of advertising.

   — — —

   The editor said **if** she **were** able to give me a salary increase, she would.

   — — —

   Had I just taken the time to listen, this tragedy might not have happened.

3. **To express doubt or uncertainty after *as though* and *as if.***

   The sports reporter acted **as though** he **were** unsure of what question to ask next.

   — — —

   "He acts **as if** he **were** a beginner," the news director complained.

4. **Without an *"s"* ending for third-person singular verbs.**

   The new publisher told all department heads that it is necessary that she **approve** *(not approves)* all raises.

   — — —

   She also said it is important that she **check** *(not checks)* all advertising sales figures at the end of each week.

   — — —

   She also recommended that the regional vice president **read** *(not reads)* the monthly financial statements.

5. **In clauses beginning with the word *that,* use *be* instead of *is* or *are* to show parliamentary motion, to give a mild command and to state a necessity.**

   The City Council member moved **that** the resolution **be** adopted.

   In this parliamentary motion, **is/are** cannot be used in place of **be** because **is** or **are** would indicate that the resolution already had been adopted.

   — — —

   "I order **that** he **be** present in the courtroom," the judge said.

   The judge can't say **is** because the court session he is referring to has not happened yet.

   — — —

"It is important **that** you **be** silent during the ceremony," the minister told his congregation.

Are would not make sense because the ceremony hasn't taken place yet.

6. **With the helping verbs *would* and *could* to express speculations or conditions contrary to fact.**

Had conditions **been** favorable, we ***would*** have finished the story in time for the final edition, the editor said.

— — —

If we had started just 30 minutes earlier, we ***could*** have made the deadline.

Verbals

They look much like verbs.

They act much like verbs.

They can have modifiers the same as verbs.

They can have objects the same as verbs.

But they are not verbs and cannot serve as verbs.

"They" are **verbals,** verbs' curious but commonly used offspring that work their way into sentences as adjectives, adverbs or nouns. Verbals is the collective name for ***gerunds, participles*** and ***infinitives.*** Gerunds serve as nouns, participles as adjectives, and the versatile infinitives as adjectives, adverbs and nouns.

Gerunds

Let's consider gerunds first because they are the easiest. Gerunds are formed from words commonly used as verbs but with the addition of an ***ing*** (present participle) ending. Play**ing**, hop**ing**, feel**ing**, swimm**ing**, walk**ing** and think**ing** are but a few examples. Gerunds may be used in any way that a noun can function in a sentence.

(Subject) **Swimming** is good exercise.

— — —

(Appositive) My least favorite chore, **typing,** has been made less burdensome now that I have a computer.

— — —

(Predicate complement) My only exercise is **walking.**

— — —

(Object of preposition) The graduate student sets aside five hours a day for **studying.**

— — —

(Direct object) Most journalists enjoy **reading.**

— — —

(Indirect object) The sports editor gave **rowing** top coverage in today's newspaper.

Like all other words, the way a word with an ***ing*** ending functions in a sentence determines its part of speech. Words that end in ***ing*** serve frequently as verbs with the help of an auxiliary. We can say correctly that **we *cheer* for our favorite team,** but we cannot say correctly that **we *cheering* for our favorite team.** The verb is incomplete without a helper such as *are, am, is, was, were* or *have/has/had been.*

Participles

Like gerunds, participles serve exclusively as one part of speech, and they also have ***ing*** endings. But unlike gerunds, participles do not have to end in ***ing,*** and that fact alone makes them more complicated.

As adjectives, participles have only one function—to modify nouns and pronouns. But because they most often work within phrases instead of alone, participles are more difficult to learn and use than ordinary adjectives.

Agriculture experts are concerned about the ***increasing*** population.

The participle **increasing** functions alone as an adjective to modify the noun **population.**

— — —

***Applying* for the third time,** Cassels finally was accepted by the graduate school.

The participial phrase ***applying* for the third time** serves as an adjective to modify the noun **Cassels.**

— — —

The peace talks, ***complicated* by the refusal of one leader to participate,** start today in Paris.

The participial phrase ***complicated* by the refusal of one leader to participate** modifies the noun **talks.**

Infinitives

Like gerunds, infinitives can function as nouns. Like participles, infinitives can function as adjectives. Unlike either gerunds or participles, however, infinitives also can perform the functions of adverbs.

Except for when the word **to** is not expressed, infinitives are easy to identify. When **to** is followed by the present principal part of the verb *(to run, to talk, to listen, to help, to deny),* it is an infinitive. When **to** is followed by a noun or a pronoun object *(to the room, to the meeting, to the class, to the office),* it is a preposition.

Infinitives may work alone *(to go, to fail, to imagine)* or in a phrase (*to go* to the conference, *to fail* the examination, *to imagine* winning the lottery).

Haggerty asked **to speak.**

The infinitive **to speak** functions as a **noun** by serving as the object of the verb **asked.**

— — —

***To prepare* for a career in mass communications** is a worthwhile ambition.

The infinitive phrase ***to prepare* for a career in mass communications** functions as a **noun** by serving as the subject of the sentence.

— — —

The photographer stopped **to reload.**

The infinitive **to reload** serves as an **adverb** by answering the question *why* and modifying the verb **stopped.**

— — —

She went to her boss ***to ask* for a raise.**

The infinitive phrase **to ask for a raise** functions as an **adverb** by answering the question *why* and modifying the verb **went.**

— — —

The advertising director complained that she had too much **to do.**

The infinitive **to do** functions as an *adjective* by modifying the pronoun **much.**

— — —

Writing ***to please* the editor** is not as satisfying as writing to please yourself.

The infinitive phrase ***to please* the editor** modifies the gerund ***writing.***

Infinitives with To *Not Expressed*

Spotting infinitives becomes more difficult when the word **to** does not have to be expressed. Just like the understood subject **you** in an imperative sentence ([***You***] Check out the final edition, please), the word **to** is present in an infinitive even when it is not expressed. Consider the following examples:

My news source made just one demand: ***(to)* Keep** his identity confidential.

To may be expressed or unexpressed in this example.

— — —

The photographers volunteered to help me ***(to)*** **watch** for the president's car to arrive.

Expressing ***to*** would be awkward in this example.

— — —

Please help me ***(to)*** **think** of an idea for this advertising campaign.

The sentence reads better with ***to*** unexpressed.

* * *

Beware of "Dangling" Verbals

"Dangling" sentence elements—whether they are verbals, dependent clauses, or prepositional phrases—create confusion about which word is being modified. This problem is discussed extensively in the **Syntax** section on pages 163–168. The following are examples of dangling verbals:

(**Dangling participle**) **Being a write-in candidate,** McKinney's name will not appear on the ballot.

Name is not the candidate; **McKinney** is.

(Correct) **Being a write-in candidate,** McKinney will not have his name on the ballot.

Now the participial phrase correctly modifies the subject, **McKinney.**

(Correct) **Because he is a write-in candidate,** McKinney will not have his name on the ballot.

A dependent clause that modifies the subject, **McKinney,** is substituted correctly for the participial phrase.

— — —

(**Dangling infinitive**) **To succeed as an editor,** a thorough knowledge of your employees' duties is required.

Knowledge is not trying to succeed; a ***person*** is.

(Correct) **To succeed as an editor,** you must have a thorough knowledge of your employees' duties.

Now the infinitive phrase correctly modifies the subject, **you.**

(Correct) **If you are to succeed as an editor,** you must have a thorough knowledge of your employees' duties.

A dependent clause that modifies the subject, **you,** is substituted correctly for the infinitive phrase.

— — —

(Dangling gerund) Instead of **writing my report,** my professor accepted a recording of it.

The **professor** is not writing the report.

(Correct) Instead of **requiring me to write my report,** the professor accepted a recording of it.

Now we correctly have the **student** completing the paper and the **professor** accepting it.

(Correct) Instead of **writing my report,** I received permission from my professor to record it.

This sentence also makes clear that the **student** is doing the report, not the **professor.**

* * *

Verbals May Have Modifiers and Objects

Although verbals cannot function as verbs, as verb forms they retain characteristics of verbs. That means they can be modified and take objects. The following examples illustrate the point:

Participial Phrases

The most valuable player was Merrick, ***selected*** **by a committee of writers and broadcasters.**

The participle ***selected*** is modified by the prepositional phrases **by a committee** and **of writers and broadcasters.**

— — —

Having **a big tax refund,** I paid cash for the computer.

Refund is the object of the participle ***having.***

— — —

Feeling **sick,** I asked my photography chief to excuse me from work.

Sick serves as an **adverb** to modify the participle ***feeling.***

Gerund Phrases

Interviewing **all the candidates** will take most of the week.

— — —

All the candidates serves as the object of the gerund ***interviewing.***

— — —

Typing **slowly** is my worst fault.

Slowly modifies the gerund ***typing.***

Infinitive Phrases

Unlike most journalists who like to work on assignments out of the office, Hixson loves ***to edit*** **copy.**

Copy serves as the object of the infinitive ***to edit.***

— — —

To write **clearly** is my main objective.

Clearly modifies the infinitive ***to write.***

(You may test yourself on the material in this chapter or section by connecting with the following Web site: www.mhhe.com/arnold.)

chapter 11

SUBJECT–VERB AGREEMENT

Rules Eliminate Guess Work

Singular subjects require singular verbs and plural subjects require plural verbs. That's simple enough. And when we write sentences in which the subject and the verb are side by side, we have few problems making them agree in number. However, in many sentences we place phrases and clauses between the subject and the verb. This complicates the situation considerably.

To make things even tougher, we frequently use as subjects collective nouns that are usually singular but can be plural depending on their intended meaning. Furthermore, some nouns that look plural because they end in ***s*** are singular in meaning and take singular verbs. Additional complicating factors will be considered in this section.

Regardless of how simple or how complex the subject–verb relationship is in any sentence, we can take comfort in knowing that there is no guesswork involved. Specific rules cover virtually every circumstance. Some are simple; some are difficult. The following pages contain rules, examples and explanations that should help clarify the decision-making process.

Singular Subjects

If the subject is singular, use a singular verb.

The **fire** ***is*** under control, the chief said.

Fire is a singular subject; therefore, use the singular verb ***is,*** not the plural verb ***are.***

Plural Subjects

If the subject is plural, use a plural verb.

Union **members** ***are*** to vote Tuesday on the contract proposal.

Members is a plural subject; therefore, use the plural verb ***are,*** not the singular verb ***is.***

Compound Subjects

If two or more different subjects (compound subjects) are joined by the coordinating conjunction *and,* use a plural verb.

The student **editor and** the **principal** ***discuss*** school issues each Monday at 9 a.m.

> **Editor** by itself is a singular noun, and the same is true for **principal.** But when connected by the coordinating conjunction ***and,*** **editor** and **principal** form a **compound subject** that requires the third-person plural verb ***discuss,*** not ***discusses.***

— — —

The **editor in chief,** the **managing editor** and the **editor** of the editorial page ***determine*** professional policies to be followed by the reporting staff.

> **Three singular subjects** joined by the coordinating conjunction ***and*** form a **compound subject** that requires the third-person plural verb ***determine,*** not ***determines.***

* * *

An exception to the previous rule comes in those less common instances in which a compound subject joined by *and* refers to the same person or thing and takes a singular verb.

The **producer and director** ***is*** preparing the news special for Friday night's broadcast.

> The **same person is both the producer and director** of the program; therefore, a singular verb is used. When one person is serving as the producer and another person as the director, the plural verb ***are*** would be correct. In that case, the sentence would have been written as follows: **The** producer and **the** director ***are*** preparing the news special for Friday night's broadcast.

— — —

His **brother and best friend** ***is*** in serious condition at Acme General Hospital.

> **Brother** and **best friend** are words referring to the same person; therefore, a singular verb is required. If the subjects referred to different people, the sentence would be written as follows: His **brother and his best friend** ***are*** both members of today's graduating class.

Note that even though the examples with the singular verbs are grammatically correct, they are still potentially misleading. How many readers or listeners are aware that the omission of **the** before **director** and **his** before **best friend** indicates that only one person is being referred to in each sentence?

Eliminate the potential confusion by using producer and director as a **compound noun:** The **producer-director** is preparing the news special for Friday night's broadcast. Or you could tell your readers or listeners that **the person** producing and directing Friday night's broadcast is at work preparing it. The second example can be expressed clearly as follows: His **brother,** who is also his **best friend,** is in serious condition at Acme General Hospital.

You as the Subject

The second-person personal pronoun *you* requires a plural verb regardless of whether its antecedent is singular or plural.

You *are* a talented *journalist.*

You *are* talented *journalists.*

Even though **you** refers to just **one** journalist in the first example, a plural verb is always used. A plural verb is required in the second example referring to the plural journalists.

The requirement of a **plural verb** with a **singular *you*** has caused endless confusion. **You *are* invited** can refer to one person or more than one. The problem has been so troublesome that people in several regions of the country have developed their own words or expressions to make clear the distinction between **you *singular*** and **you *plural.*** The next time you're tempted to make fun of someone who says "y'all," "you all," "youse" or "you'uns," remember that the people who use these terms are just trying to make up for a deficiency in the language.

Nontraditional Sentence Order

When the traditional sentence order (subject-verb-object) is not followed, look for the subject in the middle or near the end of the sentence. Do not be fooled into thinking an introductory word (such as *here* or *there*) is the subject.

Here *is* the assignment **sheet.**

The singular subject **sheet** requires the singular verb ***is.*** **Here** functions as an adverb modifying the verb and telling where the sheet is.

— — —

Here ***come*** the **editor** and her **assistant.**

The plural compound subjects **editor** and **assistant** require the third-person plural verb ***come,*** not the singular verb ***comes.***

— — —

There ***was*** a long **silence** between the prosecutor's questions.

The singular subject **silence** requires the singular verb ***was.***

— — —

*There **are*** two **meetings** to be covered before the final deadline.

The plural subject **meetings** requires the plural verb ***are.***

— — —

Making** the most money from the blizzard alert **were the **supermarkets** and the grocery **stores.**

The plural compound subjects **supermarkets** and **stores** require the plural verb ***were.***

— — —

Getting** the most attention at the wedding **was the **bride,** of course.

The singular subject **bride** requires the singular verb ***was.***

Subjects Having Plural Form but Singular Meaning

If the subject has a plural form (spelling) but is singular in meaning, use a singular verb.

The **news** ***was*** not as bad as we had feared.

Even though the subject, **news,** has an *s* ending that makes it look plural, it is still **singular** because the news is considered as a whole, not one item at a time. Therefore, **news** requires the singular verb ***is,*** not the plural verb ***are.***

— — —

The **series** of documentaries ***is*** being produced by a public broadcasting station.

The subject, **series,** certainly consists of more than one documentary. But it is **only one series;** therefore, it requires the singular verb ***is,*** not the plural verb ***are.***

Do not be confused by the word **documentaries.** It is the object of the preposition **of** and has no influence on whether the verb will be singular or plural. Remember that an object of a preposition is in the **objective case** and only nouns and pronouns in the **nominative case** can serve as subjects. However, please note that an entire prepositional phrase can serve as a subject, as the following example illustrates: **To the left** is correct. Do not turn to the right.

Three minutes is considered a long time for a single item in a newscast.

Minutes usually would be a plural word because it consists of more than a single minute. However, in this example, **three minutes** is considered **one lump sum, one period of time;** therefore, the subject is singular and requires the singular verb ***is,*** not the plural verb ***are.***

— — —

"**Two million dollars** ***is*** more than the city budget can afford to allot to renovate the civic center," the mayor said.

The reasoning in this example is the same as that used in the preceding one involving the word **minutes. Two million dollars** is considered **one lump sum;** therefore, it is singular and requires the singular verb ***is,*** not the plural verb ***are.***

— — —

Eight years of college work ***has*** resulted in his earning a Ph.D.

Eight years is considered **one unit or block of time;** therefore, a singular verb is required.

— — —

Attorneys ***is*** a word whose plural form is often misspelled.

The subject, **attorneys,** is not used in this sentence to refer to two or more lawyers. It is used as **one word** that has the unusual characteristic of forming its plural by adding ***s*** to a ***y*** ending instead of dropping the ***y*** and adding ***ies.*** Therefore, **attorneys** in this example requires the singular verb ***is,*** not the plural verb ***are*** that usually would accompany it. If we were using **attorneys** as a plural to refer to more than one attorney, a plural verb would be required: The **attorneys** ***are*** meeting in San Francisco.

— — —

Simple Explanations for Common Writing and Editing Problems **is** the title of a book.

Regardless of how many words it contains or how many of those words are plural, the title of a book, movie, play, poem or song is singular. It is **only one title;** therefore, it requires a singular verb.

— — —

Measles ***is*** still a potentially dangerous disease, according to a warning from the American Medical Association.

Everyone knows that the disease consists of more than one spot on the afflicted body. Never in medical history has anyone had just one measle. Nevertheless, measles is **only one disease;** therefore, it requires a singular verb.

— — —

Economics ***is*** a difficult subject for most mass communications majors.

The same reasoning given in the previous example also applies to this one. Economics is **only one subject;** therefore, it requires the singular verb ***is,*** not the plural verb ***are.***

Compound Subjects that Form One Unit

If the members or parts of a compound subject are considered one item, one unit or one substance, use a singular verb.

Vinegar and oil *is* a popular salad dressing.

Previously, you were told that if two or more subjects are joined by **and,** you are to use a plural verb. This is an exception to that rule. In this example, **vinegar and oil** are mixed to form **one salad dressing;** therefore, the subject is considered **one substance** and requires the singular verb ***is,*** not the plural verb ***are.***

— — —

"**Liver and onions** *is* a meal people either love or hate," the chef explained.

Liver and onions is **one meal** or **one menu item;** the liver and the onions are not served and eaten separately. Therefore, the subject is singular and requires the singular verb ***is,*** not the plural verb ***are.***

Number, Variety and *Majority* as Subjects

When the words *number, variety* and *majority* are preceded by the definite article *the,* the verb is singular; when *number, variety* and *majority* are preceded by the indefinite article *a,* the verb is plural.

The publisher told the editing staff that ***the*** **number of** *errors* in last month's edition of the magazine ***is*** more than he will tolerate.

The **number** of *students* studying mass communication in college ***has*** increased in recent years.

— — —

A **number** of *protesters* ***are*** expected outside the capitol when the governor arrives to give his State-of-the-State address tonight.

The chancellor said ***a*** large **number** of financial *problems* ***are*** keeping some qualified students from attending college.

— — —

The **variety** of *courses* ***was*** designed to attract as many students as possible.

A* variety** of *courses **are available to experienced journalists who want to continue their education.

— — —

The* majority** of the *vote **has been cast in favor of the incumbent.

A* majority** of the *delegates **are expected to arrive throughout the weekend.

The definite article ***the*** refers to a group or a collection considered as **a unit** and requires a ***singular*** verb. The indefinite article ***a*** refers to **individual members or parts** of the group or collection and requires a ***plural*** verb.

Sentences with Predicate Nouns

Predicate nouns have no influence on the number of the verb. If the subject is singular, use a singular verb; if the subject is plural, use a plural verb.

Video display *terminals **are*** my favorite **invention.**

The subject, **terminals,** and the predicate noun, **invention,** are the same thing. The job of the singular predicate noun is to provide more information about the subject. The fact that **invention is singular** has no influence on the verb. **Terminals** is a plural subject; therefore, it requires the plural verb ***are,*** not the singular verb ***is.***

— — —

My favorite *invention **is*** video display **terminals.**

In this example, **invention** becomes the subject and **terminals** the predicate noun. **Invention** is singular and requires the singular verb ***is,*** not the plural verb ***are.*** The predicate noun, **terminals,** plays no role in the decision.

One Subject Used Affirmatively and the Other Subject Used Negatively

When one part of a compound subject is used affirmatively and the other is used negatively, the verb agrees with the one used affirmatively. The affirmative subject is almost always listed before the negative one.

The **mayor,** ***never** his assistants,* **appears** before the television cameras to announce news voters will welcome.

His **assistants,** ***never** the mayor,* **appear** before the television cameras to announce news voters will dislike.

— — —

I told the editor that **Elizabeth,** ***not I,*** **is** responsible for persuading the governor to release the information.

I told the editor that **I,** ***not*** *Elizabeth,* **am** responsible for persuading the governor to release the information.

Each and *Every* Preceding Compound Subjects

If compound subjects are preceded by *each* or *every,* use a singular verb.

Each **camera** and ***each*** **lens** ***was*** inspected by the chief photographer.

This is another example of compound subjects joined by **and** but requiring a singular verb. The singular verb ***was*** is used instead of the plural verb **were** because a separate action was used to inspect **each** camera and **each** lens. If the reference had been to the cameras and the lens as a group, the verb would have been plural: The **cameras** and the **lens** ***are*** inspected regularly.

— — —

Note that if **each** follows a compound subject, it has no influence on the number of the verb:

The **5 p.m. news program anchor** and the **6 p.m. news anchor** ***each*** **have** separate reporting staffs.

However, even though the rule is worth knowing, why use it? Simply write or say that the **5 p.m. news anchor** and the **6 p.m. news anchor** ***have*** separate reporting staffs.

Every **reporter** and ***every*** **editor** ***was*** given a pay raise.

The reporters and the editors are dealt with **individually;** therefore, a **singular** verb is used. Had the editors and the reporters been dealt with **as a group,** the verb would have been plural: The **reporters** and the **editors** ***were*** given a pay raise.

Either/Or and *Neither/Nor* before Compound Subjects

If two (or more) subjects are joined by the correlative conjunctions *either/or* or *neither/nor,* the verb agrees with the nearer subject.

Either the *senator* from Vermont **or** the *governor* of New York ***is*** expected to give the keynote address.

The decision is easy. Both subjects, **senator** and **governor,** are **singular;** therefore, the verb is **singular.**

— — —

Neither the *politicians* **nor** the *reporters* ***were*** surprised by the small number of voters.

This one is equally easy. Both subjects, **politicians** and **reporters,** are **plural;** therefore, the verb is **plural.**

— — —

Neither the *mayors* **nor** the **governor** ***wants*** to raise taxes. **Neither** the **governor nor** the *mayors* ***want*** to raise taxes.

These two examples, unlike the two easy previous ones, require a decision. One subject, **governor,** is **singular;** the other, **mayors,** is **plural.** The rule requires the verb to match the number of the **closer** subject. **Governor** *wants* in the first example and **mayors** *want* in the second are both grammatically correct.

However, the rule fails to consider the effect on the reader or listener when the singular subject follows the plural one. **Neither the mayors nor the governor** *wants* "reads" awkwardly and "sounds" strange. The solution: When one subject is singular and the other is plural, **place the *plural* one last and follow it with a *plural*** verb.

Indefinite Pronoun as the Subject

Use a singular verb when the subject is one of the following indefinite pronouns that are always singular:

anybody	each	everyone	neither	nothing	something
anyone	either	everything	nobody	somebody	such
anything	everybody	much	no one	someone	

Anybody studying journalism ***is*** expected to understand subject–verb agreement.

— — —

"**Any one** of the three applicants you want to hire ***is*** all right with me," the director told her assistant.

— — —

Each of us ***is*** applying for the job of editorial assistant.

— — —

Neither of the applicants ***has*** a job.

Anybody and **any one** take singular verbs because each subject represents only one person. The same is true for **each** and **neither** in the last two examples. The temptation to use a plural verb is strong in the last two examples because the last word before each verb is plural. Just remember to select the "true subject" and not be tempted by objects of prepositions like **us** and **applicants.** Remember that objects of prepositions are in the objective case and that only nominative case nouns and pronouns may serve as subjects.

To review noun–pronoun number and gender problems associated with indefinite pronouns, turn to the section on noun–pronoun agreement on pages 84–89.

Subject and Verb Separated by Phrases or Clauses

Do not be confused by words that separate the subject from the verb. Some that create singular-plural confusion include *accompanied by, along with, as well as, in addition to, including, of, for, not to mention, that, together with, who, which* and *with.*

When trying to determine the number of the verb, the writer or the broadcaster usually can **disregard wording between the subject and the verb.** Regardless of how many words come between the subject and the verb, if the subject is singular, the verb will be singular, and if the subject is plural, the verb will be plural.

One of the commissioners ***is*** a Republican and the other two are Democrats.

One is the singular subject and requires the singular verb ***is,*** not the plural verb ***are.*** **Commissioners** is the plural object of the preposition **of** and has no influence on the number of the verb. As has been pointed out several times previously, an object of a preposition is in the objective case and cannot serve as a nominative case subject.

— — —

The police **chief,** along with three of his assistants, ***visits*** several schools each month to warn students about the dangers of taking drugs.

Chief is the singular subject and requires the third-person singular verb ***visits,*** not ***visit.*** **Assistants** is the plural object of the preposition **along with** and cannot serve as the subject.

— — —

Three **assistants,** along with the chief of police, ***visit*** several schools each month to warn students about the dangers of taking drugs.

This example is the reverse of the previous one. Now the subject is the plural **assistants,** which takes the third-person plural verb ***visit,*** not ***visits.*** **Chief** cannot serve as the subject because it is the singular object of the preposition **along with.**

— — —

Dr. Orlando E. Francisco, who gave great lectures, ***is*** retiring at the end of the term.

The subject is the singular **Dr. Francisco. Lectures** is the plural direct object of the verb ***gave.*** Because direct objects are in the objective case, they can't serve as nominative case subjects.

Collective Nouns as Subjects

If collective nouns (team, group, family, etc.) and pronouns (none, some, most, etc.) are considered as one unit, they require singular verbs. If the members or units of such words are considered individually, they require plural verbs.

The **team** ***is*** undefeated.

A **team** certainly consists of more than one member, but all members combined form **only one team.** Therefore, team is one "collection" of members and is considered **singular.**

— — —

The mayor's **family** ***is*** present for the ceremony.

The individual members of the family are considered to be acting as **one group** attending a ceremony. Therefore, **family** is a **collective unit** requiring a **singular** verb.

— — —

The mayor's **family** ***are*** arriving throughout the weekend.

In this example, **family** is considered to mean **several individuals acting independently** from one another. They are not arriving together as a unit but separately at different times throughout the weekend. Therefore, **family** is used in a plural sense and requires a **plural** verb.

Note that using such words as **family, faculty** and **jury** as ***plurals*** is quite awkward for Americans. Mass communicators would serve their readers and listeners better when a plural is needed by substituting ***family members*** for **family,** ***faculty members*** or ***teachers*** for **faculty,** and ***jurors*** or ***members of the jury*** for **jury.**

Words that Can Be Singular or Plural

"**Most** of the *work* on the special edition ***is*** completed," the publisher reported.

Most is collective singular in this example and requires the singular verb ***is.*** To determine why, ask yourself what the antecedent of **most** is. In other words, what noun does the pronoun **most** replace? As you can see, the pronoun **most** would make no sense by itself. **Most of what?** The answer is **work,** the object of the preposition **of. Work** is considered **a lump sum** or **one unit** and is **singular.** As the pronoun substitute for the noun **work,** the subject **most** has to agree with **work** in **number. Most,** therefore, is singular and requires the singular verb ***is,*** not the plural verb ***are.***

— — —

Most of the *delegates* ***are*** seeking re-election.

Most is ***plural*** because its antecedent, **delegates,** is plural. The delegates are seeking re-election **separately, not as a group.** Because **delegates** is plural, the subject **most** also is plural.

— — —

Because it had spoiled, **none** of the *corn* ***was*** edible.

The subject, **none,** is ***singular*** because its antecedent, **corn,** is considered **a lump sum** or a **unit.**

— — —

Because **none** of the academic *advisers* ***were*** available, the students left the building.

The subject, **none,** is ***plural*** because its antecedent, **advisers,** refers to **individuals** and not to one unit.

Remember that when **none** is used to mean ***not one,*** it is *singular.* When **none** is used to mean ***not any,*** it is *plural.* When the potential for confusion is great, don't use **none.** Use ***not one*** for *singular* and ***not any*** for *plural.*

* * *

Keep one other factor in mind to avoid potential confusion. Previously in this section on subject–verb agreement, you were told that the object of a preposition usually has no influence on whether a verb will be singular or plural. The exception occurs with collective nouns and pronouns. In the above examples, **work, delegates, corn** and **advisers** are all objects of prepositions that influence the number of the verb. Just remember that **they do so not because they are objects of prepositions** but because they serve as **antecedents** for the pronoun subjects ***most*** and ***none.***

Half of the *equipment* ***is*** outdated.

The subject, **half,** is ***singular*** because its antecedent, **equipment,** is considered **a single quantity.**

— — —

Half of the *computers* ***are*** new.

The subject, **half,** is ***plural*** because its antecedent, **computers,** refers to **several units,** not just one.

— — —

Two-thirds of the wheat *crop* ***has*** spoiled.

The subject, **two-thirds,** is ***singular*** because its antecedent, **crop,** is considered **one amount.**

— — —

Two-thirds of the *students* ***plan*** to attend college.

The subject, **two-thirds,** is ***plural*** because its antecedent, **students,** refers to **individuals.**

— — —

Relative Pronouns as Subjects

A relative pronoun serving as a subject assumes the number of its antecedent.

Relative pronouns (primarily **who, which** and **that**) have no number of their own. They assume the number of their antecedent. If the antecedent is singular, the relative pronoun will be singular; if the antecedent is plural, the relative pronoun will be plural.

The *news director,* **who *has*** been on the staff only six months, *is* making drastic changes in personnel.

The antecedent of **who** is *news director,* the *singular* subject of the independent clause. Because *news director* is *singular,* the relative pronoun **who** is also **singular.** Therefore, **who** requires the third-person singular verb ***has,*** not ***have.***

— — —

They are the *editors* **who *are*** interviewing me this morning.

The plural predicate noun, **editors,** from the independent clause serves as the antecedent of the relative pronoun **who.** Because *editors* is *plural,* **who** also is **plural** and takes the plural verb ***are,*** not ***is.***

* * *

If the antecedent is the last word before the relative pronoun, determining the number of a relative pronoun is usually easy. That's why the two previous examples present no challenge. However, when the antecedent does not directly precede the relative pronoun, or when the relative pronoun is preceded by more than one noun or pronoun that could serve as its antecedent, determining number becomes more complicated.

Ralston is *one* of the advertising **directors who *try*** to be patient with inexperienced copywriters.

Several directors try to be patient. That rules out the singular subject *Ralston* and the singular predicate noun *one* as potential antecedents for **who.** The plural **directors** is the antecedent; therefore, **who** also is plural and takes the third-person plural verb ***try,*** not ***tries.***

— — —

Ralston is *the only* **one** of the advertising *directors* **who *tries*** to be patient with inexperienced copywriters.

This example tells us that there is only **one** director who tries. That rules out the plural **directors** as a potential antecedent for **who. One** is ***singular;*** therefore, **who** also is ***singular*** and requires the third-person singular verb ***tries,*** not ***try.*** Give special attention to the difference in wording between **one of** and **the *only* one. One of** tells us that both the antecedent and the relative pronoun will be plural. **The *only* one** tells us that both the antecedent and the relative pronoun will be singular.

Plurals and Singulars from Other Languages

Some foreign words used frequently by Americans have retained their traditional plural spellings; others have not. Check your stylebooks and dictionaries.

(Traditional) Radio is a news medi**um (singular).** Radio, television, newspapers and magazines are referred to jointly as news med**ia (plural).**

— — —

One female graduate is an alumn**a (singular).**

— — —

Two or more female graduates are alumn**ae (plural).**

— — —

One requirement is a criteri**on (singular).**

— — —

Two or more requirements are criter**ia (plural).**

(Changed) In addition to its own stadi**um (singular),** a football team plays in five or six other stadi**ums (plural)** during the season.

— — —

The county clerk explained that the referend**um (singular)** on property taxes is only one of four referend**ums (plural)** scheduled this year.

Other words used traditionally include:

Singular	Plural
alumnus	alumni
bacterium	bacteria
curriculum	curricula
datum	data
memorandum	memoranda
phenomenon	phenomena
vertebra	vertebrae

Although **datum** represents one and is singular, and **data** more than one and is plural, **data** is accepted as a singular in some circles when it is used to represent a lump sum or a quantity: The **data** collected in the five-year study ***is*** kept in the Acme University library.

(You may test yourself on the material in this chapter or section by connecting with the following Web site: www.mhhe.com/arnold.)

ADJECTIVES

chapter 12

Functions

If the preceding sections on verbs seemed tedious, **adjectives** may provide brief relief. They're comparatively simple and take much less time to study. In this section, we will consider descriptive and limiting adjectives in the attributive, appositive and predicate positions.

Adjectives are not less important than other parts of speech, but we can cover them by citing a few basic rules and applying a little common sense.

Think for a moment about the following:

1. **Why we need adjectives.**
2. **How we use them.**
3. **Where they are located in sentences.**

First, we need adjectives **to describe** nouns and pronouns:

- A **big** headline
- A **little** camera
- A **red** fire truck
- An **intelligent** writer
- An **awkward** interview
- An **angry** news source
- An **award-winning** copywriter

Second, we need adjectives **to limit** or **to quantify** nouns and pronouns:

- **All** news directors
- **Five** deadlines
- **The** report
- **His** newspaper
- The **first** subpoena

- The **50th** anniversary
- **Several** Pulitzer Prizes

If your college roommate ever asked you to agree to go on a blind date with his or her friend, you undoubtedly started asking for adjectives without giving a thought to parts of speech **(good looking? tall? short? fun? intelligent? nice?).** You could have saved yourself a bunch of questions by just facing your roommate and saying, **"Let's hear some *descriptive adjectives!*"**

If you wanted to know how long the date would last, you would ask your roommate for **limiting adjectives** (**four** hours or **every** evening during the weekend).

Attributive

Because adjectives modify only nouns and pronouns, that's where we usually find them—hanging around nouns and pronouns. Adjectives most often come **before** the noun or the pronoun they modify. They also can come **directly after** the noun or the pronoun they modify, and they can come **after a nonaction verb and modify the subject.**

Adjectives that come before the noun or the pronoun they modify are in the **attributive** position.

> **The** governer gave **a** copy of **his lengthy** speech to **each** reporter in **the huge** auditorium.
>
> (Every boldface adjective is **attributive** because each comes **before** the noun or the pronoun it modifies.)

Appositive

Adjectives that come **directly after** the noun or the pronoun they modify are in the **appositive** position:

> The public relations staff members, **tired** and **hungry** after answering reporters' questions for two hours, were glad when the conference ended.
>
> (The boldface adjectives are in the **appositive** position because they come **directly after** the noun they modify.)

Predicate

Adjectives that come **after a nonaction verb and modify the subject are predicate adjectives.**

> The public relations staff members were **tired** and **hungry** after answering reporters' questions for two hours.
>
> (The boldface adjectives are in the **predicate** position because they come after the nonaction verb ***were*** and modify the subject, ***members.***)

Helpful Questions

Adjectives are rarely difficult to find because the nouns and pronouns they modify are usually prominent in sentences. However, in addition to being helped by the positions adjectives occupy in relation to the words they modify, you may ask several questions to help locate them: **which, what, what kind of** and **how many.**

"**This** interview is crucial," the news director said.

The bold adjective answers the question **which.**

— — —

"The election story is **outdated,**" the editor complained.

The bold adjective answers the question **what.**

— — —

The **advertising** campaign took the staff three months to develop.

The bold adjective answers the question **what kind of.**

— — —

Seventeen journalists accompanied the president on his speaking tour.

The bold adjective answers the question **how many.**

Proper or Common

Keep in mind that, like nouns, adjectives can be **proper** or **common.** Although usually common (and therefore not capitalized), adjectives become proper (and therefore capitalized) when words normally used as proper nouns are adapted for use as modifiers.

Recall that although words may have a traditional part of speech, the way they function in a sentence determines whether they are nouns, pronouns, adjectives and so forth. For example, a specific place such as London is usually a ***proper noun.*** But if London is used to modify another noun (as in London broil), it becomes a ***proper adjective.***

Possessive forms of nouns and pronouns are used as **adjectives** (**his** desk, **its** guidelines, **Anthony's** photographs, **my** computer). In addition to ***possessive*** pronouns **(his, her, its, their),** ***demonstrative*** **(this, that, these, those),** ***interrogative*** **(which, what, whose)** and ***indefinite*** **(few, several, many,** etc.) pronouns also may function as adjectives. If you need to refresh your memory, turn to the numerous examples provided in Chapter 8, beginning on page 62.

Coordinate Adjectives

When several words are used to modify the same noun or pronoun, the writer must decide whether to place commas between them. If the adjectives are coordinate, they modify the noun or the pronoun equally and commas go between them. If they are not coordinate, no commas are used.

Two simple tests will tell the writer whether commas are appropriate. If the coordinating conjunction **and** makes sense between the adjectives, commas are needed. If the words can be **interchanged,** commas are needed.

(Not coordinate) The producer's **blue cotton** sweater always hangs from a hook on her office door.

Blue and **cotton** are not coordinate adjectives. ***And*** makes no sense between them, and they cannot be interchanged.

— — —

(Coordinate) Her **spelling, punctuation** and **grammar** skills are highly developed.

Spelling, punctuation and **grammar** are coordinate adjectives. ***And*** makes sense between them, and they can be **interchanged** without affecting the meaning of the sentence.

See pages 35 and 177 for additional information on coordinate adjectives.

Participles and Infinitives as Adjectives

Participles always serve as adjectives, and infinitives sometimes do. Members of the verbal family, participles and infinitives are more complicated than regular adjectives because they often come in phrases.

Smiling, the editorial page editor obviously was pleased with the cartoon she had selected for Sunday's edition.

The participle **smiling** modifies the noun subject, **editor.**

— — —

The election, ***won*** **by the reform candidate,** attracted 60 percent of the eligible voters to the polls.

The participial phrase **won by the reform candidate** modifies the subject, **election.**

— — —

The interns have talent **to burn.**

The infinitive **to burn** modifies the direct object, **talent.**

— — —

From the time he was in the seventh grade, Zimmerman had only one goal: ***to become*** **a journalist.**

The infinitive phrase ***to become*** **a journalist** modifies the noun **goal.**

See pages 108–111 for additional information on participles and infinitives.

(You may test yourself on the material in this chapter or section by connecting with the following Web site: www.mhhe.com/arnold.)

ADVERBS

chapter 13

Functions

Like adjectives, **adverbs** are ***modifiers.*** In fact, these two parts of speech are the only ones that can serve as modifiers. But unlike adjectives, which modify only nouns and pronouns, adverbs are considerably more complicated. Of all parts of speech, perhaps only verbs require more effort to learn than adverbs.

To understand adverbs, you must be a good detective. Although many adverbs are obvious, others "hide" themselves in unsuspected places in sentences. Once you find them, figuring out what purpose they serve in the sentence is not too difficult. To help you in your search, remember that adverbs tell the following:

1. The **time** ***(when)***
2. The **direction** or the **location** ***(where)***
3. The **reason** or the **cause** ***(why)***
4. The **manner** ***(how)***
5. The **degree** ***(how much or to what extent)***

Some Clues

Here are some clues that should help your search:

Many Adverbs End in ly. This is one of their most obvious characteristics.

The company's communications director looked **critical*ly*** at the new employee's first report.

Critically is an **adverb** modifying the **verb** ***looked.***

— — —

The **fresh*ly*** painted newsroom made working conditions pleasant.

Freshly is an **adverb** modifying the **adjective** ***painted.***

— — —

Because she felt tired following an allergy attack, the star of the basketball team played **bad*ly.***

Badly is an **adverb** modifying the **verb** ***played.***

Finding Adverbs

Adverbs Usually Hang Around Verbs. This makes sense because the primary function of adverbs is to modify verbs. But don't forget that the versatile adverb also modifies adjectives and other adverbs. That's when they can be difficult to find.

The new cartoonist **draws (verb)** ***well (adverb modifying the verb).***

— — —

The water supply **is shrinking (verb)** ***rapidly (adverb modifying the verb).***

— — —

Time **passes (verb)** ***fast (adverb modifying the verb)*** between deadlines.

— — —

She is ***quite (adverb modifying the following adjective)*** **good (adjective)** at getting her employees to do their best work.

— — —

The ***bright (adverb modifying the following adjective)*** **red (adjective)** car attracted the crowd's attention at Saturday's race.

— — —

"The ***drastically (adverb modifying the following adjective)*** **declining (participle/adjective)** population is causing a severe revenue problem," the governor said.

— — —

Each pianist plays ***very (adverb modifying the following adverb)*** **well (adverb),** but only one will win the championship.

— — —

On her first day out of the hospital, the mayor applied her weight ***most (adverb modifying the following adverb)*** **cautiously (adverb)** on her injured foot.

— — —

When the weight-conscious journalists came to the dinner table, their host jokingly warned them that the chocolate cake "tastes ***deliciously (adverb modifying the following adjective)*** **sinful (adjective).**"

See pages 199–204 for rules governing hyphenated words such as "weight-conscious."

Adverb Questions

***As was explained previously, adverbs answer five questions:* when, where, why, how, *and* how much *or* to what extent.**

1. "We'll design the advertisement **later,"** the graphic artist said.

The **adverb** *later,* which modifies the **verb** ***design,*** tells the **time** by answering the question **when.**

— — —

2. Reporters go **everywhere** in search of stories.

The **adverb** ***everywhere*** modifies the **verb** ***go*** and tells the **place** by answering the question **where.**

— — —

3. It rained; **therefore,** the game was postponed.

The **conjunctive adverb** ***therefore*** tells the **cause** by answering the question **why. Therefore** serves as a **connective** between the two independent clauses.

— — —

4. The editor sings **horribly** at the annual office party.

The **adverb** ***horribly*** tells the **manner** by answering the question **how. Horribly** modifies the **verb** ***sings.***

— — —

5. The commissioner admitted that he was **somewhat** mistaken in his budget estimates.

The **adverb** ***somewhat*** modifies the **predicate adjective** ***mistaken*** and tells the **degree** by answering the questions **how much** or **to what extent.**

Adverbial Objectives

***When a word that is usually a noun is used as an adverb, it is called an* adverbial objective.**

After working late on election day, the reporters immediately went **home.**

Home, usually a noun because it is a **place,** is used as an **adverb** answering the question **where.** It modifies the **verb** ***went.***

— — —

The president's State of the Union address is scheduled **Wednesday.**

Usually a noun because it is a **thing,** ***Wednesday*** modifies the **verb** ***is scheduled*** and is used as an **adverb** answering the question **when.**

— — —

Enrollment at the state's colleges and universities has increased by 10 percent this **year.**

Usually a noun because it is a **thing,** ***year*** modifies the **verb** ***has increased*** and is used as an **adverb** answering the question **when.**

Interrogative Adverbs

Like interrogative pronouns, **interrogative adverbs** ***ask questions. Consider the following examples.***

Why is this course required?

— — —

Where will mathematics help me in my career?

— — —

When will I be able to put to use what I've learned?

— — —

How should I study?

These adverbs answer their own questions (**why, where, when, how**). They may seem a little strange because the normal sentence order (subject-verb-object) is changed when questions are asked. If you turn each of the sentences around, though, each adverb would appear in its usual place—after the verb. (This course is required **why?** Mathematics will help me **where** in my career?)

Conjunctive Adverbs

An Adverb That Also Serves as a Conjunction Is Called a Conjunctive Adverb. It is used to hold two independent clauses together and often shows a cause-and-effect relationship. Note that long sentences may be split with the second sentence beginning with the conjunctive adverb.

The candidate's plane was delayed in Oklahoma; **therefore,** his speech had to be postponed.

The **conjunctive adverb** ***therefore*** joins the two sentences and tells **why** the speech had to be postponed.

— — —

The company president said she wanted to give copywriters a salary increase; **however,** she said a small profit margin in the past fiscal year made raises impossible.

The **conjunctive adverb *however*** joins the two sentences and tells **why** no raise will be given.

— — —

The governor said he supports a pay increase for teachers; **consequently,** faculty members are optimistic about receiving a raise.

The **conjunctive adverb *consequently*** joins the two sentences and tells **why** the teachers are optimistic.

Parenthetical Adverbs

***Adverbs can be used parenthetically to provide emphasis or to help make the transition smoother. Parenthetical words include* however, therefore, nevertheless, consequently, subsequently, moreover *and* furthermore.**

"I can tell you, **however,** that the election will be won by my party," the mayor said.

However is used **parenthetically** to show a **contrast** to what the speaker had said previously and to make the **transition smoother.**

— — —

Although the citizens had no vote on the ordinance increasing sewage fees, they will, **nevertheless,** have to pay the extra money.

Nevertheless is used **parenthetically** to show a **contrast** and to make the **transition smoother.**

Avoiding Confusion

Warning No. 1: **Do not confuse parenthetical adverbs with conjunctive adverbs.** Because words such as **however, therefore, nevertheless** and so forth **can be used either as *parenthetical adverbs* or as *conjunctive adverbs,*** they can cause punctuation problems. To avoid confusion, remember three guidelines:

1. ***Parenthetical adverbs*** are used **within one sentence.** They are preceded by a **comma** and are followed by a **comma.**

   "An adjustment is necessary, **however,** because we don't have sufficient funds for the project," the city treasurer said.

2. ***Conjunctive adverbs*** **join two independent clauses** that can stand alone as separate sentences. They are preceded by a **semicolon** and followed by a **comma.**

The governor provided the necessary funds from his emergency reserves; **consequently,** enough money has been appropriated to build the bridge.

3. After following these two steps, if you still are unsure whether you have a ***parenthetical adverb*** or a ***conjunctive adverb,*** apply the following visual test:

Look at all the words **to the left of the adverb** in question. Then look at all the words **to the right.** If the words to the left make **a complete sentence** that could stand on its own, and if the words to the right make **another sentence** that could stand on its own, you have a ***conjunctive adverb.*** It requires a **semicolon before it** and a **comma after it.** (See pages 187–189 for an explanation of the uses of semicolons.)

Look again at the words **to the left** and **to the right** of the adverb in question. If **one** or **both** sets of words **fail to constitute a sentence** that could stand alone, you have a ***parenthetical adverb.*** Put a **comma before it** and a **comma after it.**

Be aware that some authorities suggest that the **commas are not necessary with *parenthetical adverbs* unless a pause is intended;** however, in most instances, **the writer does intend for the reader to pause.** Most writers use the commas because neither parenthetical words nor conjunctive adverbs have to be used. Note in all the previous examples that the adverbs in question could be deleted. The meaning would still be the same; it would just be harder to discern.

Confusion with Adjectives

Warning No. 2: **Don't use an adjective to do an adverb's job and vice versa.** People who wouldn't think of eating soup with a fork routinely commit the grammatical equivalent of using an adjective to do a job intended for an adverb or vice versa. Consider how often you hear the following:

1. He really plays the banjo **good (*well*).**
2. She sings **terrible (*terribly*).**
3. They did **wonderful (*wonderfully*)** on their tests.
4. We feel **badly (*bad*)** about your being hurt in the accident.
5. That plant smells **horribly (*horrible*).**

In No. 1, the **adjective *good*** is incorrect because it has no noun or pronoun to modify. The **adverb *well*** is needed to answer the question **how** and to modify the **verb *plays.*** Nos. 2 and 3 have the same problem.

In No. 4, the **adverb *badly*** is used incorrectly to modify the **pronoun subject *we.*** The **adjective *bad*** is needed because only an adjective can modify a pronoun.

In No. 5, the **adverb *horribly*** is used incorrectly to modify the **noun *plant.*** Only an adjective (**horrible**) can do that job.

All these errors are avoidable if you remember the abilities and limitations of the only two modifiers in the language and if you carefully analyze the sentence. Is the verb a linking verb connecting the subject to a word (an adjective) that tells more about the subject? Or is it an intransitive verb followed by a word (an adverb) that tells more about the verb? If a hunter thinks his hound *smells* **bad,** that means the dog stinks. But if the hunter claims his hound *smells* **badly,** that means the dog has an impaired ability to recognize scents.

Infinitives as Adverbs

One verbal family member, the infinitive, can serve as an adverb (see **verbals** on pages 109–110). Infinitives are more complicated than regular adverbs because they often come in phrases.

Thomasson worked hard ***to complete*** **the advertising campaign.**

The infinitive phrase ***to complete*** **the advertising campaign** serves as an adverb and modifies the verb ***worked.***

— — —

Damron apologized ***to ease*** **his guilt.**

The infinitive phrase ***to ease*** **his guilt** serves as an adverb and modifies the verb ***apologized.***

(You may test yourself on the material in this chapter or section by connecting with the following Web site: www.mhhe.com/arnold.)

chapter 14 COMPARISON OF ADJECTIVES AND ADVERBS

A track coach has three **fast** runners but can enter only one in the conference championship meet. Undoubtedly, he will not be concerned about grammar when he makes his decision, but he will compare the runners' abilities by using adjectives and adverbs.

One of his three runners is **fast (*adjective*).** Another runs **more rapidly (*adverb*)** and the third is the **most competitive (*adjective*).**

To make comparisons, we put **er** and **est** on the end of adjectives and adverbs or place ***more*** and ***most*** or ***less*** and ***least*** in front of them. One runner is fast, but a second is fast**er,** and a third is the fast**est.** One runner is competitive, a second is ***more*** or ***less*** competitive, and the third is ***most*** or ***least*** competitive.

Positive Degree

We have three degrees of comparison: the *positive,* the *comparative* and the *superlative.*

The ***positive degree*** is the simple or root form of the word:

fast

smart

little

bothersome

rapidly

conscientious

Comparative Degree

The ***comparative degree*** is used **to compare two** persons, places or things. Usually, if the word has **one or two syllables,** we **put *er* on the end of it** to form the comparative degree. If it has **three or more syllables,** we usually **place *more* or *less* in front of it.** We use ***more* to show an increase** in the comparison and ***less* to show a decrease:**

fast**er**

smart**er**

littl**er**

more/less bothersome

more/less rapidly

more/less conscientious

Between the **two** typists, Becker is fast**er.**

— — —

Of the **two** public relations experts, Amsbary is smart**er.**

— — —

The evening newscast is ***more/less*** bothersome than the night edition.

— — —

The sportscaster talks ***more/less*** rapidly than the news anchor.

— — —

The teacher is ***more/less*** conscientious than the student.

Superlative Degree

The ***superlative degree*** is used **to compare three or more** persons, places or things. If the word has **one or two syllables,** we usually **put *est* on the end of it** to form the superlative degree. If it has **three or more syllables,** we **put *most* or *least* in front of it.** We use ***most* to show an increase** in the comparison and ***least* to show a decrease:**

fast**est**

smart**est**

littl**est**

most/least bothersome

most/least rapidly

most/least conscientious

Of the **three** typists, Becker is the fast**est.**

— — —

Of the **five** public relations experts, Amsbary is the smart**est.**

— — —

The evening newscast is the ***most/least*** bothersome of the three major programs televised each day.

— — —

The sportscaster talks ***most/least*** rapidly of all employees who appear on camera.

— — —

That teacher is the ***most/least*** conscientious on the faculty.

Some Adjectives Form Comparisons Irregularly

Most adjectives, like most verbs, form their comparative and superlative degrees in a **regular** manner: **fine, fin*er,* fin*est;* courageous,** ***more/less*** **courageous,** ***most/least*** **courageous.** Some, however, are formed ***irregularly*** and, like irregular verbs, they must be memorized: **well, better, best; bad, worse, worst; good, better, best,** and so forth.

Some Adjectives Cannot Be Compared

When people say that something is **clear*er,*** **flatt*er*** or **round*er*** than something else, their message is clear; their logic isn't. **Perfect is perfect;** it can't be **perfect*er*** or **perfect*est.*** Likewise, if something is **clear,** how can it possibly be **clear*er?*** If something is **flat,** how can it be **flatt*er?*** The same can be said for **unique, round, straight, square, level, full** and **equal.**

If a couple of teams are getting ready to start a volleyball game and three balls are available, the players want to use **the one that is "round*est.*"** Actually they want to use **the one that comes closest to being round** (or the one that contains the most air). If all three were round (360 degrees), they all would be perfect.

To make distinctions, we can say that some things are ***almost*** **round,** ***nearly*** **equal** and ***virtually*** **flat.**

(Avoid) "This is the **most unique** political cartoon we've ever published," the editor said.

If something is unique, it is one of a kind. Substitute **most unusual, most creative** or another more appropriate word.

— — —

(Avoid) At her press conference, the governor provided background that made her budget proposal **clear*er.***

If something is clear, it cannot be more than clear. Substitute **easier to understand** or another more appropriate word or phrase.

Use *Other* or *Else* When Comparing Like Things

Remember that **when you are comparing persons, places or things with other persons, places or things from the same grouping or class** (newspapers with other newspapers, broadcasts with other broadcasts, photographers with other photographers), **you must remove the item being compared by using the words *other* or *else.***

(Avoid) "This newspaper is **better than any newspaper** I've ever read.

(Better) "This newspaper is **better than any *other* newspaper** I've ever read."

Because the newspaper you are referring to **cannot be better than itself,** you must remove it from the others with which you are comparing it.

— — —

(Avoid) "Last night's broadcast was **worse than any** I've ever heard."

(Better) "Last night's broadcast was **worse than any *other*** I've ever heard."

Because last night's broadcast **cannot be worse than itself,** you must remove it from the others with which you are comparing it.

— — —

(Avoid) "She can write with more flair **than anyone** I've ever known."

(Better) "She can write with more flair **than anyone *else*** I've ever known."

Because **she cannot write with more flair than herself,** you must remove her from the others with whom you are comparing her.

— — —

(Avoid) "This apple tastes better **than any** I've ever eaten."

(Better) "This apple tastes better **than any *other*** I've ever eaten."

Because **the apple could not possibly taste better than itself,** you must remove it from the others with which you are comparing it.

(You may test yourself on the material in this chapter or section by connecting with the following Web site: www.mhhe.com/arnold.)

chapter 15

PREPOSITIONS

Functions

Most textbook definitions of a preposition are more like riddles than explanations. They state that prepositions are words that link their noun or pronoun object with another word or group of words in the sentence and show the relationship between the two.

That definition is not so bad if you already are familiar with prepositions. However, if you aren't, a wonderfully simple method of finding prepositions was provided years ago by a creative elementary school teacher. She said **a preposition is "anywhere a squirrel can go"** (up, down, around, behind, over, across, etc.). Of course, not all words used as prepositions fit the "squirrel rule," but that teacher gave her students a practical way to get started.

Let's take a moment to analyze that more difficult textbook definition by working through it step by step.

(Example) The president of the advertising agency walked ***into*** **the conference** ***room.***

Into is the **preposition.**

Room is the **noun object** of the preposition.

The **preposition** ***into*** is used to show the relationship between its **noun object** ***room*** and the **verb** ***walked.*** The entire prepositional phrase **(into the conference room) serves as an** ***adverb*** **modifying the verb** ***walked*** and **tells** ***where*** **the president** ***walked.***

Common Prepositions

The most commonly used prepositions include:

Simple		Compound
aboard	from	according to
about	in	ahead of
above	inside	along with
across	into	apart from

after
against
along
among
around
at
before
behind
below
beneath
beside
besides
between
beyond
but (to mean except)
by
despite
down
during
except
for

like
near
of
off
on
onto
out
over
past
since
through
throughout
to
toward
under
until
up
upon
with
within
without

as far as
because of
in addition to
in back of
in between
in front of
in place of
inside of
in spite of
next to
out of

A Preposition Must Have a Noun or a Pronoun Object

Every preposition must have an object, and that object must be either a noun or a pronoun. In other words, that squirrel must have somewhere to go: **up** the ***tree,*** **around** the ***bush,*** **across** the ***lawn,*** and so on. Remember also that prepositions are modifiers; therefore, they perform the functions of the English language's two modifiers—adjectives and adverbs.

Consider these examples:

The firefighter climbed hurriedly **up** the ***ladder.***

Up the **ladder** is a prepositional phrase answering the question ***where*** and functioning as an **adverb** to modify the **verb *climbed.*** The preposition is **up** and its object is **ladder.**

— — —

The reporter walked **beside** the ***editor.***

Beside the **editor** is a prepositional phrase answering the question ***where*** and functioning as an **adverb** to modify the **verb *walked.*** The preposition is **beside** and its object is **editor.**

— — —

Dozens **of** public relations ***practitioners*** attended the seminar.

Of public relations **practitioners** is a prepositional phrase functioning as an ***adjective*** and modifying the **noun subject** ***dozens.*** **Of** is the preposition and its object is **practitioners.**

— — —

The agenda **for** the press ***conference*** was distributed an hour earlier.

For the press conference is a prepositional phrase functioning as an ***adjective*** and modifying the **noun subject** ***agenda.*** **For** is the preposition and **conference** is its object.

* * *

Although prepositional phrases function almost exclusively as modifiers, the following example shows that they also can serve as the subject of a sentence.

After the deadline is too late. Raise questions about libel before the deadline.

The prepositional phrase serves as the subject of the verb ***is.***

A Preposition Is Not Limited to One Word

Some prepositions consist of more than one word (**compound prepositions**). Don't be confused by them. Just learn to recognize them and ***treat them as if they were just one word***—the same as any other preposition.

In addition to the ***reporter,*** the editor and the publisher are scheduled to testify today in court.

In addition to is the preposition and its object is ***reporter.***

— — —

The number of pages had to be reduced to 24 today **because of** the ***shortage*** of paper.

Because of is the preposition and its object is ***shortage.***

— — —

The advertising director, **along with** three ***members*** of the sales staff, is attending today's meeting.

Along with is the preposition and its object is ***members.***

Don't Confuse a Preposition with an Adverb, a Conjunction or an Infinitive

Be careful not to confuse a preposition with an adverb, a conjunction or an infinitive. If there is no noun or pronoun object, the word that appears at first to be a preposition probably will be **an adverb.** If the word that appears to be a preposition introduces a clause, it will be **a conjunction.** If the word **to** is followed by a verb (to jump, to run, to talk, to attempt, etc.) instead of a noun or pronoun object, it will be **an infinitive.** The following examples should help clarify any confusion:

The judge walked **down the steps** to avoid the reporters.

Down is a **preposition** showing the relationship between its **noun object** ***steps*** and the **verb** ***walked.*** The prepositional phrase, *down the steps,* **functions as an adverb** answering the question ***where*** and modifying ***walked.***

— — —

The judge looked **down** at the defense attorney.

Down is an **adverb** answering the question ***where*** and **modifying the verb** ***looked. Down*** cannot be a preposition in this sentence because it has no object. There is a prepositional phrase—at the defense attorney—that modifies the verb.

— — —

For the next two months, the sports report on WXZZ will be extended from 15 minutes to a half hour.

For is a **preposition** and ***months*** is its **object.**

— — —

"I can't tell you to accept the new job, **for** that's a decision you must make yourself," the news director told the young reporter.

For is a **coordinating conjunction** introducing the independent clause ***that's a decision you must make for yourself.***

If the difference between **for** used as a ***preposition*** and **for** used as a ***conjunction*** still eludes you, remember that a prepositional phrase contains neither a subject nor a verb.

Objects of Prepositions Are Always in the Objective Case

Remember from the chapters on nouns and pronouns that **objects of prepositions always are selected from the *objective case.*** Nouns present no problems because they are spelled the same in both the nominative and the objective cases. However, except for the words ***you*** and ***it,*** **pronouns change their spelling from nominative to objective case (I** to ***me,*** **we** to ***us,*** **they** to ***them,*** **she** to ***her,*** etc.). Using a nominative case pronoun as the object of a preposition can be quite embarrassing to people who are supposed to know better. Consider the following examples that contain the especially tricky compound objects of prepositions:

(Wrong) The story will be edited **by** Turner or **I.**

I is a **nominative case pronoun** and cannot serve as the object of the preposition ***by.***

(Correct) The story will be edited **by** Turner or **me.**

Now it's correct. ***Me*** is an **objective case pronoun**—perfect for the object of a preposition. (You wouldn't say the story was edited by ***I,*** would you?)

— — —

(Wrong) The identity of the source is a secret **between he** and the editor.

He is a **nominative case pronoun** and cannot serve as the object of the preposition ***between.***

(Correct) The identity of the source is a secret **between him** and the editor.

Because ***him*** is an **objective case pronoun,** it may serve as the object of the preposition ***between.***

— — —

(Wrong) "I will make the trip **with she** and another graphic artist."

She is a **nominative case pronoun** and cannot serve as the object of the preposition ***with.***

(Correct) I will make the trip **with her** and another graphic artist."

Because ***her*** is an **objective case pronoun,** it may serve as the object of the preposition ***with.*** (You wouldn't say, "I will make the trip with ***she***," would you?)

Don't Use Unnecessary Prepositions

No need may exist for this final reminder, but if you make this mistake, you will be embarrassed. Do not use unnecessary prepositions, **particularly at the end of sentences.** Study the following examples, especially the first three, which most professionals conscientiously avoid:

The city editor asked, "Where's the copy **at?**"

Just ask **where's the copy?**

— — —

"Where did he go **to?**"

Just ask **where did he go?**

— — —

"What are you taking that picture **for?**"

Just ask **why are you taking the picture?**

— — —

The sales director asked me to take the layouts off **of** her desk.

Just say **off** her desk.

— — —

"That drain is clogged **up.**"

Just say the **drain is clogged.**

— — —

"The runner fell **down.**"

Just say **the runner fell.**

Can a Preposition Ever Be the Last Word in a Sentence?

You've been warned since you were in elementary school not to end a sentence with a preposition. That's good advice. It works most of the time, but there are common sense exceptions. Previously, you saw examples of prepositions used needlessly at the end of sentences. Consider, however, the usefulness of the following sentences that end with prepositions.

"That's more than **I can put *up with,*"** the exasperated advertising director complained.

Even though the sentence ends with a preposition, it sounds better than saying, "That's more than **up with which I can put.**"

— — —

The candidate claimed his opponent did not know **what he was talking *about.***

Even though the sentence ends with a preposition, it sounds better than saying, "The candidate claimed his opponent did not know **about which he was talking.**"

— — —

Following the earthquake that killed more than a thousand city residents, the mayor said, "That's a tragedy **we'll never get *over.***"

Even though the sentence ends with a preposition, it sounds better than saying, "That's a tragedy **over which we will never get.**"

Formal and Informal

Some people will argue for accepting both of the following types of examples depending on whether the circumstance is formal or informal:

(Informal) "Are you the person I'm supposed **to ride *with*?**"

(Formal) "Are you the person **with whom I am supposed to ride?**"

— — —

(Informal) "**Who** are you talking ***to*?**"

(Formal) "***To whom*** are you talking?"

— — —

(Informal) "**Who** is that present intended ***for*?**"

(Formal) "***For whom*** is that present intended?"

Of course, the potential conflict between the formal and the informal can be avoided by rewording that is both unpretentious and grammatically correct.

"Am I supposed to ride with you?"

"Who's talking?"

"Whose present is that?"

(You may test yourself on the material in this chapter or section by connecting with the following Web site: www.mhhe.com/arnold.)

Conjunctions

chapter 16

Functions

Conjunctions are ***connectors*** that can perform small jobs such as joining simple words (editor **and** reporter), or bigger tasks such as linking phrases (to the composing room **but** not to the press room). They also can take on heavy-duty assignments such as joining **independent clauses** (The reporter covered the governor's speech, **and** her story was published on page 1) or joining an independent clause to a dependent clause (The story was published on page 1 **because** it was important).

The three types of conjunctions are **coordinating, subordinating** and **correlative.** People who have difficulty with conjunctions need to review the composition and functions of phrases and clauses and study how commas are used with them. This preliminary information can be found in the appropriate chapters in this book.

Let's examine each type of conjunction and consider some examples of how each is used in a sentence.

Coordinating Conjunctions

Coordinating conjunctions join **words, phrases** and **clauses of *equal rank.*** Included are such things as compound subjects (the **editor *and*** the **reporter**), compound verbs (**write *and* edit**), compound objects (to **class *and*** to the **office**), compound modifiers (**red *and* green** uniforms), and independent clauses (**we did not take the photographs, *nor* did we complete the page designs**).

To determine what is meant by **equal rank,** consider the examples in the previous paragraph. Each of the bold words in parentheses can be used independently from the other:

She is the **editor.**

He is the **reporter.**

The uniforms are **red.**

The uniforms are **green.**

The professor went to **class.**

The news director went to the **office.**

We did not take the **photographs.**

We did not complete the page **designs.**

* * *

The most commonly used coordinating conjunctions are **and, but, or, nor** and **so. For** and **yet** also serve as coordinating conjunctions but aren't used as frequently as the others.

1. ***<u>And</u>*** is used to link things that are **similar.**
2. ***<u>But</u>*** is used to show a **contrast.**
3. ***<u>Or</u>*** and ***<u>nor</u>*** are used to link **choices.**
4. ***<u>For</u>*** is used to **give an explanation** that follows.
5. ***<u>Yet</u>*** used as a conjunction most often has the meaning of **vacillate, nevertheless,** or **still.**
6. ***<u>So</u>*** usually **links a reason with a statement.**

<u>Let's see how each is used in a sentence:</u>

The **sports editor** ***<u>and</u>*** the **chief photographer** attended the press conference.

<u>And</u> joins the compound subjects **sports editor** and **chief photographer.**

— — —

Two public relations staff members went **to their supervisor** ***and*** **to the president** to seek approval for their project.

<u>And</u> joins the two prepositional phrases, **to their supervisor** and **to the president.**

— — —

The president wanted to approve the project, ***<u>but</u>*** **she said she did not have sufficient funds.**

<u>But</u> connects two independent clauses: **The president wanted to approve the project** and **she said she did not have sufficient funds.**

— — —

He will assign the **copy desk chief** ***<u>or</u>*** the **photo editor** an office at the end of the hall.

<u>Or</u> joins the compound indirect objects **copy desk chief** and **photo editor.**

— — —

The food critic will not eat in the cheap restaurant, *nor* will he send one of his staff members there.

Nor joins two independent clauses.

— — —

The editor said she knows the identity of the city manager nominee, *for* the head of the nominating committee told her the name.

For links two independent clauses.

— — —

The president's press secretary wanted to release all the details, *yet* he knew he would be unwise to do so.

Yet joins two independent clauses.

— — —

She finished her routine stories early, *so* she could cover the senator's press conference.

So joins two independent clauses.

Subordinating Conjunctions

If we can join only "equals" with coordinating conjunctions, we must have conjunctions that connect "unequals." These are called **subordinating conjunctions.** However, because there are more subordinating than coordinating conjunctions, we will not name all of them as we did with the coordinating conjunctions. Instead, we will depend on their position and function in the sentence to help us identify them. In addition, some words commonly used as subordinating conjunctions (**before, after, since**) also are used routinely as other parts of speech. Other words used as subordinating conjunctions include **because, although, until, unless, if, when, as, where, as if** and **while.**

Subordinating conjunctions join an **independent clause** with a ***dependent clause*** (**We will attend the press conference *when the ball game ends***). The two clauses are not equal. The dependent clause (***when the ball game ends***), as its name implies, cannot stand alone. It depends on the independent clause to make its meaning clear.

If you find this explanation confusing, let's try a simpler approach. Suppose you are seated in a meeting room with several fellow employees, and the boss walks in and says, "***Before* we can make this decision,**" and then leaves the room. You would have no idea what he had in mind because he did not complete his thought. He almost said a complete sentence—he gave a **subject** (***we***) and a **verb** (***can make***), but he did not express a complete thought.

Remember that a sentence requires not only a subject and a verb but also a complete thought. What the boss said was a dependent clause (a group of related words containing a subject and a verb but not expressing a complete thought). A dependent clause must be accompanied by an independent clause to make the meaning clear.

The boss would have caused no problem if he had said, ***"Before we can make this decision (dependent clause),*** **we'll have to find out if sufficient funding is available *(independent clause).*"**

* * *

Did you notice that the only difference between the dependent clause and the independent clause is that a subordinating conjunction introduced the dependent clause, and, in effect, turned an independent clause into a dependent one? Look at the example again:

Before we can make this decision.

By deleting the subordinating conjunction ***before,*** we can turn this dependent clause into an independent one:

We can make this decision.

If you keep this thought in mind, locating subordinating conjunctions should be easier.

Now, consider **why we would want to make one part of a sentence subordinate** rather than equal to another part. The answer simply is ***because one part of the sentence is considered more important than the other.*** One part is emphasized over another, and that point should be clear to the receiver of the message.

Suppose you are a sportswriter or a sportscaster assigned to cover a basketball tournament during December. On the day of the championship game, six inches of snow covers the area. You contact the tournament director by telephone to find out if the game will be played. She says, ***"Even though snow is covering all roads,*** **the game will be played as scheduled."**

The tournament director answered your question with a complex sentence containing one independent clause and one dependent clause. She had two thoughts to convey to you: There is snow on the roads, and the game will be played anyway. One of those thoughts was much more important than the other; therefore, she stressed the important thought by de-emphasizing the less important one: "Even though snow is covering all the roads." The more important message is "the game will be played as scheduled."

Placement of Subordinating Clauses

Subordinating clauses can come at the **beginning,** the **middle** or the **end** of a sentence:

If **he is accepted,** he will attend Acme University.

— — —

Merle Jacobson said, "***If*** **I am accepted,** I will attend Acme University."

— — —

He will attend Acme University ***if*** **he is accepted.**

Don't Confuse Subordinating Conjunctions with Prepositions

We mentioned earlier that some words commonly used as subordinating conjunctions also are used routinely as other parts of speech. Let's consider **before, after** and **since** by using each as a preposition and again as a subordinating conjunction. Telling the difference is very simple. A subordinating conjunction comes in a dependent clause containing a subject and a verb; a preposition comes in a phrase containing a preposition, a noun or a pronoun object, and perhaps some modifying words.

(Preposition) **Before the meeting,** copies of the minutes from the previous session were placed on the table.

Before the meeting contains a **preposition** (***before***), and a **noun object** (***meeting***). It has no subject or verb.

— — —

(Subordinating conjunction) **Before the meeting began,** each delegate read the minutes from the previous session.

Before the meeting began contains a **subordinating conjunction** (***before***), a **subject** (***meeting***), and a **verb** (***began***).

— — —

(Preposition) **After the opening session,** we gathered in smaller groups for further discussion.

After the opening session contains a **preposition** (***after***) and a **noun object** (***session***).

— — —

(Subordinating conjunction) **After we attended the opening session,** we gathered in smaller groups for further discussions.

After we attended the opening session contains a **subordinating conjunction** (***after***), a **subject** (***we***), and a **verb** (***attended***).

— — —

(Preposition) We haven't completed an advertising sketch **since yesterday.**

Since yesterday contains a **preposition** (***since***) and a **noun object** (***yesterday***).

— — —

(Subordinating conjunction) We haven't completed an advertising sketch **since we started yesterday.**

Since we started yesterday contains a **subordinating conjunction** (***since***), a **subject** (***we***), and a **verb** (***started***).

Correlative Conjunctions

Correlative conjunctions are used in pairs: **either/or, neither/nor, whether/or, not only/but also,** and **both/and.**

Either readers will have to pay more for newspapers **or** publishers will have to reduce the number of pages in their publications.

— — —

Neither readers **nor** publishers want prices to increase.

— — —

Deciding **whether** to raise prices **or** to reduce pages is not going to be easy.

— — —

Readers and publishers want **not only** lower costs **but also** an increase in the number of pages.

— — —

Both readers **and** publishers need to recognize the complexities of the problem.

Don't Forget the Conjunctive Adverb

Remember from Chapter 13 **that the conjunctive adverb is used to join two independent clauses** and often shows a cause-and-effect relationship:

The publisher wanted to increase the number of pages in her magazine; **however,** the cost was just too much.

Note that the **semicolon** before the conjunctive adverb **joins** the two independent clauses.

(You may test yourself on the material in this chapter or section by connecting with the following Web site: www.mhhe.com/arnold.)

INTERJECTIONS

chapter 17

Functions

Because **interjections** ***show strong feeling or emotion,*** journalists usually restrict them to direct quotations in objective writing. In subjective writing such as editorials, personal columns, critiques and other works containing the writer's opinion, the use of interjections is not so restricted. Even in opinion pieces, however, journalists recognize that interjections (or exclamations) lose their effect if used too often.

Don't waste your time turning the page looking for examples of interjections other than the few that follow. Studying interjections is a mercifully brief task.

Interjections May Be Used within a Sentence or May Stand Alone

Wow!

Great! That's the news we've been waiting to hear.

Interjections May Be Followed by Commas if They Are Mild

"**Well,** we could delay the broadcast for another day," the assistant news director suggested.

"**Gee,**" the news director said. "Let's not give up on that story until just before air time."

chapter 18

Sentences and Syntax

Now that we have completed our study of parts of speech and have given considerable time to phrases and clauses, we will turn our attention to sentences as a whole. Let's define and analyze the four types of sentence **functions** and the four types of sentence **structures.**

Function refers to the purpose of a sentence. If it is **declarative,** it makes a statement; if **interrogative,** it asks a question; if **imperative,** it makes a request or gives an order; and if **exclamatory,** it expresses strong feeling or emotion.

Structure refers to the way a sentence is designed. If it is **simple,** it has one independent clause; if **compound,** it has at least two independent clauses; if **complex,** it has one independent clause and one dependent clause; and if **compound–complex,** it has at least two independent clauses and at least one dependent clause.

Sentence Functions

Function is easy to explain and to understand. Let's look at some examples and explanations of each type.

Declarative

The declarative is easily the most frequently used sentence type. In both our writing and our speaking, we make statements more often than we do anything else. All declarative statements end with a period.

Newspapers provide a record of the news.

— — —

Television can show you what's happening.

— — —

Photographers capture history on film.

— — —

Advertising pays the bills.

Interrogative

The interrogative sentence asks a question that expects or demands a response; therefore, it ends with a question mark. There's nothing tricky about them; you just have to make sure an answer is needed. Indirect questions (see page 174), rhetorical questions (see page 174), and imperative sentences that place requests in the form of a question to be polite (see imperative examples that follow) are not interrogative and do not end with a question mark. The following are examples of interrogative sentences that expect or demand a response:

Is the starting pay at least $50,000?

— — —

Do I get Saturdays and Sundays off?

— — —

Will a company car be provided?

— — —

Why are you laughing?

Imperative

The imperative sentence either makes a request or gives an order, and it ends with a period. The subject, *you,* is rarely expressed.

Please edit this feature story for me.

— — —

Tell the news director I want to talk with her.

— — —

Finish your work or turn in your resignation.

— — —

Control your temper.

— — —

"Shall we stand for a moment of silence in memory of those who were killed by the earthquake." *(This is an imperative sentence because it is a request, not a question.)*

Exclamatory

The exclamatory sentence expresses strong feeling or emotion and ends with an exclamation mark. As explained in Chapter 21, exclamations are most effective when used sparingly. In addition, news journalists must be aware of the danger of editorializing when using exclamations other than in direct quotations.

I got the job!

— — —

"I'll never resign!" the mayor shouted at petitioners demanding he quit his office.

— — —

This is the greatest honor of my life!

— — —

The headline read: Armstrong walks on the moon!

Sentence Structures

Structure is a little more complicated than function for most student journalists and for some professionals. However, it becomes simple for everyone who can distinguish between independent and dependent clauses. All you have to do is identify and count the clauses. See pages 153–154 and 179–180 for a review of independent and dependent clauses.

Simple

No matter how many or how few words it contains, the simple sentence consists of just ***one independent clause.***

Go.

The subject is the understood **you** and the verb is **go.** This meets the minimum requirements for an independent clause or a simple sentence—a subject, a verb and a complete thought.

— — —

I study three hours each night.

The subject is **I,** the verb is **study,** and a complete thought is expressed.

* * *

Do not be fooled by the following constructions, which may appear at first to be too complicated to be simple sentences.

Marcus and **I** ***wrote*** and ***edited*** the **copy** and the **headlines.**

This is a simple sentence with a compound subject (**Marcus, I**), a compound verb (**wrote, edited**), and a compound direct object (**copy, headlines**). If it were a compound sentence, it could be broken into two separate sentences.

— — —

Along with Roscoe and Simmons ***(prepositional phrase—not a dependent clause),*** I attended the convention.

— — —

Having run out of time ***(participial phrase—not a dependent clause),*** I decided to finish the research paper.

— — —

I returned to the office **to complete my assignment** ***(infinitive phrase—not a dependent clause).***

These sentences are simple because each contains only one independent clause. Notice that there is no place you can break any of the sentences into the two equal parts that would be needed to make them compound. And they cannot be complex because there is no dependent clause in any of them.

Compound

To be compound, a sentence must have at least ***two*** **independent clauses.** Theoretically, there is no limit to the number of independent clauses a compound sentence may contain. However, the longer the sentence, the more likely it will confuse the reader or the listener. Just remember that there can be no dependent clause in this construction.

The editor accepted the award, **but** *the publisher displayed it on his office wall.*

The **comma** and the coordinating conjunction **but** join two independent clauses to form a compound sentence. Each independent clause can stand alone as a separate sentence. Notice that each independent clause meets the minimum requirements for a sentence: a subject, a verb and the expression of a complete thought.

— — —

That's not a feature story; *it's a column.*

The **semicolon** joins the two independent clauses to form a compound sentence.

— — —

I wrote the ads, *Miller designed them* **and** Hapenstall sold them.

This compound has three independent clauses, but they are brief enough to form an acceptable sentence.

Complex

The complex sentence has **one independent clause** and **one dependent clause.** Remember that a dependent clause has a subject and a verb—the same as an independent clause. The difference is that a dependent clause does not express a complete thought and an independent clause does. In other words, the dependent clause depends on an independent clause to make sense.

Keep in mind that the sentence is complex regardless of whether the dependent clause precedes or follows the independent clause.

After she arrived at her office, the advertising executive saw the award on her wall.

After she arrived at her office is the dependent clause. It has a subject (*she*) and a verb (*arrived*) but it does not express a complete thought. Only by attaching itself to the independent clause does the dependent clause make sense.

— — —

The public relations director will retire *after the campaign is finished.*

After the campaign is finished is the dependent clause because it cannot stand alone. The independent clause, **The public relations director will retire,** can stand alone because it makes sense without the dependent clause.

— — —

Acme University, *which has been in operation for more than 150 years,* received a special citation from the governor.

The dependent clause, ***which has been in operation for more than 150 years,*** can be placed within the independent clause (as well as before or after it, as shown in the two previous examples).

Compound–Complex

This structure causes more problems than any of the others. But it's not difficult if you work your way through it step by step. To form the **compound** part, we need a minimum of ***two*** **independent clauses**—the same as for a compound sentence. To form the **complex** part, we need at least **one dependent clause**—the same as for a complex sentence. The only major problem we have is sentence length. If not carefully constructed, the compound–complex sentence can become so long that it is difficult to follow.

The photographer accepted the award (one independent clause), but **he dropped and broke it** (a second independent clause) ***while he was walking down the steps of the stage*** (*one dependent clause*).

— — —

Even though we wanted to offer our intern a full-time job (*one dependent clause*), **we couldn't afford to hire him** (one independent clause), and **he took a job with our competitor** (a second independent clause).

— — —

Because he wanted to earn an advanced degree (*one dependent clause*) and also ***because he couldn't find a satisfactory job*** (*a second dependent clause*), **Winston sold his car** (one independent clause), and **he used the money to return to the university** (a second independent clause).

Syntax

At one time or another, all of us have had to say, "I didn't mean that the way it sounded," or "That came out wrong." We knew what we wanted to say, and we used the right words. But the meaning wasn't what we intended.

We had a syntax problem. The words were right, but the order in which we used them was wrong and it mangled our message. The problem is common, and it is difficult to overcome because we're often unaware that we've made an error.

Some syntax mistakes are so obviously wrong that we catch them immediately. Others are so subtle that we can continue to make them for a lifetime unless we consciously check for them, or someone points them out to us.

Let's consider some obvious and some not-so-obvious syntax errors and analyze where and when we're most likely to make them. Each of the following syntax problems came from material published or broadcast. The examples have been altered to prevent the embarrassment that might result if their sources were identified.

(Wrong) "Valium and Human Memory" is the subject of a National Institute of Health grant awarded to Acme University, ***which will end this year.***

The **grant,** not Acme University, will end this year.

(Correct) "Valium and Human Memory" is the subject of a National Institute of Health grant awarded to Acme University. The **grant** will end this year.

— — —

(Wrong) The accused is expected to plead guilty to the crimes he committed ***in federal court today.***

Hardly anyone is stupid enough to commit crimes in front of a judge in a federal courtroom.

(Correct) The accused is expected to plead guilty today in federal court.

— — —

(Wrong) Police chiefs from 25 of the nation's biggest cities have been invited to a conference on crimes ***committed by repeat offenders in Los Angeles in September.***

Surely all those people aren't going to limit their study to what goes on in just one city in one month.

(Correct) Police chiefs from 25 of the nation's biggest cities have been invited to Los Angeles in September for a conference on crimes committed by repeat offenders.

— — —

(Wrong) Drug problems among teenagers, ***increasing at a rate some government officials consider alarming,*** will require more than just money to solve, according to a Senate subcommittee report.

Are we to infer from this construction that there is a surplus of teenagers?

(Correct) Increasing at a rate some government officials consider alarming, drug problems among teenagers will require more than just money to solve, according to a Senate subcommittee report.

— — —

(Wrong) The project for senior citizens, ***launched earlier this year,*** has financial backing from the federal government.

Are we to believe that the federal government is supporting an effort to launch senior citizens?

(Correct) Launched earlier this year, the project for senior citizens has financial backing from the federal government.

* * *

In presenting examples that may not be so obvious, let's also identify them by type. That may give us the increased awareness needed to spot the problems.

Misplaced Dependent Clauses

(Wrong) The student failed his final examinations this summer, ***which prevented him from graduating.***

Summer had nothing to do with his not graduating. The failed examinations did.

(Correct) Failing his final examinations prevented the student from graduating this summer.

— — —

(Wrong) Rep. Maury L. Frankel of the 10th Congressional District in Texas, who is seeking re-election, announced today he has raised $2 million in campaign funds.

Texas is not the candidate; **Frankel** is.

(Correct) Rep. Maury L. Frankel, who is seeking re-election in the 10th Congressional District in Texas, announced today he has raised $2 million in campaign funds.

— — —

(Wrong) The president said he has a plan to improve the economy ***that he has been working on for a year.***

The president has been working on a ***plan*** to improve the ***economy.***

(Correct) The president said he has been working for a year on a *plan* to improve the *economy.*

— — —

(Wrong) The documents at the capitol, ***which have been on display throughout the summer,*** already have attracted more than 250,000 tourists.

The *documents,* not the *capitol,* have been on display.

(Correct) The documents that have been on display throughout the summer at the capitol already have attracted more than 250,000 tourists.

— — —

(Wrong) The candidate will campaign in the western states in September ***where he is expected to draw large crowds,*** *his manager said.*

The dependent clause should follow *states,* not *September.*

(Correct) The candidate will campaign in September in the western states where he is expected to draw large crowds, his manager said.

Misplaced Appositives

(Wrong) Dr. John L. Springtree of the University of Arizona, ***a specialist in reading disabilities,*** will direct the summer workshop.

Dr. Springtree, not the *University of Arizona,* is the specialist.

(Also wrong) Dr. John L. Springtree, a specialist in reading disabilities ***at the University of Arizona,*** will direct the summer workshop.

We presume Dr. Springtree is a specialist everywhere, not just at the University of Arizona.

(Correct) A specialist in reading disabilities, Dr. John L. Springtree of the University of Arizona will direct the summer workshop.

— — —

(Wrong) She won first prize at the Voice of Democracy competition in Boston, ***the toughest speaking contest she said she has ever entered.***

The *competition,* not Boston, was the toughest.

(Correct) She won first prize in Boston at the Voice of Democracy competition, the toughest speaking contest she said she has ever entered.

Dangling Verbals

Because dangling verbals already have been addressed (see pages 111–112), only one example of each error will be presented here.

(Wrong) ***To be eligible for this school year*** (infinitive phrase), the financial aid forms must be completed and returned by May 10.

The *students,* not the *forms,* must be eligible.

(Correct) To be eligible for this school year, students must complete and return their financial aid forms by May 10.

— — —

(Wrong) ***Unleashing his unstoppable "sky hook"*** (participial phrase), the ball swished through the net to give Jabbar another two points.

The *basketball* didn't *unleash* itself.

(Correct) Unleashing his unstoppable "sky hook," Jabbar swished the ball through the net for another two points.

— — —

(Wrong) ***After arguing with my editor*** (gerund phrase), my story went unpublished.

The *story* was not arguing with the *editor.*

(Correct) After *arguing with my editor* (gerund phrase), I failed to get my story published.

— — —

(Also correct) Because I argued with my editor, my story went unpublished.

Misplaced Prepositional Phrases

(Wrong) ***On the air for only a few weeks,*** our viewers already are increasing in large numbers.

The *broadcasts,* not the *viewers,* are on the air.

(Correct) Although we have been broadcasting for only a few weeks, our viewers already are increasing in large numbers.

— — —

(Wrong) The Cardinals will play in Windell Stadium ***at 7 p.m.,*** the only indoor baseball facility in the state.

The *stadium,* not *7 p.m.,* is the only indoor baseball facility in the state.

(Correct) The Cardinals will play at 7 p.m. in Windell Stadium, the only indoor baseball facility in the state.

Split Infinitives

Although writers should generally keep their infinitives intact, the absolute taboo against splitting them is dead. "*To* **radically** *reduce* the possibility that the disease will recur" reads considerably better than "*To reduce* **radically** the possibility that the disease will recur" or "*To reduce* the possibility **radically** that the disease will recur."

(Wrong) That project is too important **to *not* fund.**

(Correct) That project is too important not **to fund.**

— — —

(Wrong) The front page is the one place that we never want **to *under any circumstances* run advertising.**

(Correct) The front page is the one place that we never want **to run** advertising under any circumstances.

Split Verb Phrases

(Wrong) The editorial **had, *as the editor had expected,* provoked** numerous readers to complain.

(Correct) As the editor had expected, the editorial **had provoked** numerous complaints.

— — —

(Wrong) "You **should *for better or for worse* prepare yourselves,**" the fire chief warned his crew.

(Correct) "You **should prepare yourselves** for better or for worse," the fire chief warned his crew.

Misplaced Time Elements

(Wrong) The president announced a new tax proposal that will help citizens save hundreds of dollars ***today.***

(Correct) The president announced **today** that he has a new tax proposal that will help citizens save hundreds of dollars.

— — —

(Wrong) The chancellor of the university outlined a plan to raise $25 million to help students get a college education ***this year.***

(Correct) The chancellor of the university outlined a plan to raise $25 million **this year** to help students get a college education.

"Squinting" Modifiers

"Squinting" modifiers are confusing because they can modify words both to the left and to the right of them.

(Wrong) Subscribers who complain ***needlessly*** annoy newspaper circulation managers.

The placement of the word **needlessly** makes unclear whether the writer means that the subscribers are complaining needlessly or that they are needlessly annoying the circulation managers.

(Correct) By complaining **needlessly** (without sufficient cause), subscribers annoy newspaper circulation managers.

(Also correct) By complaining, subscribers **needlessly** annoy newspaper circulation managers.

— — —

(Wrong) Reading ***occasionally*** improves a person's mind.

Does the writer mean reading ***every now and then*** can improve a person's mind, or that ***every now and then*** reading can improve a person's mind?

(Correct) By reading occasionally, a person can improve her mind.

(Also correct) By reading, a person can occasionally improve his mind.

Dangling Elliptical Elements

These errors result from phrases in which words are implied rather than written or spoken.

(Wrong) ***Although working hard for many years,*** my boss never promoted me.

The writer does not mean that the boss was *working hard* for many years.

(Correct) **Although I worked hard for many years,** my boss never promoted me.

— — —

(Wrong) ***Even though wanting to make A's in all our classes,*** our professors never gave them.

The *professors* are not the ones *wanting* to make the grades.

(Correct) **Even though we wanted to make A's in all our classes,** we never got them from our professors.

(You may test yourself on the material in this chapter or section by connecting with the following Web site: www.mhhe.com/arnold.)

PUNCTUATING

part 3

Introduction

A laugh, a fist pounding on a desk top, a raised eyebrow, a lowered voice, a frown, a pointing finger, a tapping foot—we use all these signals and many others to punctuate our spoken words.

Body language and voice inflections form important parts of our spoken messages, and we use them intuitively. We don't think about them until we need to write our thoughts. Then we turn to commas to indicate pauses, exclamation marks to express strong emotions, dashes to show dramatic effect, parentheses to promote understanding, and periods to regulate stops and starts.

The primary function of punctuation is to take the readers by their collective hand and guide them through the sentences, telling them to pause here, get excited there, contract these words, and stop briefly before going to the next part of the message.

We can't successfully convert our thoughts into written words unless we know how to punctuate. We can't punctuate unless we understand parts of speech and sentence structures and functions. That's why the punctuation section of this book comes only after a thorough discussion of grammar.

Continuing with the approach we've followed so far, let's make our discussion of punctuation as simple and as practical as we can. Some punctuation is less difficult to master than others. Periods, question marks and exclamation marks are not hard to understand and to use effectively. Slashes, dashes, parentheses, brackets, colons and semicolons present more of a challenge. And commas, apostrophes, hyphens and quotation marks test the skill of even the best writers.

(You may test yourself on the material in this section by connecting with the following Web site: www.mhhe.com/arnold.)

chapter 19

PERIODS

Periods are used to end declarative sentences, indirect questions, rhetorical questions and most imperative sentences. Periods also are used for abbreviations and to indicate that selected words have been omitted on purpose from a quotation.

How to Use Periods

1. At the end of a declarative sentence.

The final deadline is 11:15 p.m.

— — —

Johnston is retiring today.

— — —

Anita graduated in the top 10 percent of her class.

2. At the end of an indirect question.

Remember that an indirect question is revealed in a declarative sentence but requires no response.

The president asked his press secretary whether the interview with The Washington Post reporter would be on or off the record.

— — —

The editor wanted to know when the lead editorial would be ready.

3. At the end of most imperative sentences.

Have the advertisement prepared by 9 p.m., Carrie.

— — —

Please shut the door so others can't hear our conversation.

— — —

Would you please be silent during the ceremony.

In the last example, a request or a command phrased politely in the form of a question requires a period, not a question mark. No answer is expected because the person to whom the request is directed is being told, not asked, to be silent.

4. At the end of a rhetorical question.

Remember that a rhetorical question presents a suggestion or an invitation and requires no response. Therefore, a period is used instead of a question mark.

Shall we gather in the newsroom.

— — —

Will you rise for the concluding prayer.

5. With abbreviations.

Because the use of and tolerance for abbreviations vary between different forms of writing, students and professionals should check the appropriate stylebooks before abbreviating anything. For most mass communicators, the most commonly used reference is *The Associated Press Stylebook.*

115 Fifth Ave.	U.N.	Ph.D.
G.L. Overmeyer	U.S.	Mrs.
8:22 a.m.	Jr., Sr., II, III	Ms.
Lexington, Va.	Washington, D.C.	Dr.

6. As an ellipsis.

Consisting of three consecutive periods, an ellipsis is used to indicate that the writer has omitted selected words from a sentence. Although the practice is frequent in academic writing, it is rarely used in newspapers.

Barbara A. Hoskins is believed to be the person who donated funds anonymously for the town's first library. Numerous references to her generosity . . . can be found in the county newspaper published weekly from 1875 to 1900.

— — —

If the omitted material comes at the end of a sentence, a fourth period is added.

Barbara A. Hoskins is believed to be the person who donated funds anonymously for the town's first library. In the county newspaper published weekly from 1875–1900, one can find numerous references to her generosity. . . .

7. **To separate seconds from parts of seconds in athletic events.**

   (*seconds and tenths of a second*) 9.9

   — — —

   (*seconds and hundredths of a second*) 10.06

8. **To separate dollars from cents.**

   $5.25 $101.05 $5,236.37 $1,820,351.86

How *Not* to Use Periods

1. **After another period used for an abbreviation at the end of a sentence.**

(Wrong) The reception will be at the Art Gallery, 1122 First St..

(Correct) The reception will be at the Art Gallery, 1122 First St.

The period following **St.** will both abbreviate the word and end the sentence.

2. **To indicate pauses.**

(Wrong) The city manager's job is considered safe . . . at least for now.

(Correct) The city manager's job is considered safe, at least for now.

or

(Correct) The city manager's job is considered safe—at least for now.

Note that some broadcast writers use an ellipsis to indicate pauses or to separate news items.

3. **With certain well-known abbreviations.**

   FBI, NBC, mph, mpg, NCAA, MIT, JFK and many others.

To save space, journalists routinely omit many periods that would be required with abbreviations in more formal writing. Always check the stylebook(s) that guides your particular task.

4. **With an acronym** (a pronounceable word formed from the first letter of two or more other words).

   UNICEF, NATO, OPEC, MADD

Question Marks

chapter 20

Question marks follow interrogative words, phrases and clauses and tell the readers that a response is requested or demanded.

How to Use Question Marks

1. **After a direct question.**

   Is this the advertising department?

   — — —

   Are you going to seek re-election?

   — — —

   Why are you reading my notes?

   — — —

   Who? What? When? Where? Why? How?

2. **After each item in a series of questions if more emphasis is desired than could be obtained by placing only one question mark at the end of the sentence.**

   To come to work for us, you are demanding weekends off? double pay for overtime? a clothing allowance? and a new car?

3. **Enclosed in parentheses to express doubt or uncertainty about dates or numbers that cannot be verified.**

   He discovered that island July 22 (?), 1902.

Obviously, such a practice would be unacceptable in most forms of journalistic writing.

4. **In a declarative sentence that ends with an interrogative.**

   You wouldn't fire me for missing one deadline, **would you?**

5. Either inside or outside of a terminal quotation mark.

Please refer to the section on quotation marks on pages 213–214.

How *Not* to Use Question Marks

1. After an indirect question in a declarative sentence that reveals a question but requires no response.

(Wrong) The vice president wanted to know whether his speech would be written today**?**

(Correct) The vice president wanted to know whether his speech would be written today.

— — —

(Wrong) The council member asked the police chief what he planned to do with the requested funds**?**

(Correct) The council member asked the police chief what he planned to do with the requested funds.

2. After a rhetorical question in which a person attempts to be polite by putting a request, a suggestion or an invitation in the form of a question.

(Wrong) Shall we turn to page 40 in our textbooks**?**

(Correct) Shall we turn to page 40 in our textbooks.

— — —

(Wrong) Would you hand me my camera, please**?**

(Correct) Would you hand me my camera, please.

3. Enclosed in parentheses to indicate sarcasm or humor.

(Wrong) Thank you for offering me the pleasure(**?**) of listening to your recording of background noises in your newsroom.

(Correct) No, thank you. (*If you want to be polite.*)

(Also correct) No, thank you. Listening to your recording of background noises in your newsroom would give me no pleasure. (*If you do not want to be polite.*)

4. Combined with a comma between statement and attribution.

(Wrong) "Are you applying for the job**?,**" she asked.

(Correct) "Are you applying for the job**?**" she asked.

EXCLAMATION MARKS

chapter 21

The first thing writers need to understand about exclamation marks is that they are to be used sparingly and selectively. Because exclamation marks express strong feelings or emotions, they lose their effect if overused. Furthermore, to avoid editorializing, writers of objective articles restrict the use of the exclamation mark to direct quotations.

How to Use Exclamation Marks

1. **In declarations.**

   That's the greatest victory in the history of the university!

2. **In commands.**

   Get back to work now!

3. **In expressions of disbelief.**

   I can't believe you didn't get the job!

4. **In expressions of surprise.**

   It's the wrong color!

5. **With interjections expressed strongly.**

   Gosh! Darn! Great! Fantastic! Wonderful!

6. **Inside or outside of quotation marks.**

   Refer to the section on quotation marks on pages 213–214.

How *Not* to Use Exclamation Marks

1. **In combination with one or more other exclamation marks.**

(Wrong) That advertising jingle is the best I've ever heard!!

(Correct) That advertising jingle is the best I've ever heard!

Remember that emphasis is not increased by adding a second or a third exclamation mark.

2. **In combination with a comma to separate a statement from its attribution.**

Refer to the section on quotation marks on page 214.

chapter 22 COMMAS

The comma is arguably the most difficult punctuation mark to master because it is used in so many ways. However, despite its utility, the comma is not powerful. It cannot hold two sentences together the way the stronger semicolon can, and it certainly cannot bring anything to a stop or to a halt the way periods and exclamation marks can. Nevertheless, the comma is wonderfully useful when called upon for less demanding tasks.

Perhaps the best way to gain a comprehensive understanding of the comma is to start by committing to memory the rules covering its most common functions. The more difficult uses will take longer to learn and will require continual referral to the rules governing them.

How to Use Commas

1. To separate words, phrases and clauses placed in a series.

Words in a series

Club members elected a **president, vice president, secretary,** and **treasurer.**

Phrases in a series

During his college years, Sidney earned money selling used textbooks **to his professors, to his classmates(,)** and **to the manager** of the campus bookstore.

Clauses in a series

McCoy spoke for the bill, Sutherland argued against it(,) and **Madany insisted on remaining neutral.**

In the first example, president, vice president, secretary, and treasurer are separated by commas. Remember that the comma takes the place of the coordinating conjunction ***and*** (see pages 35–36).

The only decision the writer has to make is whether to put a comma after **secretary,** the last element in the series before ***and.*** In academic and other more formal forms of writing, the comma is used consistently. However, mass communicators, who are always seeking ways to save time and space, use the following test to determine whether to place a comma between the last two elements separated by ***and*** in the series: If there is no likelihood that the next-to-last word (secretary) will be confused with the last word (treasurer), the comma is omitted.

A comma is necessary in this instance because it tells readers that club members elected four people. Without the comma, readers may infer that the positions of secretary and treasurer are filled by the same person.

In the examples involving phrases and clauses used in a series, the comma placed in parentheses would remain in formal writing such as term papers, theses and essays, but most journalists would omit it because it is not needed for clarity.

* * *

When adjectives are used in a series, another step has to be considered in determining whether to use commas between them. If the adjectives are **coordinate,** either a *comma* or the coordinating conjunction ***and*** must be placed between them. If the adjectives are not coordinate, neither a *comma* nor the word ***and*** is needed.

Coordinate adjectives modify a noun or a pronoun equally. If ***and*** can be placed between them, they are coordinate and a comma may be substituted for ***and.*** If the two (or more) adjectives can be interchanged without affecting the meaning of the sentence, they are coordinate.

Consider the following example:

The **new red, yellow** and **black** signs cost $500 each.

Red, yellow and **black** are coordinate adjectives. ***And*** can be placed logically between them, and they also can be interchanged without harming the meaning of the sentence. **New** and **red,** however, are not coordinate adjectives. ***And*** makes no sense when placed between them, and the two words cannot be interchanged without harming the meaning of the sentence. Neither a *comma* nor ***and*** should be placed between adjectives that are not coordinate. (See No. 6 on pages 35–36 for additional examples.)

2. After introductory explanatory phrases and clauses.

Introductory prepositional phrase

At the end of their discussion, members of the jury announced their verdict.

— — —

Introductory participial phrase

Shifting the ball to his right hand, the team's best player made a 20-foot shot.

— — —

Introductory infinitive phrase

To prepare for his speech, the senator practiced for an hour in front of the mirror.

Introductory dependent clause

When firefighters were delayed by heavy traffic, the chief said he lost all hope of saving the building.

In each example, a pause is natural before moving on to the independent clause. In the case of the dependent clause, however, no pause (and therefore no comma) is needed if the sentence order is reversed by placing the independent clause before the dependent clause: **The chief said he lost all hope of saving the building** when firefighters were delayed by heavy traffic.

Some authorities claim that introductory material requires no comma if the end of the introduction blends without a pause into the beginning of the independent clause. Others insist that no comma is necessary unless the introductory matter is longer than three words. These two points are worthy of consideration by expert writers. For others, however, using the comma consistently should work just fine.

3. Before a coordinating conjunction that joins two independent clauses.

Remember from Chapter 16 that the coordinating conjunctions are ***and, but, or, for, nor, yet*** and ***so.*** Also recall that each independent clause connected by a coordinating conjunction is a complete sentence that can stand alone.

The temperature hit a record low of 37 at 6 a.m., **but** it climbed slowly to 69 by late afternoon.

Remember that the comma by itself is not strong enough to hold two sentences together. It must be combined with a coordinating conjunction to gain enough strength to do the job. The comma may be omitted if both independent clauses are brief:

She lectured **and** we listened.

4. To set off explanatory numbers and figures.

Alfred T. Lowell**, 65,** retired last week.

— — —

Roberta J. Smithers**, 1001 W. Lake St.,** won first place.

5. To set apart words and phrases used as appositives.

Juan L. Martinez**, secretary,** read the minutes from the last meeting.

— — —

Belinda Q. Terry**, Ph.D.,** lectured for an hour and a half.

Felix O. Danton**, Barboursville sophomore,** will coordinate the program.

— — —

The project**, directed by Barbara R. Rosenberg of Craigsville,** is completed.

— — —

Dr. Elizabeth A. Gilkerson**, professor of history and an authority on World War II,** has completed her eighth book.

Watch the closing comma in an appositive or in an appositive phrase. Writers rarely neglect to use the opening comma, but they sometimes forget or misplace the closing comma.

6. To separate direct and indirect quotations from their attribution.

Direct quotations

"Injuries have destroyed our chances for winning the conference championship**,**" the coach said.

— — —

The coach said**,** "Injuries have destroyed our chances for winning the conference championship."

Indirect quotation

Acme University will close for the holidays**,** President Basil M. Stillwater announced today.

— — —

President Basil M. Stillwater announced today that Acme University will close for the holidays.

In an indirect quotation, no comma is necessary when the attribution comes first. For more discussion of the use of commas with quotations, refer to the section on quotation marks on pages 209–210 and 213.

7. To set off a nonessential dependent clause that comes in the middle of an independent clause.

A nonessential dependent clause provides information that adds to but does not affect the meaning of the independent clause. Nonessential clauses may be omitted without harming the meaning of the independent clause.

Conversely, essential dependent clauses affect the meaning of the independent clause and cannot be omitted. Therefore, no commas are used to set off essential clauses.

The way to determine whether a dependent clause is essential is to read the sentence with the clause included and then to read the sentence with the clause omitted. If the meaning of the independent clause is unchanged by the omission, the dependent clause is nonessential and must be set off with commas. If the meaning of the independent clause is changed by the omission, the dependent clause is essential and no commas are used.

Nonessential dependent clauses

Club members, **who range in age from 21 to 90,** meet each Tuesday.

— — —

News reporters, **most of whom are notorious for their skepticism,** question whatever they doubt.

Essential dependent clauses

Club members **who arrive before 6 p.m.** will be admitted free.

— — —

All news reporters **who work for The Tri-State Herald** will be given pay raises Monday.

8. To separate the city from the state. Add another comma after the state unless the sentence ends with the state.

Many college students spend their spring break at Daytona Beach**,** Fla.

— — —

The annual convention of the Society of Professional Journalists will be in Lexington**,** Ky.**,** Nov. 12–16.

9. With dates in the following ways:

Between the day and the month and date

The meeting started Thursday**,** May 21.

— — —

Between the date and the year

The meeting started Thursday**,** May 19**,** 2004.

— — —

After the year when it is used with the month and date

The meeting started Thursday**,** May 19**,** 2004**,** in Augusta, Ga.

10. With ***yes, no, for example,*** **interjections, nouns of direct address and parenthetical adverbs.**

Yes

"**Yes,** I will write the editorial."

No

"**No,** I will not change the wording in the advertisement."

For example

"I think I can tell you, **for example,** about the time I covered a visit by President Bush."

Interjection

"**Well,** we could assign two additional photographers."

Nouns of direct address

"**Markita,** please edit my column for me."

— — —

"I want you to know, **Dr. Randolph,** that I thoroughly enjoyed my summer internship."

Parenthetical adverbs

"I can tell you**, however,** that without typing skills, you'll never be hired."

— — —

"**Moreover,** I want you to understand that you must be an accurate speller."

11. **Before every third digit from the right in numbers that contain four or more digits.**

    Enrollment at Acme University dipped to 12,250 students during the past semester, according to figures released by the registrar.

    The jury awarded $2,372,221 to the plaintiffs.

Do not use a comma after the third digit from the right in dates: **1776, 1865, 1998.**

12. **To indicate that a word or several words have been left out to avoid repetition. This use of the comma is a great space-saver.**

    The meteorologist said the winter will be milder than usual; the summer**,** hotter.

    — — —

    The seating order in the high school auditorium is arranged as follows: Seniors get the front rows; juniors**,** the middle; and sophomores**,** the back.

13. **To set off some identical words used consecutively.**

    "I want you to know **that, that** will be finished as quickly as possible."

    — — —

    Everything there **was, was** divided equally among the survivors.

A better solution would be to rewrite the sentences to eliminate the repetition.

14. **Before a question that comes at the end of a declarative sentence.**

    You hire recent college graduates, **don't you?**

    — — —

They are going to apply for the scholarships**, aren't they?**

15. Before *not* or *never* used to show a contrast.

The mistake was the publishers**, not** the writer's.

— — —

I want to work in some area of mass communications**, never** at some routine job.

16. To set off absolute phrases.

An absolute phrase consists of a noun or a pronoun followed by a participle and other modifying words. It is used to help explain the independent clause.

His parents' apprehensions notwithstanding, the college junior gave up his senior year to enter the National Basketball Association draft.

— — —

The cast featured four star performers**, each having a separate dressing room.**

— — —

Her heart pounding rapidly, the recent law school graduate waited anxiously for the results of the bar examination.

17. To prevent a misreading that might occur without a comma.

While eating**,** John read the newspaper.

— — —

From 20**,** four were selected as editors of the student newspaper.

— — —

Mary sniffed**,** her nose wrinkling in disgust.

How *Not* to Use Commas

Learning how **not** to misuse commas is almost as important as studying how to use them correctly. Classroom teachers and professional copyeditors spend about as much of their time removing commas as they do inserting them. The following are examples of how teachers and copy editors find commas misused.

1. Don't set off days of the week inside commas.

(Wrong) The playoff will begin**, Monday,** at 10 a.m.

(Correct) The playoff will begin Monday at 10 a.m.

2. Don't use a comma by itself to hold two sentences together.

This is called a **comma-splice error.** Remember from our earlier discussion that a comma is not strong enough to hold two independent clauses together. To do so, the comma must be followed by a coordinating conjunction.

(Wrong) The president said he will submit another proposal to the Board of Trustees**,** he said he hopes the members will accept it.

(Correct) The president said he will submit another proposal to the Board of Trustees, **and** he said he hopes the members will accept it.

* * *

An even worse mistake than a comma-splice error is a **run-on sentence** in which two sentences butt against each other without the benefit of any punctuation. As bad as a comma-splice error is, a writer using it at least attempts to do something to hold the two sentences together.

(Wrong) The president said he will submit another proposal to the Board of **Trustees he** said he hopes the members will accept it.

(Correct) The president said he will submit another proposal to the Board of **Trustees, and** he said he hopes the members will accept it.

(Correct) The president said he will submit another proposal to the Board of **Trustees; he** said he hopes the members will accept it.

(Correct) The president said he will submit another proposal to the Board of Trustees. **He** said he hopes the members will accept it.

3. Don't place a comma between the month and the year unless a date also is used.

(Wrong) April, 2002

(Correct) April 2002

(Correct) April 22, 2002

— — —

Don't use commas when a date is expressed in the following way:

22 April 2002

4. Don't use a comma before a coordinating conjunction that joins two independent clauses when the subject is the same in both clauses but is expressed only in the first clause.

(Wrong) Jan wanted to ask for a raise, but didn't have the courage.

(Correct) Jan wanted to ask for a raise but didn't have the courage.

5. Don't use a comma *after* a coordinating conjunction that joins two independent clauses. The comma goes *before* the conjunction.

(Wrong) The college senior wanted to attend graduate school **but,** he had to go to work to pay off his student loans.

(Correct) The college senior wanted to attend graduate school**, but** he had to go to work to pay off his student loans.

6. Don't use a comma before a coordinating conjunction that joins compound subjects.

(Wrong) The governor**,** and the state senator will compete for the seat in Congress.

(Correct) The governor and the state senator will compete for the seat in Congress.

7. Don't use commas before and after a name that follows a title.

(Wrong) President**, Roscoe B. Pippen,** approved the tuition increase at Acme University.

(Correct) **President Roscoe B. Pippen** approved the tuition increase at Acme University.

— — —

Commas are used, however, if the title follows the name.

(Wrong) Roscoe B. Pippen **president of Acme University** approved the tuition increase.

(Correct) Roscoe B. Pippen**, president of Acme University,** approved the tuition increase.

— — —

When the title is preceded by the definite article **the,** the name becomes an appositive and is set off with commas.

(Wrong) The president **Roscoe B. Pippen** approved the tuition increase at Acme University.

(Correct) The president**, Roscoe B. Pippen,** approved the tuition increase at Acme University.

8. Don't use commas with names followed by *Jr., Sr., II* or *III.*

(Wrong) Philip N. Mayberry**, Jr.,** is the program director at WXXZ radio.

(Correct) Philip N. Mayberry **Jr.** is the program director at WXXZ radio.

9. Don't use commas before and after a restrictive appositive.

(Wrong) My daughter**, Joan,** is vice president of Stanford Public Relations.

(Correct) My daughter **Joan** is vice president of Stanford Public Relations.

Joan is restrictive. The name tells which of the parent's daughters is the vice president.

10. Don't use a comma before the first adjective or after the last adjective used in a series to modify a noun or a pronoun.

(Wrong) **The, long, boring** speech produced no news worth broadcasting.

(Wrong) **The long, boring,** speech produced no news worth broadcasting.

(Correct) **The long, boring** speech produced no news worth broadcasting.

Just remember to place the commas only where you can substitute the coordinating conjunction **and.**

11. Don't use commas either before or after essential dependent clauses and phrases.

(Wrong) The horse**, that won the Kentucky Derby,** was not one of the favorites.

(Correct) The horse **that won the Kentucky Derby** was not one of the favorites.

— — —

(Wrong) The sign**, painted by the students,** won first place in the statewide competition.

(Correct) The sign **painted by the students** won first place in the statewide competition.

Remember that essential or restrictive information cannot be removed without harming the meaning of the sentence. That's why no commas are used with essential elements. Nonessential clauses and phrases, however, can be removed without harming the meaning of the sentence; therefore, they are set off with commas. See pages 9–10 and 179–180 for more information on essential and nonessential dependent clauses.

12. Don't use a comma after a relative pronoun that introduces an essential dependent clause.

(Wrong) I want to use the computer **that,** we purchased for $25,000.

(Correct) I want to use the computer **that** we purchased for $25,000.

13. Don't use a comma after a subordinating conjunction that introduces a dependent clause.

(Wrong) **Although,** the photograph was technically good, the editors rejected it as potentially libelous.

(Correct) **Although** the photograph was technically good, the editors rejected it as potentially libelous.

— — —

(Wrong) The editors rejected the photograph as potentially libelous **although,** it was technically good.

(Correct) The editors rejected the photograph as potentially libelous **although** it was technically good.

14. Don't use a comma before or after *like, such as* or *similar to.*

(Wrong) The reporters for The Messenger have computers**, like/such as/similar to** yours and mine.

(Wrong) The reporters for The Messenger have computers **like/such as/similar to,** yours and mine.

(Correct) The reporters for The Messenger have computers **like/such as/similar to** yours and mine.

15. Don't use commas before and after intensive and reflexive pronouns (the "self" pronouns).

(Wrong) The commissioner**, herself,** broke one of the rules she established when she assumed her office.

(Correct) The commissioner **herself** broke one of the rules she established when she assumed her office.

— — —

(Wrong) When the magazine designer slipped and fell in the hallway, he hurt**, himself,** seriously enough to require emergency treatment.

(Correct) When the magazine designer slipped and fell in the hallway, he hurt **himself** seriously enough to require emergency treatment.

16. Don't use a comma before an incomplete direct quotation.

(Wrong) One spectator called the governor's speech**, "wonderful and exciting."**

(Correct) One spectator called the governor's speech **"wonderful and exciting."**

Remember that incomplete direct quotations are unacceptable to some editors and in most forms of formal writing. Check your stylebooks.

Refer to the section on quotation marks on page 210 for additional information on the use of incomplete direct quotations.

17. Do not use a comma after a question mark or an exclamation mark that separates a statement from its attribution.

Refer to the section on quotation marks on page 214 for information on the use of commas with quotation marks.

SEMICOLONS

chapter 23

Considering the functions semicolons perform, an argument could be made for calling them "semiperiods." Because they contain properties of both commas and periods, semicolons perform tasks that require more than the strength of commas but less than the power of periods. For example, semicolons can hold two closely related sentences together, but they cannot bring a sentence to a stop.

Unlike colons, semicolons do not introduce anything. What they do have in common with colons is their assurance to readers that more words will follow because semicolons can't end sentences.

Semicolons are marvelous organizers, especially in sentences that already contain commas. When they are used correctly, semicolons enable us to reduce significantly the potential confusion that otherwise could occur in our writing.

How to Use Semicolons

1. To join two closely related independent clauses.

Voters don't want promises**;** they want action.

— — —

News stories are written objectively**;** editorials aren't.

— — —

"I really wanted the job**;** I just didn't get it."

As useful as they are in joining two independent clauses, semicolons do not always provide the best method to accomplish this goal. Commas and coordinating conjunctions are used more frequently (News stories are written objectively**, but** editorials aren't), as are two separate sentences (News stories are written objectively. Editorials aren't). In addition, one of the independent clauses could be subordinated into a dependent clause (**Although** news stories are written objectively, editorials aren't).

2. Between items listed in a series if each of the items is followed by appositive material.

Members of the subcommittee are Mike S. White, District 1; Pat D. Jones, District 7; Perry A. Lucas, District 14; and Regina B. Thurman, District 21.

Semicolons are used to eliminate the confusion that could result if they were replaced with additional commas. The commas and semicolons combine to make certain that readers know, for example, that Jones, not Lucas, represents District 7. Just keep in mind that anytime the number of commas in a sentence becomes potentially confusing, the writer can promote understanding by turning either to semicolons or to one or more additional sentences.

When commas and semicolons are used in a series, an additional point should be kept in mind to prevent another frequent error. You will recall from our earlier discussion that when commas are used to separate simple items listed in a series, journalists often omit the comma that precedes ***and*** (Members of the subcommittee are Mike S. White, Pat D. Jones, Perry A. Lucas **and** Regina B. Thurman). However, the semicolon before ***and*** in a series using both commas and semicolons (Lucas, District 14***;*** and) is never omitted. It is needed to close the appositive.

3. Before a conjunctive adverb.

Remember that a conjunctive adverb joins two independent clauses. For a review, turn to Chapter 13, pages 136–137.

The candidate's plane was grounded by a bomb scare**; therefore,** he will not arrive in time to speak at the convention.

4. To combine with a coordinating conjunction to join two independent clauses *if* the independent clauses already contain a potentially confusing number of commas.

In journalistic writing, this rule is rarely followed. When a sentence becomes so potentially confusing that this rule could be applied, journalists choose to divide the material into two or more sentences.

The former major, Richard E. Perkowski, a 20-year Army veteran, was offered a new military assignment in Asia**; but** he turned it down, he said, to retire in Marietta, Ga., near Atlanta.

5. Place a semicolon outside a quotation mark.

Turn to the chapter on quotation marks, page 214.

How *Not* to Use Semicolons

1. After a verb that introduces a list.

(Wrong) Team members **are; Betty J.** Cooley, Carla R. Johnson and Twila P. Raspberry.

(Correct) Team members **are Betty J.** Cooley, Carla R. Johnson and Twila P. Raspberry.

(Wrong) Schools being considered for consolidation include the following**; Ragsdale,** Summerville, Lewiston, Cartwright, Lincoln, Cross River, Twin Valley and Fargo.

(Correct) Schools being considered for consolidation include the following**: Ragsdale,** Summerville, Lewiston, Cartwright, Lincoln, Cross River, Twin Valley and Fargo.

2. In a sentence in which commas and semicolons are used for a listing *if* the sentence doesn't end with the last item listed.

(Wrong) Mike S. White, District 1**;** Pat D. Jones, District 7**;** Perry A. Lucas, District 14**;** and Regina B. Thurman, **District 21; are** the members of the subcommittee.

(Correct) Members of the subcommittee are Mike S. White, District 1**;** Pat D. Jones**,** District 7**;** Perry A. Lucas**,** District 14**;** and Regina B. Thurman**,** District 21.

chapter 24

Colons and Dashes

The sight of a colon is a certain signal to the readers that something's coming. The colon is the best sign we have to provide an introduction. Except for their most common uses such as separating hours from minutes and chapters from verses, colons are considered formal. And although their use is not rare, it is infrequent.

Dashes are less formal but much more dramatic than colons (or commas, which sometimes can be used in place of dashes). Writers use dashes to give emphasis and special attention to a word or a group of words. Skill and judgment are required to use them effectively.

Study the following uses of colons and dashes and put them to use when and where they can be most effective. Remember that if overused, these two types of punctuation, along with the exclamation mark, can lose their impact and become annoying to readers.

How to Use Colons

1. **For simple tasks such as separating hours from minutes and chapters from verses.**

   (*hours from minutes*) 8**:**15 a.m. 11**:**45 p.m.

   (*chapters from verses*) Galatians 6**:**10 Acts 28**:**16–31

2. **To relate time in athletic events.**

   (*minutes and seconds*) 10**:**2

   (*minutes, seconds and tenths of a second*) 10**:**2.4

3. **Before a listing or a series.**

   Our journalism professor gave each student a list of the following required resource books**:** a dictionary, a thesaurus and a stylebook.

4. **Before an announcement.**

   Remember to capitalize the first letter of the first word if the colon introduces a *complete* sentence.

Now hear this: The first deadline has been changed from 10:15 p.m. to 10:45 p.m.

5. **Before an explanation.**

Our publisher has only one major fault: stinginess.

6. **For emphasis.**

This much I know: Either our ratings will improve, or we will have to look for new jobs!

7. **Before some appositives.**

The weather is typical for the middle of March: rainy and cold.

Remember that most appositives are punctuated with commas.

The weather, rainy and cold, is typical for the middle of March.

8. **For quotations that cannot be introduced with a comma.**

For more than 40 years, he drilled this one point into his students' heads: "It's results, not excuses, that count in this life."

Refer to pages 214–215 in the chapter on quotation marks for additional guidance in using colons, and to page 213 for advice on using commas with quotation marks.

9. **To replace the verb between the source and the quotation in a newspaper or a magazine headline.**

Prendle: 'I'll resign if convicted'

Don't be confused by the use of single quotation marks. That's standard practice in newspaper headlines because it saves space. However, check your stylebook before using either a colon or single quotation marks as each appears in this example. Some editors follow other practices.

10. **Between a title and a subtitle.**

Recollections: My 50 years as editor of a country newspaper

11. **Outside quotation marks.**

Refer to the chapter on quotation marks, pages 214–215.

How *Not* to Use Colons

1. **After a verb to introduce a list or a series unless a pause is clearly necessary.**

(Unnecessary) The five winners **are:** Kesha V. Snow, Wade C. Canterbury, Livingston P. Stone, Travis D. Willis and Nikki A. Forrester.

(Necessary) The following states **were represented:** Alaska, Florida, New Mexico, Missouri, Vermont and West Virginia.

2. **After a preposition (regardless of whether it has one or several objects).**

(Wrong) The pitcher was blessed **with:** a strong arm, unfailing accuracy and great stamina.

(Correct) The pitcher was blessed **with a** strong arm, unfailing accuracy and great stamina.

3. **After *like, such as* or *including***

(Wrong) Network television executives depend on spectators enjoying Olympic events **like/such as/including:** gymnastics, swimming and track and field.

(Correct) Network television executives depend on spectators enjoying Olympic events **like/such as/including** gymnastics, swimming and track and field.

How to Use Dashes

1. **After an introductory list or series.**

   Professor, politician, philosopher and preacher—Roland "Robb" Franklin was all of these before retiring to his beloved Montana ranch.

2. **To end a sentence with a list or a series** (when something more dramatic but less formal than a colon is wanted).

   She is adept at spelling, writing, interviewing and working under pressure—all the skills editors, news directors and media managers want in an employee.

3. **To clarify or to emphasize appositive material** (especially if it already contains commas).

   My graduate students—15 Americans, seven Saudi Arabians, four Chinese and one Russian—have different perceptions about the meaning of free expression.

To use commas instead of dashes in this sentence would be confusing because other commas already are present. Parentheses could be used instead of dashes if the writer's intention is just to provide an explanation. Dashes are more effective if a dramatic effect is desired.

4. **Before a name used after a quotation** (especially in a headline or in a "pulled-quote").

   "I take full responsibility."

   —Mayor Francine Sill

5. **To set off an abrupt interruption in a sentence.**

   Our orders are to write all of the advertising copy—if that's humanly possible!—before our vice president meets with the client in two days.

When we won last year's top award—which still shocks the heck out of me—we had no idea we'd be selected first again this time.

5. **To provide a surprise or a dramatic end to a sentence.**

   With only seconds remaining in overtime and the quarterback raising his arm to throw a game-winning pass, the newspaper photographer had all he could wish for—except film.

Also Be Aware of the Following Punctuation Tips

- Some stylebooks require a space before and after each dash. Other stylebooks do not. Be sure to determine which rule applies to your writing.
- Only one dash is required if the sentence ends following the material preceded by the dash. Otherwise, two dashes are required.

  He had everything life had to offer—except happiness.

  The mayor will return your call—I promise—before your final deadline.
- Some newspaper and magazine stylebooks permit dashes to be used before each paragraph in a listing.
- Remember also that a dash is twice as long as a hyphen. For typewriters and computers that have no dash key, strike the hyphen key twice.

chapter 25

Parentheses and Brackets

Perhaps the best way to learn how to use parentheses and brackets effectively is to think of them as brief interruptions designed to give readers immediate explanations, clarifications, corrections, directions or missing information.

Think of the opening parenthesis or bracket as a referee's whistle signaling a time out in a basketball game. If there is just a pause to allow a substitute to enter the game, spectators usually wait patiently. However, if the referee's whistle disturbs the flow of the game too frequently, or if the time outs last too long, the fans become annoyed or angered.

Keep this lesson in mind when using parentheses and brackets. If they are used only occasionally and the information is brief, they will be beneficial. Conversely, if they are used too often, or if the information they contain is lengthy, readers will get just as annoyed with the writer as basketball fans do with the referee.

Before we examine the ways in which these two punctuation marks are used, one obvious question remains: If both perform basically the same functions, how are we to know which one to use? The answer is to use parentheses to make insertions in our own writing and brackets to make insertions in quotations from other speakers or writers.

How to Use Parentheses and Brackets

1. To insert explanations or clarifications.

In your own writing

The prosecutor said she could prove that the defendant was in the bank at the time of the robbery (Thursday, July 12 at 11:05 a.m.).

In a quotation

The prosecutor said, "I can prove that the defendant was in the bank at the time of the robbery [Thursday, July 12 at 11:05 a.m.]."

— — —

In your own writing

A reporter for the Charleston (West Virginia) Gazette broke the story that led to a congressional investigation.

In a quotation

The head of the congressional committee said, "The news story that led to our investigation was published in the Charleston [West Virginia] Gazette."

— — —

In your own writing

I am pleased to discover that the motto of the French newspaper is "La liberté de la presse est essentielle (Liberty of the press is essential)."

In a quotation

"La liberté de la presse est essentielle [Liberty of the press is essential]," the editor of the French newspaper told the visiting journalism students from the United States.

— — —

In your own writing

The first time one of my students suggested that I chill out (stay calm), I had no idea what she meant.

In a quotation

When I asked the yearbook editor if she had checked to make certain that all photo assignments had been made, she said: "Chill out [stay calm]. It's all taken care of."

2. To insert directions.

In your own writing

Opponents of the bill said they disagree with the provision changing the minimum voting age from 18 to 21 (see related story on page 10).

In a quotation

The bill's main opponent, Sen. Maribeth J. Tompkins, said: "I disagree most with the provision changing the minimum voting age from 18 to 21 [see related story on page 10]. If citizens are old enough to serve in the military, they're old enough to vote."

3. To insert missing information.

In your own writing

Since its founding 20 years ago, CROP (the Committee to Recognize Outstanding Pupils) has awarded more scholarship money than any other organization in the school system.

In a quotation

The governor said, "There is no doubt that Judge [Caroline M.] Peterson is the person best qualified for the appointment."

4. To insert corrections (applies only to brackets).

In your own writing

In more formal writing, the Latin word "sic" is inserted to indicate the person being quoted has made an error. However, journalists prefer to correct the error by paraphrasing part or all of the statement.

Journalists avoid

"All of our problems can be **contributed** [sic] to a mayor who thinks higher taxes will solve everything," Councilman James E. Withers said.

Journalists prefer

Councilman James E. Withers **attributed** all of the city's problems to what he described as "a mayor who thinks higher taxes will solve everything."

5. To insert parenthetical information inside other parenthetical material.

Although this use of brackets may be helpful on rare occasions, journalists prefer to simplify the material by rewriting it.

Journalists avoid

The retired coal miner said his respiratory disease (pneumoconiosis [commonly called black lung]) is so debilitating that talking makes him tired.

Journalists prefer

The retired coal miner said his respiratory disease is so debilitating that talking makes him tired. He suffers from pneumoconiosis, commonly called black lung.

6. Either before or after the period that ends the sentence.

Place the closing parenthesis or bracket ***before*** the period ***if*** the enclosed material comes at the end of a sentence.

To get the late-breaking news into the final edition, the story had to be "railroaded" (published without being proofread).

By placing the period outside the parenthesis, the writer is indicating that the period applies to the entire sentence, not just to the segment placed within the parentheses.

— — —

Place the closing parenthesis or bracket ***after*** the period ***if*** the enclosed material is a separate sentence.

Apologizing to the publisher for the embarrassing error, the editor explained that to get the late-breaking news into the final edition, it had to be "railroaded." (By "railroaded," the editor meant that the story was published without being proofread.)

By placing the period inside the parenthesis, the writer is indicating that the period applies *only* to the material within the parentheses.

How *Not* to Use Parentheses and Brackets

1. Frequently.
2. To insert lengthy material.
3. Interchangeably. Parentheses are used to make insertions in our own writing, and brackets are used to make insertions in quotations from other speakers or writers. Do not use one for a function performed by the other.

chapter 26

Slashes and Hyphens

Slashes will be discussed first because they have a modest number of functions, and journalists use fewer of them than many other writers. Slashes can be quite helpful if used skillfully and sparingly. Otherwise, they can be more of a hindrance than a help to readers.

Note that the slash is used neither preceded nor followed by a space except when indicating a division between lines of poetry.

How to Use Slashes

1. To show that either choice is applicable.

> The president of the state senate asked each new member to submit two copies of his/her work schedule.

Journalists prefer either to substitute the word **or** for the slash, or to reword the sentence as follows: The president of the state senate asked new **members** to submit two copies of **their** work schedules.

— — —

Jason said he will attend college and/or work full time.

Mass communicators find little favor with this use of the slash. They prefer to write the sentence as follows: Jason said he will **either** attend college while working full time **or** he will just work.

2. To express a fraction or a date in digits.

3/4 3 1/16 9/26/72

Don't forget to check your stylebook before using slashes with fractions and dates. Many editors, news directors and other media managers limit or forbid their use.

3. To show line breaks in quoted poetry.

> What the handy colon does is nice: / It keeps / Unwary writers safe from hurtful vice. / Secure behind a brace of sturdy dots / They pause / And contemplate the coming phrase or clause. / A colon gives the glib a chance to

sigh / And breathe: / The Plodding, rest: the mean, to seethe. / To some a colon is just anatomy. / I hope / If you encounter such / you'll set them right for me.

—W.E. Knight

How *Not* to Use Slashes

1. **As substitutes for hyphens in compound adjectives or compound nouns.**

(Wrong) Fashion designers hope the blue/green blend will become a popular color for summer clothing.

(Correct) Fashion designers hope the blue–green blend will become a popular color for summer clothing.

or

Fashion designers hope the blend of blue **and** green will become a popular color for summer clothing.

— — —

(Wrong) The producer/director of this play has won dozens of awards for her work.

(Correct) The producer-director of this play has won dozens of awards for her work.

or

Maggie L. Tunnelton, who is **both** producing **and** directing the play, has won dozens of awards for her work.

Hyphens

Hyphens are used primarily to reduce or to eliminate the possibility of confusion or misinterpretation. They do this in part by linking two or more words for the reader to consider as a single unit (a **last-second** victory, a **two-for-one** trade, a **producer-director**). They also ensure that a word is interpreted correctly (**re-mark,** to mark again; **remark,** to comment).

Other uses include joining compound numbers (**thirty-three**) and fractions (**one-fifth**), attaching some prefixes to root words (**ex-governor**), and showing an extension (**1-5** p.m.). Hyphens also allow for suspended compounds (**first-** and **fifth-place** finishers), and although somewhat outdated in the computer age, they provide a way to split a word from one line to the next (**hyphenat-ing**).

At first glance, hyphens appear to have simple purposes and to be easy to use. Unfortunately, some of the functions are difficult to understand because there are numerous exceptions to the rules. Consider the following complications:

- Some words such as **backup, knockout** and **cutback** do not use hyphens either as adjectives or as nouns. But **cover-up, follow-up** and **grown-up** use hyphens both as adjectives and as nouns. **Dead end, roll call** and **fund raising** use hyphens as adjectives but are spelled as two words when used as nouns. As verbs, most of these words are used as two words (**build up, follow up, knock out**).

- Most prefixes take a hyphen when used with a proper noun, but most don't take a hyphen when used with a common noun.
- As prefixes, ***self, ex*** and ***all*** are always hyphenated regardless of whether they are used with proper or common nouns.
- ***Anti*** and ***pro*** are hyphenated with some words but not with others.
- ***Pre, re,*** and ***mid*** are not usually hyphenated with common nouns unless the noun starts with the same letter that ends the prefix.

At this point in their reading or discussion of hyphens, most students and professional journalists have to fight the temptation to clasp their hands over their ears and run screaming into the streets. They do have some justification. Some of these rules and their exceptions seem unreasonable because the writer is forced to rely on memory instead of reason. And because hardly anyone can commit to memory all the examples in stylebooks and dictionaries, writers who are conscientious spend much valuable time checking and rechecking their resource books.

The solution that everyone eventually uses is to commit to memory what they use most frequently and to check the books for things they use occasionally or rarely. For the sake of consistency, this book follows *The Associated Press Stylebook.*

How to Use Hyphens

1. To form compound adjectives that come *before* the word(s) they modify.

The **three-alarm** fire destroyed an apartment building.

— — —

The city editor gave me an **I-told-you-so** look when the publisher scolded me for not following instructions.

— — —

The graphic artist was given a **well-deserved** award.

Compound adjectives should be thought of as a unit, not as individual words, because they work together to modify a noun or a pronoun instead of each doing so separately.

One helpful way to determine which adjectives are working together and therefore should be hyphenated is to try to use each separately to modify the noun or the pronoun. In the first example, the definite article **The** works alone. It makes sense to say **The fire** destroyed an apartment building. However, it does not make sense to say **The three fire** destroyed an apartment building or **The alarm fire** destroyed an apartment building. **Three** and **alarm** work as a unit to modify fire; therefore, a hyphen should be placed between them. The same is true for the other examples.

2. **To form compound *predicate* or *linking* adjectives.**

Remember that a predicate adjective comes after a verb and modifies the subject.

The award was **well-deserved.**

— — —

The accommodations were **first-rate.**

— — —

My boss is **ill-tempered.**

Do not be surprised to see many journalists ignore this rule either on purpose or because they are unaware of it. To make matters even more difficult, the hyphen is usually dropped if the sentence continues beyond the predicate adjective (My boss is **ill tempered** every morning until he drinks his third cup of coffee). The question to ask in each circumstance is whether the hyphen makes reading and comprehension easier.

The best advice is to check your stylebooks and then bring your questions to the attention of your editor, news director or media manager.

3. **To form compound nouns.**

Fayette is considered the best **singer-composer** in the business.

— — —

Grant is the company's leading **producer-director.**

Substituting ***and*** for the **hyphen** is a better choice most of the time.

4. **In compound numbers (*which journalists rarely spell out*) and with fractions used before the words they modify.**

twenty-three

one hundred sixty-six

four-fifths

one-sixteenth

5. **After a five-digit zip code followed by four additional numbers.**

25755-2622

90210-1001

6. **To replace *to* or *until* in words or figures that show an extension.**

1-5 p.m.	(*from 1 p.m. until 5 p.m.*)
Pages 111-127	(*111 through 127*)
Grades 9-12	(*9 through 12*)
January-May reporting period	(*January through May*)

7. **In suspended compounds that modify the same word.**

   The difference in earnings between **first-** and **fifth-place** finishers in the Professional Golfers Association tournament is $275,000.

   — — —

   Tuition costs will remain the same for **first-, second-** and **summer-semester** classes.

8. **To divide words at the end of a line.**

Fortunately for journalists, as well as for most others who write with computers, the machines automatically hyphenate words at the end of lines of type (although they don't always do so accurately). Nevertheless, a review of some basic rules is worthwhile.

- Unless your employer or your professor demands otherwise, don't hyphenate a word at the end of a line. Put the whole word on the next line.
- Do not hyphenate one-syllable words (write, speak, draw).
- Do not hyphenate one letter (**a-**lone, **a-**long, **a-**way).
- Do not leave just two letters on one line or carry just two letters to the next line (**re-**volt, contact**-ed**).
- Do not hyphenate at a division that could be confusing (country-man, half-back).
- Do not hyphenate proper nouns (John-son, Jackson-ville).
- Hyphenate by syllables whenever appropriate. A syllable is a unit of uninterrupted sound within a word. Most dictionaries divide syllables with periods or dots.
- Divide between double consonants (hit-ting, equip-ping, accom-modate).
- Divide between compounds (self-activating, son-in-law), but do not add a hyphen to a word that already contains a hyphen (**wrong:** self-activat-ing; **correct:** self-activating).

9. **To avoid confusion between words that mean one thing if hyphenated and something else if not.**

re-press	repress
re-mark	remark
re-treat	retreat
re-creation	recreation

10. **Between a prefix and a proper noun or a number.**

pre-World War II	anti-Castro
post-Elizabethan	mid-December
un-American	ex-New Yorker
pro-Canadian	pre-1940

11. Always after the prefixes *self, all* and *ex*.

self-help all-knowing ex-governor

12. After a prefix before a common noun if the prefix ends with the same vowel that begins the next word.

r**e-e**lected pr**e-e**xist ant**i-i**ntellectual

Exceptions include cooperate, coordinate and all common words beginning with the prefix **un** (unnecessary, unnatural, unnoticed, etc.).

13. With some verbs (*although these are rare*).

tape-record window-dress air-condition

14. Between the letters of a word to indicate its spelling.

The journalistic spelling is a-d-v-i-s-e-r.

How *Not* to Use Hyphens

1. In compound adjectives that follow an action verb.

(Nonaction verb) My journalism professor's weekend employment is part-time.

(Action verb) My journalism professor works *part time* at the local newspaper.

2. After an *adverb* that ends in *ly* or after the adverb *very*.

(Wrong) The easi**ly-**provoked coach screamed at the referee for calling a penalty on his team.

(Correct) The easi**ly** provoked coach screamed at the referee for calling a penalty on his team.

— — —

(Wrong) The **very-**talented writer was rewarded with a column of her own in the Sunday newspaper.

(Correct) The **very** talented writer was rewarded with a column of her own in the Sunday newspaper.

Most editors and teachers dislike the word **very** and either discourage or forbid its use. Their reasoning is that it is unnecessary.

3. Between a prefix and most common nouns.

pr**ea**dolescent ant**if**reeze no**nl**iteral

4. With age expressed in a compound if the age comes *after* the word(s) it modifies.

(Wrong) The new **publisher** is just 36-years-old.

(Correct) The new **publisher** is just 36 years old.

Don't forget that when age is used as a compound modifier *before* the word(s) it modifies, it is hyphenated (The 36-year-old **publisher** is the youngest in the history of the company).

5. In suspended compounds in which the dollar sign ($) is used.

(Wrong) Increases will come in **$50-** and $100 increments.

(Correct) Increases will come in **$50** and $100 increments.

APOSTROPHES

chapter 27

Most student journalists and many professionals have trouble with apostrophes—and no wonder! Apostrophes are deceptively complicated and easily confused. Few people have difficulty grasping the concept of possession, but many have problems when the following questions arise:

- Do we add an *'s* or an *s'* to the end of the word?
- What do we do with words that already end in *s?*
- What influence, if any, does the word following the apostrophe have if it begins with an *s?*
- After which word does the *'s* go in a compound?
- Can an apostrophe be used to form plurals?
- Can any pronouns use an apostrophe to form a possessive?
- Where does the apostrophe go in contractions?

These and other questions are addressed in the following list of rules. As you will see, they are relatively extensive and mastering them requires patience and persistence.

How to Use Apostrophes

1. **Add an *'s* to make possessive both singular and plural common nouns and indefinite pronouns whose spelling does not end with an *s*.**

Singular Nouns	Plural Nouns	Indefinite Pronouns	
child**'s**	children's	anyone**'s**	another's
man**'s**	men**'s**	everyone**'s**	other**'s**
woman**'s**	women**'s**	someone**'s**	everyone else**'s**
alumna**'s**	alumnae's	one's	neither's

2. **Add an apostrophe to make possessive a plural noun ending in *s, es* or *ies.***

boys'	business**es'**	agenc**ies'**
girls'	Jones**es'**	compan**ies'**
players'	witness**es'**	propert**ies'**

3. **In journalistic uses, add an apostrophe to make possessive singular proper nouns whose spelling ends in *s*.**

   Hayes' Jones' Linkous' Lucas' Sias' Willis'

   In formal writing, add an 's to make possessive singular proper nouns whose spelling ends in s.

   Hayes's Jones's Linkous's Lucas's Sias's Willis's

4. **Add an *'s* to a singular common noun ending in *s*. However, if the next word starts with an *s*, add only an apostrophe.**

   actres*s's* best role
   compas*s's* great value
   boss's biggest gripe
   actres*s' s*tand-in
   compas*s' s*teel case
   bos*s' s*ecret

Please note that journalists applying Associated Press style follow this rule for common nouns (boss' secret) but not for singular proper nouns ending in s (Hayes' speech).

5. **Add an *'s* to the last word to make compound nouns possessive.**

   brother-in-law's
   sister-in-law's
   father-in-law's
   mother-in-law's
   secretary of state's
   attorney general's

— — —

Do not confuse possessives with plurals. To make such compound nouns plural, add an *s* to the first word.

sons-in-law
daughters-in-law
attorneys general
secretaries of state

6. **Add an *'s* to the last noun to indicate joint ownership.**

   Pete and Bob's Drive-In

   Ed and Wilma's Coffee Shop

   Willard and Dean's law firm

7. **Add an *'s* to each name to indicate separate ownership.**

   Pete's and Bob's cars

   Ed's and Wilma's computers

   Willard's and Dean's offices

8. **Add the apostrophe even when the possessive *follows* the word it modifies.**

   The best drawings are usually Arleen's and Baxter's.

   Is the design Charlton's or Reginald's?

9. **Use an apostrophe to replace the missing letter(s) in a contraction.**

   couldn't (could not)
   don't (do not)
   she'd (she would)
   something's (something is)

hadn't (had not)	we'd (we would)
here's (here is)	we'll (we will)
I'm (I am)	what're (what are)
it's (it is)	won't (will not)

10. Use an apostrophe to replace a letter or a figure omitted on purpose.

'37 flood	(1937)
summer of '83	(1983)
the '40s	(the 1940s)
singin'	(singing)
wishin'	(wishing)
choc'late	(chocolate)

11. Use an apostrophe to form plurals of letters, numbers and words.

In her four years of college, she made 15 **A's, 21 B's** and seven **C's.**

— — —

Many people forget that *occurred* is spelled with two **r's.**

— — —

There are four **8's** in her birth date. She was born on the eighth day of the eighth month in 1988.

— — —

The professor had an unconscious habit of overusing a word. During one class session, students counted 27 **what's** in his lecture.

Please be aware that the *Associated Press Stylebook* does not recommend using an apostrophe to make a plural of a number (8s) multiple letters (ABCs), or words as words (*ifs, ands, buts*).

12. Use an *'s* to form the possessive of words that are spelled the same in both singular and plural form.

The mother deer**'s** (singular possessive) fawn lay hidden in the tall grass.

— — —

The lost sheep**'s** (plural possessive) owners are glad to get them back.

Please note that journalists consider this plural possessive form awkward. They prefer to say that the owners of the lost sheep are glad to get them back.

How *Not* to Use Apostrophes

1. To form the possessive of relative and personal pronouns.

(Wrong)	our's	it's	who's	your's	their's
(Correct)	ours	its	whose	yours	theirs

2. In names of organizations that are more descriptive than possessive.

(Wrong) State Secondary Schools' Athletic Committee.

(Correct) State Secondary Schools Athletic Committee.

— — —

(Wrong) The teachers' college at Acme University.

(Correct) The teachers college at Acme University.

(Wrong) Cincinnati Reds' centerfielder Jay Jackson hit three home runs in a 6–5 victory.

(Correct) Cincinnati Reds centerfielder Jay Jackson hit three home runs in a 6–5 victory.

3. To form most common plurals.

(Wrong) Our computers were purchased at Lovell Electronic's.

(Correct) Our computers were purchased at Lovell Electronics.

— — —

(Wrong) That public relations firm is owned by the Donohoe's.

(Correct) That public relations firm is owned by the Donohoes.

chapter 28

QUOTATION MARKS

Mass communicators use quotation marks in many of their stories, advertisements and public relations releases. It's their way of involving their sources or clients directly in their publications and broadcasts.

A discussion of the importance of quotations and advice for determining what to quote directly and what to paraphrase are covered on pages 6–7. In discussing punctuation and quotation marks, we have other even more challenging tasks. Learning when to use double or single quotation marks is easy; the problems come when we are making decisions about using quotation marks in combination with other punctuation.

The following pages contain rules and examples of not only how to use quotation marks but also how *not* to use them. Have patience with yourself, for they take some time to commit to memory.

How to Use Quotation Marks

1. With direct quotations but not with indirect quotations.

A direct quotation starts and ends with quotation marks to indicate to the readers that the words are those of the source, not the writer. An indirect quotation has no quotation marks because the words of the source have been paraphrased by the writer. Please understand that a paraphrase must maintain the speaker's meaning even though the writer chooses to word the message differently.

(Direct quotation) "I will answer those questions during my press conference," the president said.

— — —

(Indirect quotation) Those questions will be answered during the press conference, the president said.

or

(Indirect quotation) The president said he will answer those questions during his press conference.

2. **With the attribution following the quotation.**

   "I promise to balance the budget by the end of my first term," **the president said.**

3. **With the attribution preceding the quotation.**

   The president said, "I promise to balance the budget by the end of my first term."

— — —

The comma after **said** is not used if the quotation is not a complete sentence (see No. 6 below). Another complication with commas comes when the attribution that precedes the quotation contains a subject followed by an appositive phrase or clause. One of the necessary commas frequently is left out.

(Wrong) The president, an economist by educatio**n s**aid, "I promise to balance the budget by the end of my first term."

(Wrong) The president, an economist by education, sai**d** "I promise to balance the budget by the end of my first term."

(Correct) The president, an economist by education, said, "I promise to balance the budget by the end of my first term."

4. **With the attribution in the middle of the quotation.**

   "It might take until the fourth year of my term," **he explained,** "but I will balance the budget."

When the attribution is placed in the middle of a one-sentence quotation, care must be taken to put it at a natural breaking point. In this example, the attribution works smoothly between two independent clauses.

5. **With the attribution at the end of the first sentence in a two-sentence quotation.**

   "I realize I'm taking a big political risk by promising to balance the budget," **the president said.** "I fully understand what the cost will be to me personally if I fail."

Note that no attribution is used in the second sentence. Doing so would be redundant because the attribution in the first sentence clarifies who is speaking.

6. **Before and after an incomplete quotation** (one that does not meet the requirements for a complete sentence).

   Asked if he really intended to keep his promise, the president said "absolutely."

Although the use of the incomplete quotation is common among journalists, some mass media editors, news directors and managers dislike using them. Check your stylebook. Formal writing usually requires quotations to be placed in complete sentences.

7. At the beginning of each paragraph in a multi-paragraph quotation but at the end of *only* the *last* paragraph.

The text of the president's statement is as follows:

"Good evening, my fellow citizens.

"I am taking this opportunity to speak to you directly via television tonight to announce the formation of an exciting new educational program that will enable thousands of deserving but needy young people to attend college.

"It will work something like a domestic Peace Corps. In exchange for federal grants to finance their college educations, young people will devote two years of service to their country following graduation.

"They will be given a wide choice of services to be performed, and they will be paid a salary sufficient to live on during the period.

"Details will be available soon, and we hope to start accepting applications by the end of the year.

"Thank you and good night."

Quotation marks are placed at the beginning of each paragraph to indicate that the quotation is continuing. The quotation mark at the end of the last paragraph signals the conclusion. No other quotation mark is used at the end of the other paragraphs because that would signal a premature close to the quotation.

Keep in mind that journalists rarely use lengthy quotations unless they are extremely important or unusually interesting.

* * *

8. With the paragraph limited to only one speaker's quotation.

Journalists place only one person's quotation in a paragraph. If the speaker changes, a new paragraph is used.

> "I doubt that this television station will ever have a more talented sportscaster than Hossein Shora," said Gerrit K. Otto, vice president and general manager of WXXX. "He has the most loyal following I've ever encountered."
>
> Coach Wallin S. McCorkindale of Acme University said, "We're all going to miss Hossein when he goes into retirement next week. He treated all the coaches and all the players with great fairness, even when he had to report the negative things that happened."

Make certain that readers or listeners don't get confused about who is talking. This probably would have happened if the second paragraph had started with McCorkindale's quotation instead of his name. Refer to pages 7–8.

9. With a quotation placed within another quotation.

Use single quotation marks to indicate that the person being quoted within full quotation marks is quoting someone else. Also realize that even the most carefully constructed quotation within another quotation can be confusing to readers. Potential confusion can be reduced by either paraphrasing one of the quotations or by breaking the quotations into separate sentences.

Use a quotation within another quotation only when the meaning is clear and the construction is more effective than paraphrasing or using two sentences.

> My boss said, "Heed the words of my old chief photographer who always explained, 'The photographer has to be honest because pictures can lie.' "

10. **To show that a word or several words are used in a special way** (to indicate sarcasm, humor, a nonliteral meaning, an unfamiliar term).

> Your dog's "singing" is quite entertaining.

— — —

> When my niece described the singer as "bad," she really meant the opposite.

— — —

> His major "goal" in life is to win the lottery.

— — —

> The "prize fight of the century" turned out to be the "dud of the decade."

In both formal and informal writing, the use of quotation marks to express irony, humor, sarcasm or anything similar is discouraged. It not only can become an annoying writing habit but also can be a hindrance for readers if they infer a different meaning than the writer intended.

11. **With some titles** (such as magazine articles, songs, television programs, movies, lectures, speeches, essays and book chapters).

Stylebooks vary considerably over what titles to place within quotation marks. Journalists usually use quotation marks with magazine articles, songs, television programs and movies. But practices differ on placing titles of books, newspapers and magazines in quotation marks, italics or capital letters (for the first letter of each important word).

Check the stylebook that applies to your writing. Newspaper articles and term papers often follow different rules.

— — —

> I am referring to "Third party movements gaining popularity," an article in last month's issue of the magazine.

— — —

The victory song **"We Are the Eagles"** is sung by the fans after every athletic win by Acme University.

— — —

"The Longest Day" is considered a classic movie about World War II.

How to Use Quotation Marks with Other Punctuation

1. **Place commas and periods *inside* closing quotation marks.**

   "This is a moment I'll remember forever**,"** the winner of the Pulitzer Prize said.

   — — —

   The Pulitzer Prize winner said, "This is a moment I'll remember forever**."**

* * *

Periods and commas go inside the closing quotation mark even when the sentence ends with an incomplete quotation. This practice contrasts with rules governing the placement of question marks and exclamation marks with the closing quotation mark. Notice the difference between the use of the period and the comma in the following examples and the use of the question mark and the exclamation mark later on.

(Avoid) Asked whether she would play in the tennis tournament even though she was injured, the star player said "absolutely**".**

(Correct) Asked whether she would play in the tennis tournament even though she was injured, the star player said "absolutely**."**

— — —

(Avoid) She said playing with an injured elbow "doesn't bother me**",** and she went on to win the match in straight sets.

(Correct) She said playing with an injured elbow "doesn't bother me**,"** and she went on to win the match in straight sets.

Be aware that those outside the journalism and mass communications fields may not always place periods and commas inside quotation marks.

2. **Place the question mark or the exclamation mark *inside* the closing quotation mark *if* it pertains only to the words between the quotation marks.**

(Inside) "If you are elected, will you raise taxes**?"** the reporter asked.

(Inside) "I won**!"** she yelled.

— — —

Place the question mark or the exclamation mark *outside* the closing quotation mark if it pertains not only to the words inside the quotation but also to the rest of the sentence.

(Outside) What's the name of that "fool-proof stock"**?**

(Outside) I'm thrilled to have won "the big one"**!**

In the first two examples, the question mark and the exclamation mark are placed inside the closing quotation mark to show that they refer only to the words between the quotation marks. In the last two examples, the question mark and the exclamation mark are placed outside the closing quotation mark to show they refer not only to the words between the quotation marks but also the rest of the sentence.

3. Do not use a comma after either a question mark or an exclamation mark that separates a question or a statement from its attribution.

(Wrong) "Are you working this weekend**?,**" she asked.

(Correct) "Are you working this weekend**?**" she asked.

— — —

(Wrong) "My boss scheduled me to work every weekend this summer**!,**" she shouted in disbelief.

(Correct) "My boss scheduled me to work every weekend this summer**!**" she shouted in disbelief.

The comma in each of the wrong examples is superfluous. The question mark and the exclamation mark not only signal a question or an exclamation for the preceding material but also separate the question or the statement from its attribution.

4. Place a comma before a quotation of only one sentence.

Throughout his 40-year teaching career, my professor said**,** "It's results, not excuses, that count in this life."

Place a colon before a quotation of more than one sentence.

My professor always said**:** "It's results, not excuses, that count in this life. Please don't bother telling me why you couldn't get the story."

Please note that this use of the colon is seldom followed by journalists. They use a comma.

5. Place semicolons and colons *outside* the closing quotation mark.

I didn't deprive you of your "opportunity of a lifetime"**;** you just didn't earn it, the advertising director told the disappointed employee.

— — —

This message is for the person chosen "Employee of the Month"**:** Your check is in the mail.

6. **If a paragraph ends with a quote that constitutes a complete sentence, no closing quotation mark is required if the quotation extends to the next paragraph.**

My professor always said not to bother telling him why we couldn't get the story. He said: **"**It's results, not excuses, that count in this life.

"Your future employers aren't going to put up with your excuses," he said, **"**and neither will I. I'd be doing you a disservice if I were to demand less from you than your employer will expect when you graduate and go to work full time."

— — —

If the paragraph ends with a quotation that does not form a complete sentence, place a quotation mark at the end of the paragraph even if the quotation continues in the next paragraph.

My professor said that after 40 years in journalism, he knew what editors and news directors expect from recent college graduates. He said he didn't want to hear any of us say he was **"**too demanding.**"**

"It's results, not excuses, that count in this life**,"** he said. **"**Please don't bother telling me why you couldn't get the story. Your future employers will not put up with your excuses. Don't expect anything less from me."

7. **Even if you are quoting the same person, do not end one paragraph with a quotation and start the next paragraph with another quotation *if* the source did not say them consecutively.**

Writers knowledgeable in the use of punctuation know that a closing quotation mark signals the end of the quotation. They also know that omitting the closing quotation mark in one paragraph and starting the next paragraph with a quotation mark signals the continuation of the quotation. This much knowledge they probably can expect from the majority of readers.

However, most readers' knowledge of punctuation is strained by writers who end a paragraph with a quotation mark to signal the conclusion of that quotation and then start the next paragraph with another quotation mark to indicate the beginning of a different quotation from the same source.

When things get that complicated between quotations, writers need to provide some transition for the readers.

An acceptable way to show that a quotation extends from one paragraph to the next.

President Charlotte S. Mulloy said increased giving by alumni will enable Acme University to help more students with their financial needs. She said: **"**Tuition waivers will increase from 300 to 500 for the next school year. This means that every student with a grade point average of 3.5 or higher will attend tuition free.

"We are most grateful to our alumni for their generosity, and we pledge to use the money the way they directed."

* * *

An unacceptable way to separate two quotations given at different times in the interview by the same source.

President Charlotte S. Mulloy said increased giving by alumni will enable Acme University to help more students with their financial needs. She said, "We are most grateful to our alumni for their generosity."

"We are hopeful that next year's alumni giving will be even higher," Mulloy said. "Even with the extra funds raised this year, we are still unable to help all deserving students."

— — —

For the last example to be acceptable, the writer must provide some transition that will make clear to the reader that the quotations were not said one after the other by the source. Appropriate transition needs to be inserted after the first paragraph in which Mulloy is quoted.

After explaining that the funds will be spent to reward students who excel in academics, Mulloy said: "We are hopeful that next year's alumni giving will be even higher. Even with the extra funds raised this year, we are still unable to help all deserving students."

SENSITIVITY IN LANGUAGE

chapter 29

We start with the presumption that both student and professional mass communicators want to avoid language that is insensitive, stereotypical or in any other way derogatory. We also presume that when we use language that discriminates against race, religion, ethnicity, age, gender, marital status or physical and mental ability, most of us do so not from a mean spirit but because we are unaware or careless.

Although professional media managers have a right to expect a reasonable level of awareness and sophistication from their veteran employees, college teachers and their students face more fundamental challenges. Like other civil people, most students are aware of and avoid language generally recognized as the most repugnant or insensitive. But they frequently are surprised when apprised of the more subtle forms offensive language can take.

Many people who use "gyp" as a synonym for "cheat" have never even thought about the connection of that derogatory word to Gypsies. Likewise, a student from a region inhabited by few Native Americans gave no thought about the insensitive nature of "Indian giver" when he put that term in a headline. Another student learned from embarrassment that when **people of color** won't fit into a headline, ***colored people*** is not an acceptable substitute.

Student journalists are receptive when told to select fire**fighter** over fire**man,** author or writer over author**ess,** astronaut over **female** astronaut, nurse over **male** nurse, and—whenever possible—last names unaccompanied by **Mr./Mrs./Ms.** They also accept omitting, unless clearly relevant, references to a person's age, race, ethnicity, gender, marital status or religion.

However, when the discussion progresses to waiter/waitress/server/waitperson—an occupation shared by numerous students during their college years—they raise questions. And when students follow *The Associated Press Stylebook* and refer to academic leaders as "chairman" or "chairwoman," they find that the commonly used word on many campuses is just "chair" for both men and women.

"That's silly," a few students in each class counter. "Are we really expected to call people 'waitpersons' and 'chairs' and things like that?"

The question is logical, and one answer is that students must understand and accept that language constantly evolves. As it does, some changes, such as fireman to firefighter, are obvious improvements because they not only eliminate gender bias, but they also describe much more accurately what employees of the fire department do. **Chair** may sound like an awkward word for an academic leader, but it inarguably eliminates the gender problem.

Waitperson? Well, how about ***server*** as a compromise?

Another consideration for student and professional journalists is that the rules they must follow will be made by the media organizations for which they work. Whether it is a newspaper, magazine, radio or television station, public relations firm or advertising agency, every company has a stylebook. And the people who direct businesses will demand compliance, regardless of whether individual employees agree with each guideline. Either through their own enlightenment or in response to pressure, company officials are quite aware that language sensitivity is not only the respectful and right thing to do, but it is also the smart thing to do. No company ever increased its subscribers, advertisers, listeners, viewers or clients by insulting them.

A Few Guidelines

Race, Age, Sex, Religion, Ethnicity, Gender, Marital Status, Physical Appearance or Mental Ability. In a report about a pedestrian struck by a car on a downtown street, relevance of any of these factors is unlikely. However, there is relevance in reports about a missing person, an escaped criminal, a person appointed to an important position in a religious organization or the newly elected president of the American Association of Retired Persons.

Gender. Masculine gender pronouns are no longer used to refer to both males and females. The following is such an example: Everyone should complete **his** application by the noon deadline. Changing to **his/her** substitutes awkwardness for the gender problem. The solution is to use the plural form of the noun that the pronoun **everyone** replaces. **Students** should complete ***their*** applications by the noon deadline.

When referring to government officials, substitute member of Congress or representative for congress**man,** council member for council**man** or city **father,** police officer for police**man,** and so on. Word endings that cause writers and broadcasters to become entangled in gender arguments can be avoided easily.

Ethnicity. We have more to guide us than stylebooks, precedent and common sense. When in doubt about how to refer to people, ask them! When ethnicity is pertinent to the story, ask if a person prefers **black** or **African American; Hispanic, Latino/Latina,** or **Chicano;** or **Native American, American Indian** or a specific tribal name. Also be aware that some terms no longer considered acceptable have been retained in names of organizations such as the National Association for the Advancement of **Colored** People, and the United **Negro** College Fund.

Before emphasizing that someone is the first woman/black/Asian American to accomplish something, ask yourself if that's the most important element in the story—or whether it even needs to be included.

Discriminatory Descriptions. Print and broadcast news reporters are trained to avoid descriptive words that editorialize. That should help keep them from referring to women as "perky," older people as "youthful," large people as "gentle giants," and small people as "little dynamos." When personality, energy and size have nothing to do with the communication, leave them out.

Illness, Physical Impairment. Be careful about labeling people "victims" just because they have an illness or a physical impairment. The same advice applies to the use of "handicapped" as a synonym for incapable.

Marital Status. Whether a person is divorced or has never been married is usually irrelevant. Do not identify or refer to women differently from the way you would men. "Wife of" and "widow of" (or "husband of" or "widower of") should be used only when pertinent. To start a news story with "The wife of the president of Acme University announced her retirement from the faculty" clearly would be inappropriate. In a story about her death, information about her surviving husband and children should be included. Care should be taken not to present women in a context that might make them appear to be property of men.

Military Background. In a story requiring biographical details or in an article about Veterans Day activities, military background obviously is included. Careful consideration should be given before reference is made to a person's military background or the absence of one if doing so would raise questions about whether a person is either patriotic or humane.

Team Nicknames. Be aware that in recent years, pressure has been applied to athletic teams to change nicknames or mascots considered offensive by ethnic groups. Some, such as Miami (Ohio) University and Stanford University have responded by changing their nicknames from Redskins to RedHawks and Indians to Cardinal, respectively. Professional football's Washington Redskins and baseball's Cleveland Indians have retained their names. Some media organizations refuse to print or broadcast such nicknames, preferring instead to refer to the teams by the name of the city. In addition, many of the nation's college and university women's sports teams have dropped the use of "Lady" before the school nicknames.

Avoid	**Substitute**
actress, authoress, aviatrix, heroine, poetess	actor, author, aviator/pilot, hero, poet
boy/girl	use man/woman if 18 or older. Specific references such as student, participant and applicant are even better.
businessman	business executive/owner/professional
cameraman	camera operator, photographer
career woman	lawyer, physician, dentist, etc.
chairman	head of, leader, moderator, coordinator, chair
coed	student

Avoid	Substitute
congressman	representative or member of Congress
everyone is to file ***his*** story	**reporters** are to file ***their*** stories
female jockey	jockey
fireman	firefighter
foreign student	international student
foreman	supervisor
handicap	disability, impairment
Indian	American Indian, Native American
layman	layperson
mailman	mail carrier
male model/nurse	model/nurse
man-hours	hours of work
mankind	humans, humanity, people
man-made	handmade, synthetic, manufactured, produced
man/woman-on-the-street interviews	people-on-the-street interviews
newsman/newswoman	reporter or journalist
Oriental	Asian
policeman	police officer
salesman	sales clerk, salesperson, sales representative
spokesman	representative, spokesperson, liaison
wheelchair bound/confined	wheelchair user

* * *

Writers and broadcasters also should be sensitive about misusing trademarks. A few examples follow:

Avoid	Substitute
Astroturf	artificial grass or artificial turf
Band-Aid	bandage
Coke	soft drink, soda, pop
Kitty Litter	cat box litter
Kleenex	facial tissue
Laundromat	coin-operated laundry
Levi's	jeans
Q-Tips	cotton swabs
Rolodex	business card file
Windex	glass cleaner
Xerox	photocopy

QUICK REFERENCE

part 4

Introduction

This section is designed not only to provide students and professional mass communicators with a study guide but also to give them a fast-check reference to use as they approach their deadlines.

Each reference guide is arranged in alphabetical order. Together they offer guidance in the following areas:

1. **Words frequently confused.** Brief definitions and example sentences are given for confusing sets of words such as **lay** and **lie,** ***acute*** and ***chronic,*** **profit** and **revenue,** *affect* and *effect,* **anxious** and **eager,** and more than 300 others.
2. **Words frequently misspelled.** For those who have never placed first in a spelling bee, there is a list of 650 of the words most commonly misspelled by students and by professional journalists. The trouble spot(s) in each word is set in boldface type.
3. **Irregular verbs.** Sw*i*m has a sw***a***m but sw*i*ng has no sw***a***ng. Dr*i*nk has a dr***a***nk, but you can't put *have, has* or *had* in front of it. Sla*i*n has a sl***ew*** even though it's rarely used. And bu***r***st has no **bust** even though many people say it.

   Irregular verbs are formed inconsistently and often illogically. Because few people have all of them committed to memory, a listing of about 150 is provided.
4. **Wordiness and trite expressions.** Experienced copy editors are always on the alert for wordiness and trite expressions. Approximately 300 of the most common examples are listed in this section.
5. **When to use a hyphen, one word, or two words.** As was pointed out in the chapter on hyphens, both students and professional journalists have problems determining which words are hyphenated or used as one word or two words. To complicate things further, many of these words change their pattern if they switch in use from an adjective to a noun, and most change if they switch from either an adjective or a noun to a verb.

> Perhaps even more troubling is the inconsistency from one stylebook or dictionary to another. This reference section lists more than 300 examples from *The Associated Press Stylebook,* the guidebook used by most mass communicators.

Not all editors, news directors, media managers or mass communications professors will agree with every listing under this reference section. That's why each company has a stylebook or a style guide of its own. Most of the examples, however, provide standard information generally accepted throughout the media.

REFERENCE 1 WORDS FREQUENTLY CONFUSED

How many times have you caught yourself or someone else adding one of the following to a statement or to an attempted explanation? "You know what I mean?" "You understand what I'm saying?" "Did I make myself clear?" "Did you catch my drift?"

We ask these questions when we're not certain our message has been understood. Such miscommunication occurs for numerous reasons, but perhaps the most common is that we don't always choose the most effective word or phrase. We settle for **a** word or **a** phrase that we think is sufficient instead of **the** word or **the** phrase that expresses the exact meaning we intend.

One veteran city editor always insisted that making sure that writing is understood is not enough. Writers must make sure they are not **mis**understood, he argued. Writers who thought such word pairs as **can** and **may, eager** and **anxious, uninterested** and **disinterested,** and **since** and **because** were interchangeable received corrections shouted across the newsroom for all their colleagues to hear.

Choosing the precise word or phrase is a challenge to all writers and speakers, but it is a special problem for mass communicators because of deadline pressure. Novelists and poets usually have days or months for research and contemplation; journalists and other mass communicators often have only minutes or seconds.

This reference section on words frequently confused is organized and designed specifically for mass communications students and professionals working under deadline pressure. The word pairs are common. The order is alphabetical. The definitions and examples are brief.

There is room for disagreement with some distinctions made in the examples that follow. A section designed for quick reference has little time or space for debate. However, those who raise questions will be better off if they take the time for further research.

A, An, Per

Use the articles **a** and **an** except in the few circumstances in which **per** would be more appropriate.

New Year's Eve party tickets and hotel room reservations will sell for $100 **a** ***(not per)*** couple, the entertainment director said.

The demonstrators said they will attempt to march 15 miles **a** ***(not per)*** day.

Per may be used in **miles per gallon** ***(abbreviated mpg)*** and in **miles per hour** ***(abbreviated mph).***

Per also is used correctly when placed before a term such as **per capita** or **per diem**. Even then, however, journalists would serve their readers and listeners better by using the more commonly understood **for each person** ***(per capita)*** and **a day** ***(per diem).***

Also avoid such expressions as "**per** your directions," "**per** your orders," and "**per** your instructions."

About, Almost, Approximately, Around

About means nearly, approximately ***(but not around).***

Almost means very nearly, not exactly.

Approximately means nearly exact, much like.

Around means on all sides of.

"**About** ***[or approximately, but not around]*** 5,000 people attend the concerts each weekend," the civic center director said.

"The fire went undetected for **almost** ***[or about or approximately, but not around]*** 15 minutes," Chief Michael F. Neilson said.

Approximately ***(or about, but not around)*** 10,000 fans escaped safely when fire broke out last night during a rock concert at the civic center.

The mile event will require each participant to run **around** ***(not about)*** the indoor track 10 times.

Abridged, Unabridged

Abridged means condensed by selectively leaving out some content without harming the overall work (such as a dictionary or some other reference book).

Unabridged means the work has not been shortened and therefore is the comprehensive version.

The reporters' desk dictionaries are the **abridged** ***(condensed)*** versions because they are sufficient for everyday use. The much larger and much more expensive **unabridged** ***(complete, comprehensive)*** dictionary is available to all reporters in the company library.

Absent, Without

Absent means not being present, missing.

Without means not having, excluding.

The editorial writer criticized the council member for being **absent** ***(not present)*** for the important vote.

Without ***(not having)*** a college degree, the applicant had little chance of getting the job.

Although both **absent** and **without** can be used to mean ***not present*** or ***missing,*** avoid the awkwardness in using absent in the following context:

"**Without** ***[not absent]*** the anonymous $2 million contribution, construction of the library would have been delayed for another year," the school superintendent said.

Without ***(not absent)*** its star pitcher, the Hawks are given little chance of winning the series.

Accept, Except

Accept means to receive.

Except means to exclude or to omit.

The director of the United Way campaign **accepted** ***(received)*** a $20,000 contribution from the City Improvement League.

Every incumbent **except** ***(excluding)*** Victoria M. Crouse won re-election to the House of Delegates.

Acronym, Homonym, Synonym

An **acronym** is a word formed from the first letters of other words **(NASA, RADAR, NATO).**

A **homonym** is a word pronounced the same as another but different in meaning ***(flower/flour, blue/blew, bear/bare).***

A **synonym** is a word that has the same meaning, or nearly the same meaning, as another word ***(intelligent/smart, beautiful/pretty, wealthy/rich).***

Acute, Chronic

Acute means intense, of great or of crucial importance, or a situation that has become immediately critical.

Chronic means prolonged, recurring or continuing over a considerable time.

The editorial writer urged readers to relieve the **acute** ***(critical)*** shortage of blood by donating the next day at the local Red Cross center.

He also urged Red Cross officials to work with civic and business organizations to develop a plan that would eliminate the agency's **chronic** ***(continuing over a long time)*** shortage of blood donors.

Adage, *not* Old Adage

If an expression, a rule or a custom could become an **adage,** a **cliché,** a **tradition,** a **habit** or a **maxim** overnight, distinguishing between the old and the new might be necessary. However, because considerable time is involved in their development, to use the adjective ***old*** before them is as unnecessary as saying someone has given birth to a ***new*** baby.

Adapt, Adopt, Adept

Adapt means to adjust to a changed situation.

Adopt means to accept as your own.

Adept means skillful.

When the news director transferred from the company's Florida television station to the affiliate in Montana, she had to **adapt** ***(adjust)*** to the colder climate.

Local news reporters sometimes **adopt** ***(accept as their own)*** story ideas from the national media.

Veteran political cartoonists are **adept** ***(skillful)*** at exaggerating the faults of their subjects.

Admitted, Said

Journalists must be extremely careful in selecting the verbs they use in attributing remarks to sources. **Said** is a neutral word, but **admitted** is not. **Admitted** should be used only when sources have unmistakably acknowledged that they are wrong or guilty.

The city treasurer **said** ***(not admitted)*** his report will be two weeks late. ***(He could have an acceptable reason for being late.)***

Just before the trial was scheduled to start, the defendant **admitted** she was guilty. ***(This is clearly an admission.)***

Adverse, Averse

Adverse means unfavorable.

Averse means opposed or having a distaste for.

Adverse ***(unfavorable)*** weather caused the city's street-treatment supplies to reduce to an insufficient level.

The mayor said she is **averse** ***(opposed)*** to the concept of deficit spending. (Use familiar words like opposed, not averse.)

Advice, Advise

Advice is a ***noun*** meaning recommendation.

Advise is a ***verb*** meaning to counsel.

The reporter took the editor's **advice** ***(recommendation)*** that she complete her college education.

Several experienced reporters also **advised** ***(counseled)*** the young woman to earn her degree in journalism.

Advise, Inform

Advise means to counsel.

Inform means to provide information, to relate facts or opinions.

During his College Day remarks, the advertising director **advised** ***(counseled)*** the high school students to improve their writing skills.

The director also **informed** ***(related the fact)*** the students that they could schedule tours of the advertising agency offices by contacting his assistant.

Affect, Effect

Use **affect** as a ***verb*** meaning to influence.

Use **effect** as a ***noun*** meaning result.

The boisterous crowd obviously **affected** ***(influenced)*** the concentration of the players on the visiting team.

How much **effect** ***(result)*** the noisy fans had on the outcome of the game is difficult to determine, the coach of the home team said.

Effect can be used as a ***verb*** when the meaning is to cause.

The City Council has **effected** ***(caused)*** many changes in the summer recreation program.

However, avoiding the use of **effect** as a ***verb*** could result in a sentence better suited for a mass audience:

The City Council has **made** ***(not effected)*** many changes in the summer recreation program.

Affect/Effect/Influence, *not* Impact

Affect and **effect** are defined in the previous example.

Influence refers to the ability to cause desired effects or results.

Impact means to strike or to collide against; to fill; to wedge in.

Letters of recommendation are most desirable when those who write them have **influence** ***(the ability to cause results).***

Both cars were demolished by the **impact** ***(collision)*** of the crash.

An unexpectedly large number of fans **impacted** ***(filled, wedged into)*** the small concert hall. (Even though **impacted** is used correctly in this sentence, either **wedged into** or **crowded into** will sound more familiar to a mass audience.)

Avoid using **impact** when there is no force, striking or wedging.

The bad weather will **affect/influence** ***(not impact)*** the number of people who will vote today, the secretary of state said.

After, When

Print and broadcast journalists sometimes mistakenly use **after** instead of **when** in spot news stories about accidents.

If a victim is injured, the journalist should write or broadcast that Luther N. Craycraft was injured **when** ***(not after)*** he was hit by a car at the corner of Fifth Avenue and 10th Street.

If a victim died instantly, the journalist also should write or broadcast that Luther N. Craycraft died **when** ***(not after)*** he was hit by a car at the corner of Fifth Avenue and 10th Street. If the person did not die during the accident, then **after** is the appropriate word to use: Four hours **after** being hit by a car at the corner of Fifth Avenue and 10th Street, Luther N. Craycraft died in a city hospital.

Afterward, *not* Afterwards

Use **afterward** exclusively.

There will be no celebration **afterward** ***(not afterwards),*** the cost-conscious winner of the election said.

Aggravate, Annoy, Irritate

Aggravate means to make worse, more troublesome. Use it to refer to ***things.***

Annoy means to irritate or to make angry, usually through repeated efforts. Use it to refer to ***people***.

Irritate means to provoke to impatience or anger, or to annoy.

The meteorologist warned that the warmer-than-expected temperature would further **aggravate** ***(make worse)*** the threat of floods by causing the snow to melt faster.

News sources **annoy** ***(irritate, anger)*** reporters when they deny having said words quoted directly by the journalists.

The mayor was so **irritated** ***(impatient with or angered)*** by the personal nature of the reporters' questions that he scolded them for their "lack of professionalism."

Aggregate, Total

Aggregate should not be substituted for **total.** It means a gathering or a collection of distinct things that form a mass or a whole.

Total refers to the sum, amount or number of persons or things that have been added.

A mass media chain or group is the **aggregate** ***(gathering or collection of distinct parts considered as a sum or as a whole)*** of many newspapers and radio and television stations under the ownership of one company.

The gate receipts from the championship game **total** ***(add up to)*** more than $1 million, according to a news service report.

Agnostic, Atheist

An **agnostic** thinks the human mind is incapable of knowing whether God exists.

An **atheist** does not believe God exists.

Because of the sensitive nature of these words, journalists should take extreme care to use them appropriately and precisely.

Agree To, Agree With

Use **agree to** to refer to ***things.***

Use **agree with** to refer to ***people.***

The news director **agreed to** the **changes** ***(things)*** suggested by the producer.

She **agreed with** the **producer** ***(person)*** that ratings could improve if the changes were made.

A Hold, *not* Ahold

Use neither when the meaning is **to speak with.**

There is no such spelling as **ahold,** and **a hold** should be used to mean ***to grip*** or ***to grasp.*** Reporters attempt to speak with numerous people each day, but they rarely try to grip or grasp ***(get a hold of)*** a source.

Aid, Aide

Aid means to help or to assist.

An **aide** is a person who serves as an assistant.

The governor said he will provide **aid** ***(help or assistance)*** to people in any county affected by last month's flood.

The governor selected Maria J. Rodiquez as his **aide** ***(assistant)*** for secondary education.

Aisle, Isle

An **aisle** is a passageway between two rows of seats.

An **isle** is a small island.

Watch the spelling. Definitions are too different to present much of a problem.

All *as a singular,* All *as a plural*

See **None** ***as a singular,*** **None** ***as a plural,*** pages 34 and 291.

All Ready, Already

All ready means everyone or everything is prepared or available.

Already means previously and refers to time.

The players are **all ready** ***(everyone is prepared)*** for the championship game, their coach said.

The team's plane **already** ***(previously)*** has departed.

All Right, *not* Alright

Use **all right** exclusively.

The public relations director said extending the deadline half an hour was **all right** ***(not alright)*** with her.

After returning to work following a week's sick leave, the account executive pronounced himself **all right** ***(not alright)*** and ready to get busy.

Allude, Elude

Allude means to make indirect or casual mention of something without referring to it directly.

Elude means to avoid, evade or escape.

In today's faculty meeting, the university president **alluded** to ***(mentioned indirectly)*** the new scholarship program, but he provided no details.

"I heard the president's words, but his meaning **eluded** ***[escaped]*** me," the head of the Department of English said.

He **eluded** ***(evaded)*** the police for three days before he was captured.

Allude, Refer

Allude means to make an indirect or casual mention of something without referring to it directly.

Refer means to mention something directly, specifically.

The president permitted his speech writers to **allude** to ***(mention indirectly)*** his war record, but he instructed them not to **refer** to ***(mention directly or specifically)*** the event that earned him the Medal of Honor.

Allusion, Delusion, Illusion

An **allusion** is an indirect mention.

A **delusion** is to deceive or to be deceived, to believe something even when evidence shows it is false.

An **illusion** is a false or a misleading idea or image.

In his State-of-the-State address, Gov. Roberto L. Martinez made an **allusion** ***(an indirect mention)*** to a tax increase, but he declined to answer reporters' questions about it.

Alchemists' belief that they could turn base metals into gold was a **delusion** ***(a belief that something is true even when evidence shows it is false).***

With his loud talk and bizarre gestures, the actor tried to provide the **illusion** ***(false image)*** of reality for the audience.

Almost, Most

Almost means nearly.

Most means the largest amount or the greatest number.

Almost ***(nearly)*** defeated in the previous election, the senator was careful not to take strong positions that might cost him votes during the next campaign.

The magazine publisher's speech is **almost** ***(nearly)*** finished, according to her assistant.

Most ***(the greatest number)*** of the reporters are college graduates.

Most ***(the largest amount)*** of the debris left by the hurricane was cleared from the beaches before the summer tourist season began.

Avoid using **most** in place of **almost** in examples like the following:

Almost ***(not most)*** every consumer knows not to take all advertising messages literally.

The mayor has two hours of open time **almost** ***(not most)*** every day to hear citizens' suggestions and complaints.

A Lot, *not* Alot

A lot must be used as two words.

A lot ***(a piece of property)*** in downtown Tokyo is worth many millions of dollars in today's economy.

Avoid using **a lot** ***(meaning much)*** when a more appropriate or a more precise word is available.

Students must study **at least four years** ***(more precise than*** **a lot*****)*** to earn a degree in journalism.

Altar, Alter

An **altar** ***(noun)*** is an elevated place at which religious ceremonies are performed.

Alter ***(verb)*** means to change or to modify.

The religious leader prepared the **altar** ***(elevated place, table)*** for the service later that evening.

Planning Committee members had to **alter** ***(modify)*** their design for the proposed building when the budget was reduced.

Alternative, Choice

Alternative refers to a choice limited to one possibility.

Choice refers to a selection that is not limited to one possibility.

The **alternative** ***(choice between two)*** to living is dying.

"You have three **choices** ***[not alternatives],*** " the judge informed the jurors.

Because the use of **alternative** is limited to one possibility, avoid being redundant by not writing or broadcasting the ***only*** alternative or the ***other*** alternative.

Overcome the temptation to use **alternative** as a plural even though "everyone else does."

Although, While

Although means ***despite*** the fact that.

While means ***during*** the time that.

Resist the temptation to use **while** in place of **although** ***when the purpose is to show a contrast.***

(Avoid) **While** ***(during the time that)*** the university president said he wants to obtain a special appropriation from the Legislature, he said he has little hope of getting it.

(Better) **Although** ***(despite the fact that)*** the university president said he hopes to obtain a special appropriation from the Legislature, he said he has little hope of getting it.

Altogether, All Together

Altogether means wholly.

All together means every person or thing at the same place.

At his retirement dinner, the publisher remarked that journalism today is an **altogether** ***(wholly)*** different business from what it was when he began his career 52 years ago.

The last time members of the 1960 state championship team were **all together** ***(all at the same place)*** was at the class reunion in 1980.

Alumna, Alumnae, Alumnus, Alumni

Use **alumna** to refer to one female.

Use **alumnae** to refer to two or more females.

Use **alumnus** to refer to one male.

Use **alumni** to refer to two or more males or collectively to all of a school's former students, both male and female.

She is an **alumna** ***(one female)*** of Acme University.

Anissa, Heather and LaDonna are **alumnae** ***(two or more females)*** of Carson College.

He is an **alumnus** ***(one male)*** of Breckenridge State.

John, Juan and Ivan are **alumni** ***(two or more males)*** of Midwestern University.

All of the **alumni** ***(both women and men)*** are encouraged to make annual contributions to the university's scholarship fund.

Amateur, Novice, Professional

An **amateur** may be a beginner or have extensive experience. What makes him or her an amateur is that the activity is not pursued as a vocation or as a profession for financial profit.

A **novice** is a beginner, a person who lacks experience. A novice may or may not receive money for the activity in which he or she is involved.

A **professional** earns a living from his or her activity.

College journalists who serve summer internships are considered **novices *(beginners)*** by the professionals with whom they work.

All interns, however, are eager to trade their **amateur** status for their first paycheck.

When students graduate from college and obtain their first job, they become **professionals.**

Amid, *not* Amidst

Use **amid** exclusively.

Amid *(not amidst)* the debris of the wreckage, searchers found evidence that the passenger plane had been bombed.

Among, Between

Use **between** when two people, places or things are involved.

Use **among** when the number is three or more.

The general election contest **between** the incumbent and the challenger ***(two of them)*** is expected to be close, most political experts agree.

The winner probably will divide government jobs **among** members of the campaign staff ***(three or more).***

If three or more persons, places or things are considered one pair at a time, **between** may be used instead of **among.**

Discussion of the proposed teacher pay raise bill is expected **between** the legislators and committees from the Board of Trustees, university administrators, and representatives of the Teachers Union.

Amount, Number

Amount is an indefinite quantity (water, flour, sand, grass) that ***cannot be counted.***

Number consists of a quantity of people or things that ***can be counted.***

The **amount** of **news** ***(quantity that cannot be counted)*** published and broadcast each day is amazing.

The **number** of **reporters** ***(quantity that can be counted)*** covering the convention won't be known for another week, the press officer explained.

Amuse, Bemuse

Amuse means to entertain or to hold someone's attention. It has a pleasant meaning.

Bemuse means to bewilder, to confuse or to become lost in thought.

Editorial cartoonists try to **amuse** ***(entertain)*** as well as to inform newspaper and magazine readers.

The advertising copywriter seemed **bemused** ***(bewildered)*** by her client's negative reaction to her proposal. (Mass communicators may prefer more familiar words like **confuse** or **bewilder.**)

And, *not* While

Avoid using **while** (meaning during the time that) in place of **and** (a continuation or an addition) in examples such as the following:

Johnson is a graduate of Acme University, **and** ***(not while)*** his opponent for the City Council seat graduated from Riley College.

Beckwith coaches basketball at Reynolds High School, **and** ***(not while)*** her brother coaches at rival Baker High School.

Anecdote, Antidote

An **anecdote** is a brief recounting of an interesting incident or experience.

An **antidote** refers to a substance administered or an action taken to counteract the effects of something harmful or negative.

Feature writers depend on **anecdotes** to make their articles more interesting.

The physician administered an **antidote** to the camper bitten by a poisonous snake.

The gubernatorial candidate said she had the **antidote** for the budget deficit. She said she would reduce the number of state employees.

Angel, Angle

The sign in the grocery store read: "**Angle** food cake $2.99." This won't seem too tasty to people who know which of these words refers to a winged figure in a white robe and which refers to lines and measurements. The problem is spelling, not definition.

> **Angels** ***(not angles)*** often served as God's messengers, according to The Bible.

Anticipate, Expect

Use **anticipate** when preparation has been made for something that is expected to happen.

Use **expect** when no preparation has been made.

> The 5,000 spectators remained dry and warm because the civic center director had **anticipated** ***(planned for)*** the rain and had moved the concert indoors.
>
> "We **expected** a large crowd, but we were not prepared for the 2,000 additional people who showed up during the last hour before the concert," the civic center director said. ***(Had the director been aware that as many as 2,000 additional people might attend, she could have made preparations to accommodate them.)***

Anxious, Eager

Overcome the temptation to use **anxious** and **eager** interchangeably, even though "everyone else does."

Use **anxious** to indicate concern or worry.

Use **eager** to show impatient desire.

> The city engineer said he is **anxious** ***(concerned, worried)*** about tonight's debate on the proposed sewage-treatment plant.
>
> However, he said he is **eager** ***(has an impatient desire)*** to argue his case before opponents of the project.

Anybody, Any Body

Use **anybody** as a single word when the reference is to a group of people but not to any individual in particular.

Use **any body** as two words only when the reference is to a body such as a corpse, a body of water, a corporate body and so forth.

> The publisher said she would speak to **anybody** ***(no person in particular)*** about any issue at any time.

"**Any body** ***[corpse]*** found in the rubble must be removed quickly to the morgue," the coroner said.

(Additional information is available on page 31.)

Anymore, Any More

Use **anymore** as one word when the meaning is any longer.

Use **any more** as two words when the meaning is any additional.

The angry reporter said he would not work at this newspaper **anymore** ***(any longer).***

He said he would not write **any more** ***(additional)*** articles for "such an insensitive boss."

Anyone, Any One

Use **anyone** as a single word when the reference is to a group but not to any specific person.

Use **any one** as two words when the reference is to an individual.

Anyone ***(no particular person)*** may try out for a role in the Community Players' production of "Cat on a Hot Tin Roof," the director said.

The police chief said **any one** ***(emphasis on the individual)*** of the three people questioned could be the suspect being sought by the FBI.

(Additional information is available on page 31.)

Anytime, Any Time

Use **anytime** as one word when the meaning is whenever.

Use **any time** as two words when referring to an amount of time.

"You may submit your applications **anytime** ***[whenever]*** during your final semester of college," the public relations director said.

"**Any time** *[amount]* you spend improving your writing skills is time well used," the editor said.

Anyway, Any Way, *not* Anyways

Use **anyway** as one word when the meaning is ***in any case*** or ***regardless.***

Use **any way** as two words when the meaning is ***method, choice*** or ***direction.***

Never use **anyways** (with an *s* at the end).

The senator said his vote would not matter **anyway** ***(regardless);*** therefore, he would not attend the committee meeting.

"I don't know why you're interested in my opinion **anyway** ***[in any case],"*** he said.

The suspect in the robbery said he was determined to provide for his family **any way** ***(by any method)*** he could.

"**Any way** ***[choice, direction]*** you travel, you're going to encounter roads under repair," the state highway commissioner warned.

The editor told the reporter she could write the story **any way** ***(method, choice)*** she wanted.

(Additional information is available on page 32.)

Appraise, Apprise

Use **appraise** to mean to determine the value of.

Use **apprise** to mean to notify or to inform.

The public relations director said he wants an expert to **appraise** ***(determine the value of)*** the old word-processing equipment before he purchases new computers for the firm.

He said he wants the staff to keep him **apprised** ***(informed)*** during the evaluation process. (Mass communicators prefer familiar words like **informed.**)

Approval, Consideration, Decision

When journalists write or broadcast that a bill, a proposal or a project will be submitted to an administrator for **approval,** they are being presumptuous. The administrator may not approve it. Substitute **consideration** or **decision,** whichever is more appropriate.

The director submitted the committee members' recommendations to the president for her **consideration/decision** ***(but not approval).***

Apt, Liable, Likely, Libel

Apt is an outdated word meaning appropriate, likely, quick to learn.

Liable means legally responsible, or likely in an undesirable sense.

Likely means probable.

Libel means a defamation (a false and harmful published or broadcast statement).

The dressing room is an **apt** ***(appropriate)*** setting for a post-game interview.

According to the radio report, it's **apt** ***(likely)*** to rain.

She is an **apt** ***(quick to learn)*** student of journalism history, according to her professor.

Journalists are **liable** ***(legally responsible)*** for virtually every story they publish or broadcast.

Journalists are **liable** ***(likely in an undesirable sense)*** to get into serious trouble if they publish or broadcast false material.

The president **likely** ***(probably)*** will change his mind, his press secretary said.

The governor charged the largest radio station in the state with **libel** ***(defamation)*** for a story in which he was accused of accepting bribes for political favors.

Arbitrate, Mediate

Arbitrate means to judge or to make a decision in a dispute.

Mediate means to bring together two or more disputing parties and attempt to help them settle their differences. A mediator does not make the decision. That is done, or at least is attempted, by the disputing parties the mediator brings together.

Because the baseball team's leading hitter and the club president could not agree in their salary dispute, they submitted the case to an **arbitrator** who ruled in favor of the player.

The team's personnel director had attempted to **mediate** the disagreement between the player and the club president, but the disputing parties could not reach an agreement.

Are, Include

Use **are** when the verb introduces a list that has the names of all the people, places or things being discussed or considered.

Use **include** when the verb introduces a list that has the names of some but not all.

The scholarship winners **are** Robert R. Wicks, Mary L. Roth, Karyn D. Fillinger, Juan A. Torres and Charles E. Klinger. ***(All the winners are named.)***

The scholarship winners **include** Mary L. Roth and Juan A. Torres of John F. Kennedy High School. ***(The three winners from other high schools are not named; therefore, the list is incomplete.)***

Arise, Raise, Rise

Arise means to get up from a reclining position such as from a bed. Its principal parts are **arise** for the present, **arose** for the past, and **have/has/had arisen** for the past participle.

Raise means to cause to move upward. It is transitive (passes an action on to an object). Its principal parts are **raise** for the present, **raised** for the past, and **have/has/had raised** for the past participle.

Rise means to move upward. It is always intransitive (does not pass an action on to an object). Its principal parts are **rise** for the present, **rose** for the past, and **have/has/had risen** for the past participle.

The press secretary cautioned the reporters to **arise** in time to board the campaign bus by 6:30 a.m.

Those who **arose** late had to miss breakfast.

The candidate **had arisen** at 5 a.m. and had taken a five-mile jog while most of the reporters were still asleep.

The reporter will **rise** ***(move upward—intransitive)*** from her seat, **raise** ***(cause to move upward—transitive)*** her hand, and hope to be recognized by the president.

She **rose** ***(moved upward—intransitive)*** eight times before getting the president's attention. She then **raised** ***(caused to be brought up—transitive)*** her question on a foreign-policy issue.

She **had risen** ***(moved upward—intransitive)*** dozens of times at previous press conferences without successfully being recognized by the president.

She **had been raising** ***(causing to be brought up—transitive)*** the same questions for so many years, the president probably was tired of hearing them.

Aroma, Smell, Odor

Aroma refers to something pleasant.

Smell is a neutral word that depends on surrounding words to make clear whether the reference is to something pleasant or unpleasant.

Odor refers to something unpleasant.

The **aroma** of perking coffee attracts journalists like a magnet.

The **smell** ***(pleasant)*** of the fall air is crisp and clean during football season.

After each game, the locker room **smells** ***(unpleasant)*** like fermenting tennis shoes.

The **odor** from the fire at the tire manufacturing plant made several firefighters sick.

As, As If, Like, Such As

Use **as** and **as if** as conjunctions to introduce clauses.

Use **like** as a preposition when comparing.

Use **such as** instead of **like** when the meaning is ***exactly*** instead of ***similar to.***

The mayor accepted a reduction in pay, just **as *(not like)*** he had promised during his campaign.

It looks **as if *(not like)*** the press conference will be brief.

"My editor still treats me **as if *[not like]*** I were a cub reporter," the young journalist complained.

"You look **like *[preposition]*** a winner," the campaign manager said.

"**Like *[preposition]*** your predecessor, you're an insightful reporter and a superior writer, but you can hardly spell your name," the editor complained.

"Fires **such as *[not like]*** the two we've fought tonight are the most difficult to control," Chief Mario L. Costello explained. **(The chief's meaning is *exactly,* not *similar to.*)**

"Fires **like *[not such as]*** these are quite common," Chief Mario L. Costello explained. **(The chief's meaning is *similar to,* not *exactly.*)**

Ascent, Assent

Ascent refers to an upward motion.

Assent means to agree or to concede.

The mountain climber's **ascent** was uneventful

The reporter reluctantly **assented** to the judge's demand that he reveal his source.

Assume, Presume

Both **assume** and **presume** are commonly used to mean ***to take for granted.*** However, writers and speakers who believe distinctions are worth preserving should be helped by the guidelines that follow.

Use **assume** to mean ***to take on*** or ***to adopt (manner of dress, character), to undertake an office or duty,*** or ***to affect*** or ***to pretend to have.***

Use **presume** to mean ***to take for granted, to accept something as being true until there is proof that it is not,*** or ***to take upon yourself without permission or through a dare.***

The lieutenant governor will **assume *(undertake)*** the governor's duties for the next two weeks.

She **assumed** ***(pretended to have)*** the identity of an actress.

The county commissioners warned the volunteer firefighters that the commission would **assume** ***(take on)*** their department's debts "this one time only."

The team's All-American center said he **presumes** ***(takes for granted)*** he will be named in the first round of the National Basketball Association's draft of college seniors.

Under pressure from critics, Police Chief Ralph E. Alderson said all he could do was **presume** ***(accept as true until he has proof to the contrary)*** that his officers did not use unreasonable force when arresting 20 spectators at the rock music concert.

"How dare you **presume** ***[take upon yourself without permission]*** to speak for me in my absence?" Councilman Albert S. Yakovich asked the council president.

Assure, Ensure

Assure means to eliminate or relieve the uncertainty, concern, worry or fear troubling a person.

Ensure (also see the **Ensure, Insure** entry on page 267) means to guarantee an outcome.

The physician **assured** the man that his wife's illness was not life-threatening.

The best camera equipment available cannot **ensure** ***(guarantee)*** good pictures if the photographer lacks skill.

Atypical, Typical

Typical means having the same characteristics as others of a kind, a class or a group.

Atypical is the opposite of typical and means unlike or uncharacteristic.

Jerome Wysong played another of his **typical** ***(characteristic or usual)*** basketball games, scoring 24 points, grabbing 11 rebounds and blocking 5 shots.

The physician had a difficult time making a diagnosis because the patient's symptoms were **atypical** ***(not characteristic)*** of appendicitis.

Avenge, Revenge

Use **avenge** as a verb to refer to punishment for morally right and justifiable reasons.

Use **revenge** as a noun to refer to punishment for retaliation or vengeance.

The police chief vowed to **avenge** ***(punish in a morally right way)*** the shooting death of the mayor by arresting and prosecuting the killers.

The governor took **revenge** ***(punished to get even)*** against the Acme Gazette for its editorial endorsement of his election opponent. The governor barred Gazette reporters from his press conferences.

Average, Mean, Median

Average and **mean** both refer to the sum of the components divided by the number of components.

Median refers to the number that has as many scores above it as below it.

The running back gained 1,200 yards in 10 games this season for an **average** ***(the sum of the yards gained divided by the number of games played)*** of 120 yards a game.

The professor told her 15 students that the **median** test score for the class was 80 ***(meaning that seven students scored higher than 80 and seven students scored lower).***

Avert, Avoid, Prevent

Avert means to turn away or to ward off.

Avoid means to keep or stay away from or to evade.

Prevent means to anticipate something negative and to make preparations to forestall or to keep it from happening.

The coach **averted** ***(turned away)*** his eyes when his kicker tried for a game-winning field goal with five seconds remaining.

When the man threatened her by reaching for his pistol, the cashier dived under the counter to **avoid** ***(evade/keep from)*** being shot, according to the police report. (She could not **prevent** him from reaching for his pistol because she did not know he planned to rob her.)

"The purpose of these vaccinations is simple," the health official said. "They **prevent** elderly and chronically ill people from getting the flu." (Prevention is achieved by anticipating a problem and taking precautionary measures.)

Awhile, A While, While

Both **awhile** and **a while** refer to a brief time. **Awhile** is used as an adverb and **a while** consists of an **article** ***(a)*** followed by a **noun** ***(while).***

While is a **conjunction** meaning during the time that.

The editor suggested that the reporter wait **awhile** outside the house before questioning the murdered man's widow. (**Awhile** ***serves as an adverb modifying the verb*** **wait** ***and answering the question how much or to what extent.***)

For **a while** the editors thought they had an exclusive story, but they sat in frustration as a local television reporter broke it on the noon news. ***(*****While** ***is a noun serving as the object of the preposition*** **for.** A ***modifies while.)***

While the reporter waited, she composed questions for the interview. (**While** ***is a*** conjunction ***meaning during the time that.***)

Backward, *not* Backwards

Use **backward** exclusively.

Overcome by the heat, the candidate for a master's degree fell **backward** ***(not backwards)*** into the arms of classmates when she fainted during the July graduation ceremony.

Bad, Badly

Even among well-educated people, you should not be surprised to hear someone say, "I feel **badly** about forgetting our appointment," or "I feel **badly** about the death of your uncle." **Bad,** not **badly,** is the correct word in these examples. To use **badly** after the word feel gives the impression that the speaker has an inferior sense of feel (is a bad "feeler").

Use **bad** as an adjective.

Use **badly** as an adverb.

"I feel **bad** ***[not badly]*** about missing the deadline," the reporter told her news director. (**Bad** ***is an adjective modifying the pronoun I.)***

"I feel **bad** ***[not badly]*** about the death of your uncle." (**Bad** ***is an adjective modifying the pronoun I.***)

Jenkins played **badly** ***(not bad)*** considering that he scored 12 fewer points than he had been averaging in each previous game. (**Badly** ***is an adverb modifying the verb*** **played** ***and telling how he played.***)

The conductor performed **badly** ***(not bad),*** and the concert was an embarrassment, The New York Times music critic wrote. ***(*****Badly** ***is an*** **adverb** ***modifying the verb performed and telling how the conductor performed.***)

Baited, Bated

Baited refers to a hook or a trap to which food is attached to lure fish or animals. It also refers to teasing, tormenting or harassing attacks that are unprovoked and often vicious (such as the outlawed "sport" of having dogs attack a chained bear).

Bated is sometimes used in the expression "waiting with bated breath," meaning that breath is being held in anticipation of something fearful or exciting. Its use is frequently sarcastic.

Fishing experts maintain that the manner in which a hook is **baited** is just as important as the bait itself.

Jew-**baiting** ***(badgering, tormenting)*** was a common practice of Nazi groups during Hitler's rise to power in Germany.

The crowd waited with **bated** ***(held)*** breath as the kicker's field goal attempt in the final seconds zoomed through the goal posts to give Acme University the national football championship.

"Would I like to hear again about the kick you made 25 years ago to win your team the national championship? I'm just waiting with **bated** breath."

Bare, Bear

Journalists rarely confuse a large furry animal with an uncovered floor, but sometimes they do use the incorrect spelling of **bare** and **bear** for less familiar definitions of the words.

Bare, of course, means ***naked.*** It also means ***without covering*** **(bare floors),** ***without supplies*** **(the cupboard was bare),** or ***merely*** **(I barely passed the test)**.

Bear, of course, is the name of a large animal. It also means ***to carry*** **(bearing gifts),** ***to undertake a burden*** **(to bear the responsibility),** or to ***put up with***.

In the accident, the victim's coat was ripped, causing her **bare** ***(naked or uncovered)*** arms to freeze before help arrived.

The walls of her one-room apartment were **bare** ***(uncovered)*** except for a small picture left by the previous occupant.

The pantry also was **bare** ***(without supplies),*** for the woman had no money with which to restock the shelves.

Bears are interesting animals to watch, but they can be dangerous if they feel threatened.

When the truck's engine failed, each of the passengers had to help **bear** the burden of carrying the load of medical supplies.

The woman said she shot her husband because she couldn't **bear** ***(put up with)*** another beating.

Bazaar, Bizarre

A **bazaar** is a marketplace where miscellaneous articles are sold.

Bizarre means strange or odd.

Describing shopping in a Middle Eastern **bazaar** ***(marketplace)*** can be a challenge for American journalists.

Although the vice president for public relations considered her new employee's personal habits somewhat **bizarre** ***(odd),*** she admired the way he performed his job.

Because, Since

Many writers and reporters give no thought to making a distinction in use between these two words. They just use them interchangeably. Those who do consider the difference sometimes become confused. Although not foolproof, the following advice will provide considerable clarification:

Use **because** to indicate a ***cause*** or a ***reason.***

Use **since** to refer to ***time,*** meaning between then and now.

The sheriff said he will not seek re-election **because** ***(reason)*** state law prevents him from succeeding himself.

The governor said she will not veto the bill **because** ***(reason)*** she knows her opponents in the Legislature will override her action.

Since ***(time)*** last Monday's meeting, several members of City Council have expressed their opinions publicly on the road-bond issue.

The demonstrators marched for the first time **since** ***(time)*** they received their permit half a year ago.

Beside, Besides

Beside means by the side of.

Besides means in addition to.

When the reporter found herself seated **beside** ***(by the side of)*** the speaker of the House of Representatives at the Kennedy Center concert, she couldn't resist asking him a few questions about the federal budget.

Besides ***(in addition to)*** the news magazine editor, three broadcast journalists and a newspaper reporter attended the conference.

Biannual, Biennial

Biannual means ***twice a year.***

Biennial means ***once every two years*** (or every other year).

Libel insurance premiums may be paid ***biannually (twice a year).***
Members of Congress are elected ***biennially (every two years).***

To avoid the possibility of confusing their audience, journalists should simply write or broadcast **twice a year** for **biannual** and ***every two years (or every other year)*** for ***biennial.***

Bimonthly, Semimonthly

Use **bimonthly** to mean ***once every two months*** (or every other month).

Use **semimonthly** to mean ***twice a month.***

Dues may be paid **bimonthly** ***(once every two months).***
Classes are available **semimonthly** ***(twice a month).***

Journalists want not only to use the correct word but also to make certain the reader or listener understands. Mass media audiences probably would be served better if journalists would substitute **once every two months** or **every other month** for **bimonthly** and ***twice a month*** for ***semimonthly.***

Bloc, Block

Bloc means a coalition of factions or parties with a particular purpose.

Block means a piece of wood or stone with one or more flat sides, or an obstruction or a barrier.

A **bloc** ***(coalition)*** of oil-producing countries is forming to combat a severe drop in market prices.

The campaign director made plans to **block** ***(obstruct)*** an attempt to deny the president his party's nomination for a second term.

Blond, Blonde

Use **blond** as an adjective in all references, and as a noun to refer to males.

Use **blonde** as a noun to refer to females.

Blond ***(adjective)*** hair is common among Nordic people.

Blond ***(noun)*** is a familiar hair color among men, and there are numerous **blondes** ***(noun)*** in the female population.

Boat, Ship

Ships are large and travel seas and oceans.

Boats are comparatively smaller and travel smaller bodies of water. **Ships** also carry **boats *(lifeboats),*** but boats do not carry ships.

Most of the American troops were transported to Europe in **ships**.

At most of the state parks, tourists may rent **boats** and row on the lake.

Both Sides, Either Side

Sometimes writers and broadcasters report that guards were stationed on **"either"** side of the door or that a basketball coach placed players on **"either"** side of the goal. **Either** provides a potentially confusing description of what these journalists are trying to report. They undoubtedly mean that guards were stationed on **both** sides of the door and that players were placed on **both** sides of the goal. **Both** eliminates the possibility of misinterpretation.

Either, in the examples above, could refer to a choice of placing guards or players on **either** one side or the other.

Both offers no choice. Guards and players will be placed not on **either** one side or the other but on **both** sides.

"A person who is a friend of both the bride and the groom may sit on **either *[a choice of one or the other]*** side of the room during the ceremony," the wedding director instructed the engaged couple.

When the president speaks to the delegates tonight, Secret Service agents will be stationed on **both sides *(not either side)*** of the podium.

Bouillon, Bullion

Bouillon is broth.

Bullion is gold or silver in bulk form.

Breath, Breathe

Spelling, not definition, is the problem in this word pair. **Breath** (rhymes with Beth) is a noun that refers to the air inhaled and exhaled during respiration. **Breathe** (rhymes with Steve) is a verb that refers to the process of inhaling and exhaling air during respiration.

Brief, *not* Short *(in reference to time)*

When referring to time, use **brief *(not long-lasting),*** not **short *(not long or tall).***

McComb's reign as heavyweight boxing champion was **brief *(not short).***

Bring, Take

Bring means to carry or to lead toward someone or something.

Take means to carry or to lead away from someone or something.

"**Bring** ***[carry toward]*** me a copy of your news release before you make it public."

"**Take** ***[to lead away from]*** the news release from the press office to the governor's secretary."

Burglary, Robbery

Burglary refers to breaking into a building to steal. The victim(s) is either not present or not confronted.

Robbery is the unlawful use of force or threat of force to acquire something belonging to another.

The **burglary** ***(theft by breaking into a building)*** was discovered by cleaning crew members when they arrived for work at 6 a.m.

The **robbery** ***(stealing of property with use of unlawful force or threat of force)*** resulted in the death of the victim.

Buses, Busses

Both **buses** and **busses** can provide moving experiences, but a journalist who confuses these plural spellings can be quite embarrassed.

Buses are motor vehicles.

Busses are kisses ***(although the term is outdated).***

Passing stopped school **buses** is against the law.

The **busses** that grandparents give don't come equipped with wheels.

Callous, Callus

Callous is an adjective that refers to a hardened attitude, indifference or insensitivity.

Callus is a noun and refers to hardened skin caused by friction.

The city editor seemed **callous** ***(insensitive, unsympathetic)*** when he scolded the young reporter in front of his colleagues in the newsroom.

The Boston Red Sox pitcher developed a **callus** ***(hardened skin caused by friction)*** on his middle finger after throwing thousands of curve balls.

Can, May

Use **can** for ability to.

Use **may** for permission.

Any eligible student **may** ***(have permission to)*** enter the mile run in Saturday's track meet, the athletic director said.

However, he said he doubts any runner **can** ***(has the ability to)*** break the record set two years ago.

Cancel, Delay, Postpone

Cancel means to eliminate or never to reschedule.

Delay means to stop or detain temporarily.

Postpone means to put off until another date.

Superintendent Roberta L. Cooke **canceled** ***(eliminated, never to be rescheduled)*** school for three days because of the flu epidemic.

The baseball game was **delayed** ***(stopped temporarily)*** 45 minutes by rain.

Because of the rain, the outdoor concert was **postponed** ***(put off until another date)*** until Thursday.

Cannon, Canon

A **cannon** is a mounted weapon.

A **canon** is a church law or rule, or a set of principles such as the canons of journalism.

Cannot, *not* Can Not

Use **cannot** as one word, not two.

The photographer **cannot** ***(one word)*** cover both meetings because they are scheduled at the same time.

Can't Help, *not* Can't Help But

Use **can't help.** ***Can't*** **help** ***but*** is a double negative.

The police chief said, "**I can't help thinking** ***[not can't help but think]*** the commissioners were wrong when they reduced our budget."

Canvas, Canvass

Canvas is a strong, coarse material used to make sails, floor covering for boxing rings and so forth.

Canvass is a verb used to refer to talking with people in various locations to seek their vote, to determine how they will or have voted or to ask their opinion about any topic, product or service.

The military is a primary purchaser of **canvas** ***(strong, coarse material)*** tents.

Politicians seeking local offices consider **canvassing** ***(going door-to-door asking citizens for opinions and votes)*** their neighborhoods a primary part of their campaign strategy.

Capital, Capitol

Capital is the city where a government is located.

Capitol is the building in which government business is conducted.

Charleston is the **capital** ***(city)*** of West Virginia.

The **capitol** ***(building)*** in Charleston is considered one of the most beautiful in the nation.

Carat, Caret, Carrot, Karat

A **carat** is a unit of weight for gemstones (a five-carat diamond, for example).

A **caret** is a proofreader's symbol showing where an insertion is to be made.

A **karat** is a unit for measuring the degree of gold (commonly 10, 14, 18, and 24, the latter being pure gold).

A **carrot,** of course, is a vegetable.

Cement, Concrete

Cement is a powder used as an adhesive ingredient in **concrete**.

The **concrete** ***(not cement)*** pavement is six inches thick.

In addition to making clear the distinctions between **cement** and **concrete,** journalists also should be careful not to misuse **cement** as a verb.

The ambassadors **improved/strengthened** ***(not cemented)*** the relationship between their countries by signing a trade agreement.

Censor, Censure

Censor means to prohibit or to restrict.

Censure means to condemn.

Journalists object strenuously when government officials attempt to **censor** ***(restrict)*** material that by law is supposed to be available to the public.

Members of the Senate Ethics Committee **censured** ***(condemned)*** a colleague for accepting illegal campaign contributions.

Most people pronounce cens**or** the same as cens**er**. However, **censer** ***(with an* e)** has a vastly different meaning. It is a container in which incense is burned.

Center On, *not* Center Around

On and **around** are not interchangeable in these two sets of words. Something may **center on** but never **around.**

"The legislative debate will **center on** ***[not around]*** tax reform," Sen. Maxine C. Perkowski said.

Character, Reputation

Character refers to the sum of a person's behavior, moral standards and value system.

Reputation refers to the perception others have of a person ***(in other words, the good, bad or indifferent impression that comes to mind when they either see or hear about some individual).***

An honorable **character** is essential for news reporters. Without it, they can't earn a good **reputation.**

Chord, Cord

Chord commonly refers to three or more musical notes sounded simultaneously to provide a harmonic result. **Chord** also refers to feeling or emotion.

Cord refers to strands woven or twisted into string, rope or insulated wires.

To relax from her strenuous schedule, the president of the advertising agency took guitar lessons, but she quit in impatience after learning only a few **chords.**

The music critic could not remember where he had heard the song before, but the melody struck a **chord** ***(feeling emotion)*** of sadness in him as he listened to it.

The reporter tripped over the computer **cord** when she rushed to answer the telephone on another writer's desk.

Cite, Sight, Site

Cite means to quote an authority or to refer to something as an example.

Sight means seeing, or a view that is seen.

Site means location, where something is positioned.

The reporter **cited** ***(referred to)*** the mayor's speech several times in a news story.

The Grand Canyon presents a majestic **sight** ***(view)*** for tourists.

The **site** ***(location)*** selected for the building project upset some residents whose houses would have to be condemned.

Cliché, *not* Old Cliché

See **Adage,** not **Old Adage,** page 226.

Climate, Temperature, Weather

Climate is weather conditions established over a long time in a specific area.

Temperature is heat or cold as measured in degrees on a thermometer.

Weather is atmospheric conditions (temperature, moisture, cloudiness).

The **climate** ***(indigenous weather conditions)*** is ideal for people who enjoy cold-weather sports.

The **temperature** ***(degrees of heat or cold)*** will rise today from a low of 45 degrees to a high of 68, the meteorologist said.

The **weather** ***(atmospheric conditions)*** will be colder for the next three days.

Coarse, Course

Coarse refers to something or someone rough, unrefined.

Course refers to a route, a program of study or a field or track for athletic competition.

The star athlete complained that his new uniform felt **coarse** ***(rough)*** against his skin, and he refused to wear it.

The criminal's language was too **coarse** ***(unrefined)*** to be used in a sound bite on the 6 p.m. newscast.

The **course** ***(route)*** the new magazine writer thought would save traveling time actually took longer.

The race **course**/golf **course** ***(ground, area)*** is new.

Collide, Hit

At least two moving objects (cars, planes, trains) are necessary for a **collision** to occur.

Use **hit** when explaining that one moving object (car, plane, train) ran into something stationary such as a tree, a mountainside or a truck stalled on railroad tracks.

The early morning **collision** involving two cars and a truck ***(three moving objects)*** killed three people.

Lightning ***(a moving object)*** **hit** the big oak tree ***(a stationary object)*** in front of the university, but no one was injured.

Compared To, Compared With

Use **compared to** to liken one person, place or thing to another. **Compared to** is used for similarities.

Compared with is used more frequently, and its purpose is to provide a more concrete and factual comparison of similarities and differences.

"The director of advertising **compared** my typing speed **to** the flow of molasses on a winter's day." **(Compared to *is being used to show how one slow thing is like another slow thing.*)**

"When today's professional athletes are **compared with** those of 25 years ago, similarities in desire and commitment are evident, but vast differences exist in salary and pension benefits," the veteran sports columnist explained. ***(A more concrete and factual comparison is being made of similarities and differences.)***

Complement, Compliment

Almost identical in spelling, **compl*e*ment** and **compl*i*ment** are quite different in meaning.

Complement means to complete or to supplement.

Compliment means to praise.

The drama critic described the play as "brilliantly written and **complemented** ***[completed or supplemented]*** by an exceptionally talented cast."

The playwright said she considered the critic's remarks "an unexpected **compliment** ***[praise]***."

Complexion, *not* Complexioned *or* Complected

Complexion is a **noun** and refers to the color and skin of a person's face.

Complexioned should be avoided because making an **adjective** from this **noun** is awkward.

Completed is an American colloquial expression for the same thing as complexion. Avoid using **complected.**

(Avoid) "The suspect is light **complected,**" the police chief said.

(Avoid) "The suspect is light **complexioned,**" the police chief said.

(Use) "The suspect has a light **complexion,**" the police chief said.

Comply With, *not* Comply To

Use **comply with** exclusively.

Reporters had to **comply with** ***(not comply to)*** the judge's gag order until they could file an appeal.

Compose, Comprise

The simple way to explain the difference in use between **compose** and **comprise** is to caution writers and broadcasters never to use ***of*** directly after **comprise.** That's because **comprise** is a **transitive** ***(action)*** **verb** that always has a **direct object.** If ***of*** follows **comprise,** a **direct object** is not possible. Conversely, **compose** can be **transitive** ***(with a direct object)*** or **intransitive** ***(without a direct object).***

Use **compose** when the meaning is to create or to put together.

Use **comprise** when the meaning is to include or to consist of.

Francis Scott Key **composed** ***(created)*** the words in the national anthem.

A university is **composed** of ***(put together of)*** several colleges.

The House of Representatives **comprises** ***(includes, contains)*** 435 members.

The choir **comprises** ***(consists of, is composed of)*** 15 men, 12 women and 10 children.

Remember that **comprise** is always a **transitive** ***(active voice)*** verb requiring a **direct object:** ***The House of Representatives comprises 435 members.*** **Comprises** is an **action verb** and **members** is a **direct object** answering the question **whom** or **what** comprises. Because **comprise** is transitive, it can never be used correctly in the following construction: ***The House of Representatives is comprised of 435 members.*** There is no direct object. **Members** in this construction is the **object** of the **preposition** ***of.***

Compose can be either **transitive** or **intransitive.** ***Key composed the words*** is **transitive** because there is a **direct object** ***(words). A university is composed of several colleges*** is **intransitive** because there is no **direct object.**

Journalists should consider whether **compose** or **comprise** is the best choice of words for the thought they are expressing. Other possibilities include **consists of, constitutes, includes** and **is made of.**

Contemporary, Modern

Contemporary means existing or occurring at the same time, and it may be used to refer to any time in history. However, unless otherwise specified, **contemporary** usually means now.

Modern refers to present and recent times.

Benjamin Franklin was a **contemporary** ***(lived at the same time as)*** of George Washington's.

Modern ***(present time)*** bank buildings are simple and streamlined in appearance in contrast to the elaborate, highly ornamental structures built in the early part of the past century.

Contemptible, Contemptuous

Contemptible means deserving of contempt, scorn or disgrace.

Contemptuous means to express contempt or scorn.

Perjury is a **contemptible** act ***(deserving of scorn),*** the judge warned the witness.

The judge looked **contemptuously** ***(scornfully)*** at the witness, who admitted under severe questioning from the defense attorney that he had committed perjury.

Continual, Continuous

Continual means to repeat on a somewhat regular basis.

Continuous means uninterrupted or unceasing.

The president's speech was interrupted **continually** ***(repeatedly)*** by applause.

The flow of water over Niagara Falls is **continuous** ***(unceasing).***

Convince, Persuade

Convince means to cause someone to believe.

Persuade means to cause someone to do something, to take some action.

In his State-of-the-Union address, the president said he hopes to **convince** ***(cause people to believe)*** Americans that Congress should not pass a tax increase.

He said he also hopes he can **persuade** ***(cause people to act)*** Americans to express their opposition to a tax increase by contacting their representatives in Congress.

"I disagree with the president," Rep. Charles B. Hairston, D-Ohio, said. "But I don't think I can **convince** ***[cause to believe]*** my constituents I am right. I'll never **persuade** ***[cause them to act]*** them to support a tax increase."

Corps, Corpse

Spelling and pronunciation present the problems for this word pair. Their definitions are extremely different.

Corps ***(pronounced core)*** refers to a group of people acting together under a common direction ***(Marine Corps, press corps, Corps of Engineers).***

Corpse refers to a body (usually a dead human body).

Fifteen members of the high school graduating class joined the Marine **Corps.**

The **corpse** was found lying in shallow water under the 27th Street Bridge.

Could Have, Should Have, Would Have, *not* Could Of, Should Of, Would Of

Journalists who write **could of** instead of **could have** are confused by the contraction **could've.** The pronunciation of **could've** sounds like **could of,** but the second word is **have.**

The same reasoning applies to **should have,** *not* **should of; may have,** *not* **may of; might have,** *not* **might of;** and **must have,** *not* **must of.**

Council, Counsel

A **council** is a group of people elected or appointed to serve in a legislative or an administrative capacity.

Counsel means to advise. Lawyers and religious leaders, among others, engage in such activity.

"If we don't receive approval from the City **Council** ***[legislative body],*** our project is dead," the fire chief said.

"Calm, rational **counsel** ***[advice]*** is needed during this time of crisis," the president said.

Credibility, Credulity

Credibility means believability.

Credulity means to be gullible, to believe without adequate evidence, to be unsuspecting.

A journalist's **credibility (believability)** is essential.

"Journalists must be skeptical," the veteran editor cautioned the student reporters, "or they will inevitably be the victims of their own **credulity** ***[gullibility]."*** (Mass communicators may prefer a more familiar word like gullibility.)

Credible, Creditable

Credible means reliable, capable or worthy of belief.

Creditable means praiseworthy.

If a reporter lacks a **credible** ***(reliable)*** source, the story will not be believable.

"The search committee did a **creditable** ***[praiseworthy]*** job," the university president said.

Currently, Now, Presently

Journalists frequently use **currently** and **now** unnecessarily, and **presently** inappropriately.

To write that James N. Plunkett is mayor of Clairborne is sufficient. There is no need to insert **now** or **currently** before ***mayor*** unless there is some disagreement about who is mayor.

Because **presently** can mean **soon** or **after a while,** to write that Plunkett is **presently** mayor could be misleading.

(Avoid) James N. Plunkett is **now/currently/presently** mayor.

(Use) James N. Plunkett is mayor.

Cynic, Skeptic

A **cynic** is a person who doubts or denies the goodness of human nature and does so in a sarcastic manner.

A **skeptic** is a person who has a doubting, questioning attitude and wants to be shown proof.

Skepticism in a journalist is considered an admirable quality; **cynicism** is not. Journalists are supposed to doubt and question rather than to accept information at its face value. But journalists are not supposed to let their personal feelings or beliefs prejudice them against the information or the people from whom it comes.

Cynics ***(people who doubt the goodness of human nature)*** include in their ranks those who say they never vote "because all politicians are crooks."

When the president told a gathering at the National Press Club that he would balance the budget before his term ended, he knew he was talking to **skeptics** ***(people with a doubting, questioning nature).*** Everyone immediately asked for proof.

Damage, Damages

Damage is the harm done.

Damages is the word used to describe the amount of financial loss (or gain in the case of a court award) involved in repairing or compensating for the harm.

The **damage** ***(harm)*** from the hurricane is extensive.

The plaintiff was awarded $150,000 in **damages** ***(financial assessment).***

Damage, Demolish, Destroy

Use **damage** when repairs can undo the harm caused by a fire, an automobile accident and so forth.

Use **demolish** and **destroy** when the harm is beyond repair.

Remember that **demolish** indicates destruction undertaken for reasons that are usually positive such as demolishing a building to make room for a children's playground. **Destroy,** however, should be used to indicate negative destruction such as floods, fires, hurricanes, war, riots and pestilence.

The **damage** ***(can be repaired)*** consisted of three cracked windows and a broken doorknob.

The 15-story building was **demolished** ***(razed)*** to make room for a hospital.

The three-alarm fire **destroyed** ***(cannot be repaired)*** the warehouse.

Also remember that **destroy** and **demolish** mean ***totally*** and ***completely;*** therefore, to write or broadcast that something was **completely destroyed** or **totally demolished** is redundant. Something can be **almost destroyed,** but a better expression would be **severely damaged.**

Desert, Deserts, Dessert

Can you imagine eating a bowl of chocolate-flavored **desert?** Or riding a camel across a sandy **dessert?** Stranger things have resulted from the mishandling of words almost identical in spelling but extremely different in meaning.

Just remember that you eat the one with **two** ***s's*** and you get thirsty in the one with **one** ***s.***

Remember also that when the accent is on the second syllable in **desert,** the word means to leave permanently without permission: The solder **deserted** his unit before the expected battle.

Deserts, which also is accented on the second syllable, means to deserve either positively as in a reward or negatively as in a punishment: When the writer received the Nobel Prize, she received her just **deserts.** When the student was disqualified for cheating on an examination, he received his just **deserts.**

Device, Devise

Device is a noun meaning a mechanical apparatus, a scheme or a design.

Devise is **verb** meaning to plan or to work out by thinking.

Time-saving **devices** ***(noun subject)*** are always of interest to journalists rushing to meet deadlines.

The photographers tried to **devise** ***(verb)*** a way to protect their cameras during a hailstorm.

Diagnosis, Prognosis

A **diagnosis** is the decision reached following a medical examination of the symptoms of a patient's illness.

A **prognosis** is the proposed treatment for a diagnosed illness and a prediction of the likely outcome.

Dr. Pamela S. Ridenour's **diagnosis** is acute appendicitis.

Her **prognosis** is a complete recovery.

Differ From, Differ With

Differ from means to be different.

Differ with means to disagree.

American spellings **differ from** ***(are unlike)*** English spellings in such words as honor/honour, center/centre, and civilization/civilisation.

The two candidates **differ with** ***(disagree)*** each other on such issues as gun control, sales taxes and legal gambling.

Different From, Different Than

Although some authorities plead for the use of **different *than*** in one or two circumstances, journalists generally use **different *from*** exclusively.

The minister's proposal offered solutions **different from** ***(not than)*** those made earlier.

"Our state university system is not much **different from** ***[not than]*** yours," the representative from California told his counterpart from Wisconsin.

Discomfit, Discomfort

Discomfit means to confuse, to defeat completely, to frustrate.

Discomfort is the opposite of comfort, meaning to feel disturbed, hardship, mild pain.

The senator was **discomfited** by his continuing drop in the polls. (Mass communicators may want to use more familiar words like confused and defeated.)

The Minnesota Viking's wide receiver found his broken arm **discomforting** ***(mildly painful),*** but he was even more **discomfited** ***(frustrated)*** by having to miss playing in the championship game.

Discover, Invent

Discover means to find or to reveal something that already exists.

Invent means to create, design or cause something new.

After gold was **discovered** ***(found)*** in California, many people rushed there to seek their fortune.

R.J. Gatling **invented** ***(created)*** a machine gun that made his name famous in the 19th century.

Discreet, Discrete

Discreet means being tactful in relationships with others and being especially careful or confidential about what is revealed.

Discrete means separate, distinct, not attached.

The marriage counselor told the couple they should be **discreet** ***(tactful, not reveal confidential information)*** when discussing their problems with family members or friends.

Publications that feature celebrities frequently contain articles about an actress who claims to have had several **discrete** ***(distinct, separate)*** lives.

Disinterested, Uninterested

Disinterested describes a person who is impartial (unbiased, has not taken sides or made a choice).

Uninterested describes a person who is not interested, bored.

"A jury should be composed of **disinterested** ***[impartial]*** individuals," the judge explained to visiting school children.

The judge said he was pleased that none of the students appeared to be **uninterested** ***(not interested)*** during the three-hour court session.

Disprove, Dispute

Disprove means to prove to be false or in error.

Dispute means to oppose, doubt or question the truth of.

City Council member Tonya M. Jeffries **disputed** ***(questioned the truth of)*** Mayor Jackson P. Keel's statement.

City Council member Tonya M. Jeffries **disproved** ***(successfully demonstrated the falsity of)*** Mayor Jackson P. Keel's statement.

Except when writing editorials and other opinion articles, journalists should avoid using **disproved** unless they attribute it to a source. For a journalist to write that ***Jeffries disproved Keel's statement*** requires an editorial **judgment.** (For a source to say **disprove** requires only an **opinion.**)

For a journalist to write that ***Aaron disputed the mayor's statement*** requires only that the journalist be certain there was a disagreement. The journalist then would be making no judgment about who proved or disproved anything.

The same advice applies to **rebut** ***(dispute)*** and **refute** ***(disprove).***

Dissociate, *not* Disassociate

Disassociate may seem the logical development from **associate,** but the preferred word is **dissociate** when describing what people do when they remove themselves from an affiliation.

When Johnson discovered that the organization discriminated against women in its membership requirements, he **dissociated** ***(not disassociated)*** himself from it.

Dived, Dove

Use **dived** exclusively for the past tense of **dive.**

After winning the Olympic championship, Simpkins said she had **dived** ***(not dove)*** competitively for the last time.

Doctor—*a title, not a profession*

Avoid writing or broadcasting that a person is a **doctor.** Refer instead to that person's profession (physician, minister, dentist, professor and so forth).

Because most readers and listeners will think of a member of the medical profession when **doctor** is used, clarification is required when the story is about people who have earned doctoral degrees in other disciplines.

Remember that **doctor** ***is a title,*** not a description of a profession. Therefore, avoid using **doctor** generically. Use physician, minister, professor, chemist, dentist and other more specific descriptions.

She has been a **physician** ***(not a doctor)*** for five years.

Robert T. Fuqua, a **neurosurgeon** ***(not a doctor),*** was named the Kiwanis Club's "Outstanding Young Professional of the Year."

Dr. Cynthia K. Wheelwright, **professor** ***(not doctor)*** of English at Acme College, is a former Rhodes Scholar.

Doubtful, Dubious

To be **doubtful** is to be uncertain or unclear, or to think that more evidence or proof is needed.

To be **dubious** means much the same but often stresses the questionable or suspicious elements.

"I am **doubtful** ***[uncertain]*** that the levy will pass this year," the superintendent of schools said.

"I can't support the candidacy of someone with such a **dubious** ***[questionable]*** reputation," the leader of the majority party said.

Dragged, *not* Drug

Use **dragged** as the past tense of **drag** to mean to pull along with considerable effort.

Use **drug** in the present tense to refer to a medicine or some other chemical substance.

The fullback **dragged** ***(pulled along)*** the linebacker 10 yards into the end zone. *Do not used* ***drug*** *to mean to pull along.*

The physician will **drug** ***(administer a chemical substance)*** her patient to alleviate his pain. *Please note that* ***drug*** *is more commonly used as a noun: The physician will prescribe a* ***drug*** *to alleviate the patient's pain.*

Dreamed, *not* Dreamt

Use **dreamed** exclusively for the past tense of **dream**.

"Winning $5 million in the lottery is something I've **dreamed** ***[not dreamt]*** of but never thought would happen," she said as she accepted her first of 20 annual checks.

Dual, Duel

Dual means composed of two.

Duel refers to a contest or a battle between two persons.

Senator McElhinny's bill has a **dual** ***(two)*** purpose: to establish a center for senior citizens in every county and to provide a method of funding them.

Alexander Hamilton was killed by Aaron Burr in one of the most famous **duels** ***(battles between two persons)*** in American history.

Dumb, Ignorant, Stupid

In informal conversations, many people use these words interchangeably to mean unintelligent, inappropriate, embarrassing, silly and many other things. Writers and broadcasters should be more precise.

Dumb refers to people who cannot or will not speak. (Its unfortunate use as a synonym for **stupid** is extremely common but should be avoided by mass communicators.)

Ignorant refers to being unaware or having a lack of knowledge. It should not be used as a synonym for **stupid** because even the most knowledgeable scholars are ignorant about some topics outside their fields of study.

Stupid refers to people who lack normal intelligence or understanding. It also refers to foolish or irrational thoughts or behavior.

When she heard her name called as the winner of the scholarship, the recipient was speechless. A few minutes later, she said, "I was so surprised by the announcement that I was struck **dumb** ***[incapable of speech]***."

"How could I be so **ignorant** ***[lacking in knowledge]***?" the contestant asked after missing the bonus question.

"Calling a person **stupid** ***[lacking normal intelligence or understanding]*** is unkind and thoughtless," the elementary school teacher cautioned his students.

Dyeing, Dying

Dyeing is the process of coloring a variety of materials.

Dying is the ending of life.

Each *or* Every, *not* Each and Every

A journalist may refer to **each** news source or to **every** news source but **not to each and every** news source. To use both **each** and **every** is redundant.

Senator Cline said he wants to assure **each/every** ***(not each and every)*** voter that he will keep his campaign promises.

Each Other, One Another

Use **each other** when two people, places or things are involved.

Use **one another** when three or more are involved.

Gov. Mark E. Nicely said he and Lt. Gov. Beverly J. Carson have known **each other** ***(two of them)*** for more than 20 years.

Gov. Mark E. Nicely said he, Lt. Gov. Beverly J. Carson and their seven office staff members have been working with **one another** ***(three or more)*** for five years.

Either **each other** or **one another** may be used if the number is infinite:

"As Christians we must do all we can to encourage **each other/one another,**" the Rev. Charles F. Easterly said.

As a rule, however, **one another** should be used for three or more.

Ecology, Environment

Ecology and **environment** are not synonymous; therefore, they are not interchangeable.

Ecology is the branch of biology concerning the relationship between living organisms and their environment.

Environment refers to surroundings or being surrounded. Scientifically, it refers to all the conditions influencing the development of organisms.

After years of abusing the **environment** ***(surroundings),*** people throughout the world are becoming concerned about the effects of harmful industrial and manufacturing practices on the **ecology** ***(the relationship between living organisms and their environment).***

Elder, Older

Both **elder** and **older** may be used to refer to people, but only **older** may be used to refer to things. Many people use **older** exclusively when referring to age or time. (**Elder**, of course, also is the term used to refer to a church leader.)

The president's **elder/older brother** ***(either is correct)*** is writing a book about the family's early years.

Emerge, Immerge

Emerge means to rise or to develop from obscurity or confinement.

Immerge means to plunge into or to disappear into.

Pendleton **emerged** from the ranks of the also-rans to become a serious candidate for Congress.

After losing the election, Pendleton **immerged** quickly back into the ranks of the obscure.

Emigrate, Immigrate

To **emigrate** is to leave a country to establish permanent residence in another.

To **immigrate** is to enter a country to establish permanent residence after having resided in another country.

To distinguish correctly between the two words, remember that the one that starts with an ***e*** means to ***exit*** and the one that starts with an ***i*** means to come ***into.***

Stephen T. Morrison, his wife Rebecca and their three children **emigrated** from New Zealand ***(left New Zealand to establish permanent residence in another country).***

The number of people who **immigrate** illegally into the United States ***(enter the U.S. to establish permanent residence)*** each year is causing some concern among members of Congress.

Eminent, Imminent

Eminent means prominent.

Imminent refers to something immediately threatening.

David Brinkley is an **eminent** figure in the history of broadcast journalism.

The residents of Florida, Georgia and South Carolina are being warned that the arrival of the hurricane is **imminent.**

Enormity, Enormous

Even some nationally prominent journalists have been known to confuse **enormity** with **enormous**. When journalists refer to a crime by describing the **enormity** of the act ***(that it was wicked or heinous),*** they use the word correctly. But when they refer to the **enormity** ***(meaning size or extent)*** of an earthquake or some other natural disaster, they use the word inappropriately. The word they want is **enormous** ***(huge or vast).***

(Inappropriate) "The **enormity** ***[size, extent]*** of the hurricane is only now being determined," the network correspondent reported.

(Appropriate) "The **enormity** ***[wickedness, heinousness]*** of the crime committed by the terrorists cannot be overstated," the president said.

Ensure, Insure

Use **ensure** when the meaning is to guarantee or to make certain.

Use **insure** when the meaning is to purchase protection for life, health or property.

The best camera equipment available cannot **ensure** ***(guarantee)*** good pictures if the photographer lacks skill.

The publisher **insured** ***(purchased protection for)*** her company against financially ruinous libel suits.

Enthusiastic, *not* Enthused

Use **enthusiastic** ***(inspired, intensely interested)*** exclusively. Do not write or broadcast that the director of the Center for the Arts is **enthused** about the opening of the new building. Write or say instead that he is **enthusiastic.** Better still, don't use either word; let sources' remarks about the particulars of the opening demonstrate their **enthusiasm.**

(Incorrect) The director said he is **enthused.**

(Better) The director said he is **enthusiastic.**

(Best) The director of the Center for the Arts said he thinks the new building is "the answer to every dream art lovers in the city have ever had."

Envelop, Envelope

Envelop means to surround or to cover completely.

Envelope refers to a paper wrapper or a covering for a letter.

Mud from the collapsing hillside **enveloped** ***(surrounded or covered)*** farmland for five miles in all directions.

The **envelope** ***(paper wrapping)*** was torn, but the letter was not damaged.

Estimate, Opinion

Estimate refers to calculating without mathematical certainty.

Opinion refers to an unproved conclusion that seems real or believable to its holder.

The contractor's **estimate** ***(calculation)*** of the project's completion date proved to be quite accurate.

"In my **opinion** ***[unproved conclusion],*** legislation approving riverboat gambling would do the community more harm than good," the mayor said.

Everybody, Every Body

Use **everybody** as a single word when the reference is to several or many people but not to any one of them in particular.

Use **every body** as two words when the reference is to a specific body such as a corpse, a body of water, a corporate body and so forth. If you can substitute ***each*** for **every,** use **every body** as two words.

> **Everybody** ***(no one person in particular)*** met the deadline, the editor noted.
>
> **Every body** ***(emphasis is on each single body and not all the bodies collectively)*** found after the flood was taken to the temporary morgue in the high school gymnasium.

Everyday, Every Day

Everyday as a single word is an **adjective** used to refer to days in general without emphasizing any specific day.

Every day used as two words includes an **adjective** ***(every)*** and a **noun** ***(day)*** and emphasizes the individual day. If you can substitute ***each*** for **every,** use **every day** as two words.

> Winning an advertising director's praise is not an **everyday** experience. **(Everyday** ***is used as an*** **adjective** ***to modify the noun*** **experience** ***and does not refer to any specific day.)***
>
> "**Every day** provides a new experience in the public relations business," the retiring vice president said. ***(*****Every** ***is used as an*** **adjective** ***to modify the*** **noun subject day** ***and the emphasis is on each specific day.)***

Everyone, Every One

Everyone, like **anyone, anybody** and **everybody,** is used as one word when the reference is to several or many people but not to any one of them in particular.

Every one is used as two words when referring to an individual.

> "I want to interview **everyone** ***[no one in particular]*** who graduated in the top 10 percent of the class," the personnel director said.
>
> "**Every one** of you ***[emphasis is on the individual]*** has a responsibility to seek and publish or broadcast the truth," the commencement speaker told the graduating class of journalists.

Every Place, *not* Everyplace

Use **every place** exclusively as two words.

Every place she went, the Oscar-winning actress encountered people who wanted her to sign autographs.

Evoke, Invoke

Evoke means to cause something to appear, such as a memory.

Invoke means to call on in prayer or to declare to be in effect.

Watching his daughter being sworn in as a police officer **evoked** ***(caused to come forth)*** the captain's memories of his days at the academy.

The minister **invoked** ***(called on in prayer)*** God's help as firefighters attempted to save residents of the burning apartment building.

The journalist **invoked** ***(declared to be in effect)*** the state's shield law when the prosecutor demanded she reveal the identity of her confidential source.

Expect, Suppose, Suspect

Expect implies confidence or anticipation that something will happen.

Suppose means to imagine, to believe or to presume to be real or true without proof.

Suspect means to distrust or to presume guilty, often with little or no evidence to support the suspicion.

"I **expect** ***[am confident there will be]*** a close vote in the presidential race," the incumbent's campaign manager said.

"I **suspected** ***[presumed his guilt]*** he was the murderer at least three months before the police had enough evidence to arrest him," the prosecuting attorney said in a press conference following the trial.

"I **suppose** ***[presume to be true]*** that you **expect** ***[are confident]*** to receive a political appointment for helping me in my campaign?" the candidate remarked. "I've **suspected** ***[presumed in a negative sense]*** for some time that you had ulterior motives for becoming involved in politics."

Do not use **suspect** in examples like the following:

"Considering the talent you have, I **expected** ***[not suspected]*** that your design would win the advertising competition," the agency president said.

The weather forecaster said she **expects** ***(not suspects)*** some severe hailstorms will strike the area today even though experts at the National Weather Service disagree.

Faculty *as a singular*, Faculty *as a plural*

Save yourself from awkwardness by using **faculty** only as a collective singular:

The **faculty is** ***(collective singular)*** delighted with the 12 percent salary increase, according to the president of the Faculty Senate.

You could use **faculty** as a plural if the reference is to the teachers individually rather than collectively:

The f**aculty are** ***(plural)*** meeting with students throughout the campus.

To many readers and listeners, **faculty** as a **plural** seems awkward. This awkwardness is easily avoided by adding **members** after faculty or by substituting **professors** or **teachers.**

Famous, Infamous, Notorious

Famous means to be well known for favorable reasons.

Infamous and **notorious** mean to be well known for unfavorable reasons.

She became **famous** ***(for favorable reasons)*** as a character actress in movies made in the 1960s.

Without question, Hitler will be remembered as one of the most **infamous/notorious** ***(for unfavorable reasons)*** figures in history.

Farther, Further

Use **f*a*rther** to refer to distance.

Use **f*u*rther** to refer to degree or extent.

After completing half of his statewide walking campaign for Congress, the 55-year-old candidate said he couldn't go one mile **farther** ***(distance)*** without rest.

However, he said that at 7 a.m. he would speak **further** ***(degree, extent)*** with reporters about the resumption of his trip.

Faze, Phase

Faze means to disturb or to bother.

Phase refers to something that occurs in a series of stages or steps.

After 25 years of working in noisy newsrooms, Maurice N. Johnston claims that being in the same room with his five active grandchildren doesn't **faze** ***(disturb)*** him.

After the new administration took control of the state capitol, the governor kept his campaign promise by stopping construction of the $5 million office complex even though work had progressed to the third of five proposed **phases** ***(stages or steps).***

Fewer, Less

See **More Than, Less Than,** page 290.

Figuratively, Literally

Figuratively means symbolically.

Literally means actually or exactly.

The gubernatorial candidate apologized by explaining that he was speaking **figuratively** ***(symbolically)*** when he said his opponent had "the brain of a gnat."

However, the candidate said he meant what he said when he declared his opponent's economic plans to be "**literally** ***[actually]*** disastrous for the people of the state."

Fiscal, Physical

When writing about budgets for the first time, some journalists have been known to refer to the **physical** year. **Fiscal** is the word they want to use when referring to the financial account for a 12-month period.

The budget for the **fiscal** ***(not physical)*** year has been reduced by $5 million.

Flack, Flak

Journalists and their sources sometimes use **flack** instead of **flak** to mean ***bombarded with criticism.*** **Flack** is a slang word used disparagingly to refer to a press agent or to the publicity from a press agent.

Offended by the criticism from his opponent, the candidate for the House of Delegates described the remarks as "distortions and lies dreamed up by **flacks** ***[press agents].***"

"Because I've taken about all of the **flak** ***[bombardment of criticism]*** that I can stand, I'll just hire me some **flacks** of my own and strike back," the candidate vowed.

Flair, Flare

Flair refers to talent or ability.

Flare refers to a sudden but brief outburst of flame, emotion or trouble.

Advertising agency directors want to hire writers who have a **flair** ***(talent, ability)*** for developing expressions that will become popular with the public.

Employees of public relations firms serving political candidates are constantly watching for problems that inevitably **flare** up ***(burst out)*** during a campaign.

Flammable, Inflammable, Nonflammable

Both **flammable** and **inflammable** mean something that will burn easily and quickly.

Nonflammable means something that will not burn.

Because some readers and listeners think ***in*flammable** means ***non*flammable,** journalists should take care to make certain they will not be misunderstood. They can avoid the possibility of confusion by eliminating **inflammable** and using just **flammable** and **nonflammable.**

Gasoline is **flammable** ***(capable of burning, bursting into flame).***

Sand is **nonflammable** ***(incapable of burning).***

Flaunt, Flout

Flaunt means ostentatious display, showy.

Flout means to express scorn for, to scoff.

Flout is not a word a reader will see every day in the newspaper or hear frequently on radio or television. Because it is unusual, it sometimes is misused for **flaunt.** The following examples should eliminate the confusion.

The flamboyant entertainer **flaunted** ***(ostentatiously displayed)*** his wealth by wearing diamond rings on three fingers of each hand and draping several thick gold chains around his neck.

Many drivers **flout** ***(show their contempt for)*** the speed limit by driving too fast.

Flier, Flyer

The *Associated Press Stylebook* makes this distinction:

Use **flier** to refer to an aviator or a handbill.

Use **flyer** as the proper name of some trains and buses.

Flounder, Founder

Flounder means to flail or to struggle with stumbling or plunging movements.

Founder means to fail, to go lame or to sink down. Of course, founder also refers to the person or the organization that establishes something, such as a new school, a sports team or a church.

The researcher **floundered** ***(struggled helplessly)*** in the flood of data contributed by scientists throughout the world.

The publisher's plans for a new building **foundered** ***(collapsed)*** when the expected funding was withdrawn.

Forbear, Forebear

Forbear means to refrain from, to hold back.

Forebear refers to an ancestor.

Journalists usually **forbear** ***(refrain from)*** using words like **forbear,** preferring more commonly used words like *abstain from* or *keep from.*

Forebear is not commonly used either because *ancestor* is a more familiar word.

Forego, Forgo

Forego means to go before, to precede.

Forgo means to give up, to refrain.

The **foregoing** ***(preceding)*** guest speaker was so boring that the students sighed with relief when he finished.

Gov. Adrian E. Leffingwell said he would **forgo** ***(give up, refrain from)*** seeking another term.

Foreword, Forward

Foreword refers to introductory remarks preceding the text in a book.

Forward means moving toward a point ahead, eager to send or advance.

By reading the **foreword** ***(introductory remarks)***, readers can enhance their understanding of the book.

The candidate's campaign manager said she looks **forward** ***(eagerly)*** to the election.

After the wreckage was cleared from the highway, the police officer directed drivers to move **forward** ***(ahead).***

While the sports editor was on vacation, he had his staff **forward** ***(send)*** his mail to him.

The new chairman of the board said he hopes to move the company's profits **forward** ***(to advance them).***

Formally, Formerly

Formally means in a manner established through customs or rules.

Formerly means previously.

Winners will dress **formally** ***(according to custom)*** for the journalism awards ceremony.

She **formerly** ***(previously)*** was program director for WKWW-TV.

Former Student, *not* Former Graduate

The person who placed a sign of welcome in front of city hall meant well. "Welcome **former** FHS **graduates**," the message read. What was meant, of course, was "Welcome, **former** FHS **students**" or "Welcome FHS graduates" or "Welcome FHS Alumni."

A person's student status changes eventually, but a graduate remains a graduate forever.

The senator is a **graduate** of Acme University. He **formerly** was a student at Washington High School.

Fortunate, *not* Fortuitous

Mass communicators rarely, if ever, use **fortuitous,** and that is good judgment because it not only sounds pretentious but also is thought by many to be synonymous with **fortunate** ***(unexpected luck).*** It isn't. **Fortuitous** refers to something happening accidentally or by chance.

A **fortuitous** circumstance led to Ida Mae's hiring at The *New York Times.* She saved the publisher's daughter from drowning.

Forward, *not* Forwards

Use **forward** exclusively.

When the school bus got stuck in the snow, the driver rocked it **forward** ***(not forwards)*** and backward several times until he got it back onto the asphalt surface.

Funny *(humorous)*, Strange *(odd, unusual)*

Although both **funny** and **strange** have several meanings, journalists should not interchange the two referred to below.

Funny refers to something that causes laughter or amusement.

Strange refers to something odd or unusual.

Humorists like to write material that is **funny** ***(causes laughter).***

Just before suffering a fatal heart attack, the senator complained that he felt **strange** ***(you certainly would not want to use* funny *in this context).***

Gantlet, Gauntlet

Gantlet means a severe test or an ordeal (not necessarily a flogging while running between two rows of enemies as in olden days).

Gauntlet has come to mean to issue a challenge or to accept a challenge (not necessarily to a physical fight as was done in olden days).

The angry parent threw down the **gauntlet** ***(issued/presented a challenge)*** when he dared the Board of Education members to debate those opposing the teaching of sex education in the public school.

When the board members refused to pick up the **gauntlet** ***(accept the challenge),*** they had to run a **gantlet** of jeers and insults as they squeezed their way down the aisle and out the door.

Garnish, Garnishee

Garnish means to decorate, or to provide something that adds flavor.

Garnishee means to legally attach the wages or property of a person to satisfy a debt.

The cook **garnished** ***(decorated)*** the potato salad with paprika.

The mayor was embarrassed when news of his wages being **garnisheed** ***(legally attached)*** was published.

Gentlemen, Ladies *versus* Men, Women

Whether a person is a **man** or a **woman** can be established as fact; whether a man is a **gentleman** or a woman is a **lady** is a matter of opinion. Journalists are safe and accurate in referring to individuals as either men or women, but they must be more prudent in describing people as gentlemen and ladies.

Every president of the United States has been a **man.** ***(That is a fact. Whether each was a gentleman is a matter of opinion.)***

The president said, "I respect the right of every **lady** and **gentleman** in the Congress to disagree with me." (The president is expressing his opinion—or showing his courtesy—by calling each member of Congress a lady or a gentleman. That's all right for a source to say, but for journalists to express the same opinion would be editorializing.)

Good, Well

As a rule, **good** is used as an *adjective* and **well** as an *adverb.*

"He is a **good** baseball player for a rookie," Manager Chuck Barkley said. ***(The adjective* good *modifies the predicate noun* player.)**

"He certainly is **good,**" the batting coach agreed. ***(The predicate adjective* good *modifies the pronoun subject* he.)**

"He plays defense as **well** as any first-year player I've ever seen," the team owner said. ***(The adverb* well *modifies the verb* plays *and tells how he plays.)***

"He runs **well**, too," the owner said. ***(The adverb* well *modifies the verb* runs *and tells how he runs.)***

Confusion in using **good** and **well** usually centers on the question of which to use when referring to a person's health. "I feel **good**" and "I am **well**" are both acceptable. Remember that when **well** is used to refer to someone's health, it serves as an ***adjective,*** not as an ***adverb.*** In the sentence "I am **well,**" **well** modifies the subject **I. I** is a ***pronoun,*** and the only part of speech that can modify pronouns is an ***adjective;*** therefore, in this example, **well** must function as an ***adjective.***

Gorilla, Guerrilla

A **gorilla** is an animal.

A **guerrilla** is a member of a small group of fighters whose tactics emphasize surprise attacks that harasss the enemy.

Graduated, Graduated From

Students **graduate** ***from*** or **are graduated** ***from*** high school or college. They do not **graduate** ***high school*** or **graduate** ***college.***

When the guest speaker said she **graduated** ***high school*** in 1975, several of the students whispered to one another that she should have said she **graduated** ***from high school*** in 1975 or that she **was graduated** ***from high school*** in 1975.

Guarantee, Guaranty

A **guarantee** is a promise that something of a defined quality will work properly for a specified time.

A **guaranty** is a promise or a warrant given as security that another's obligation will be met.

Hangar, Hanger

A **hangar** is a structure in which airplanes are kept.

A **hanger** is a device on which clothes are hung.

Hanged, Hung

The present tense **hang** presents no problem. A person may **hang** almost anything. The difficulty arises in choosing between the past tense **hanged** ***(executed)*** and **hung** ***(placed)***. The solution is to use **hanged** to refer to executions and **hung** for everything else.

The governor refused a last-minute appeal, and the criminal was **hanged** ***(not hung)*** at 6 a.m.

The paintings were **hung** ***(not hanged)*** carefully on the walls of the gallery.

Hardly, Can Hardly, *not* Not Hardly, Can't Hardly

Not hardly and **can't hardly** are double negatives. Use **hardly** and **can hardly.**

Kingston said he is **hardly** ***(not not hardly)*** able to pay his office staff following reductions in the city budget.

Since becoming a publisher, McDonald said she **can hardly** ***(not can't hardly)*** find time to write editorials.

Healthful, Healthy

Healthful refers to something (food, exercise, rest) that promotes good health.

Healthy refers to being in good physical and mental health.

The president jogs because he believes regular exercise is **healthful** ***(promotes good health).***

Two weeks after being treated for problems with his allergies, the president resumed jogging and said he is feeling **healthy** ***(in a state of good health).***

Height, *not* Heighth

If you can have **wid*th*,** why not **heigh*th*?** Well, there is no such word even though many people insist on using it instead of the correct **heigh*t*.** Watch both the spelling and the pronunciation.

When college and professional basketball coaches recruit players, one of their most important criteria is **height *(not heighth).***

Historic, Historical

Historic refers to something well known or significant in history.

Historical means pertaining to or based on history, not legend or fiction.

The creation of the Bill of Rights is **historic *(significant in history).***

The debate over the wording of the First Amendment is part of the **historical *(based on fact)*** record.

That George Washington was the first president of the United States is **historical** fact ***(is based on fact, not legend or fiction).***

The claim that George Washington confessed to chopping down a cherry tree is **legend *(not based on historical fact).***

History, *not* Past History

An interviewer on a national radio program asked actress Sally Field about her ***past* history** in the theater. Fortunately, he didn't also ask about her ***future* hopes.** Both **past** and **future** in these instances not only are unnecessary but also are rather silly. The same thinking also applies to ***past* experience, *prior* experience** and ***previous* experience.** All history and experience are in the past, and all hopes are in the future.

The subject's **history *(not past history)*** is important to a reporter doing an investigative story.

The magazine editor's **hopes *(not future hopes)*** were dashed when the publisher announced that his contract was not being renewed.

Hopefully, I Hope, It Is to Be Hoped

Hopefully, you will never use the word as it appears in this sentence. Do not use **hopefully** to mean **to hope.** It means full of **hope.**

One reasonably effective way to avoid the error is to refrain from starting a sentence with it. **Hopefully** is most often misused by people who begin sentences with it. Another way to avoid an error is to say **full of hope** to yourself every time you want to use **hopefully.** You will find out immediately whether the word works.

No guesswork is involved in using **hopefully** correctly—at the beginning of a sentence or anywhere else. Just decide whether you're trying to say **I hope/it is to be hoped** or **full of hope.**

(Incorrect) "**Hopefully,** we will win the election," the challenger said.

(Correct) "**I hope** we will win the election," the challenger said.

(Correct) She approached the election **hopefully.**

(Correct) **Hopefully,** the candidate turned on her television set to hear results of the election.

Identical With, *not* Identical To

Use **identical with** exclusively.

The reporter for The Associated Press wrote a lead almost **identical with** ***(not identical to)*** the one written by the representative from United Press International.

If, Whether

Use **if** as a ***conjunction*** to mean in case that, on condition that, or supposing that.

Use **whether** as a ***conjunction*** to introduce an indirect question (a statement that reveals a question but does not ask one).

If ***(in case that)*** the commissioners approve the request, five new fire trucks will be purchased and distributed to volunteer departments throughout the county.

One commissioner asked **whether** ***(to introduce an indirect question)*** the need was so great that all five of the requested purchases had to be made.

Imply, Infer

The one who gives the message (the speaker or the writer) **implies.**

The one who receives the message (the listener or the reader) **infers.**

"I ***[the speaker]*** am not **implying** that your motives are unjust," the judge said.

"I am sorry that you ***[the listener]*** **inferred** that I was."

In, Into, In To

Use **in** to indicate a location, to mean within or to be inside of.

Use **into** to indicate motion, to mean to advance from the outside toward the inside ***(within).***

Use **in to** as two words when **in** is used by itself as an ***adverb*** and **to** is used as an ***infinitive.***

The reporter was **in *(within, inside of)*** the courtroom when the judge declared a mistrial.

The reporter walked **into *(advanced from the outside toward the inside)*** the courtroom just moments before the verdict was announced.

"Get **into *[not in]*** the car without resisting arrest," the police officer cautioned the suspect.

"Let me **in to** hear the verdict," the reporter demanded. ***(*In *is being used by itself as an* adverb *and* to *is being used as an* infinitive.*)***

In Behalf Of, On Behalf Of

***In* behalf of** means for the benefit of.

***On* behalf of** means in place of.

The school's fund-raiser is **in behalf of *(for the benefit of)*** the band, whose members need new uniforms.

Speaking **on behalf of *(in place of)*** her client, the attorney entered a plea of not guilty.

Indefinite, Infinite

Indefinite means not precise, vague.

Infinite means without limits.

"The trial will require us to assign our best reporter to the courthouse for an **indefinite *[undetermined]*** period," the editor said.

"Developing our own energy resources is **infinitely *[without limits]*** preferable to depending on foreign countries to supply us," the senator from Louisiana said.

Ingenious, Ingenuous, Disingenuous

Ingenious refers to something cleverly inventive and is characteristic of genius.

Ingenuous means sincere, innocent, candid, naïve.

Disingenuous means insincere, lacking in frankness.

Many of the innovations in computer technology are **ingenious** ***(cleverly inventive).***

The director of the Acme Valley chapter of the Red Cross made an **ingenuous** ***(sincere)*** plea for donations following six days of flooding in the southern part of the state.

The candidate made a **disingenuous** ***(insincere)*** claim that his criticism of his opponent's personal life was "for the public good."

Mass communicators may want to be cautious about using **ingenuous,** which is rarely said by journalists and their sources, and **disingenuous,** which has gained some popularity recently, especially in a political context. Some of the synonyms listed above may promote clarity. Conversely, **ingenious** is commonly used and understood.

Inquire, *not* Enquire

Use **inquire** and **inquiry** exclusively when the meaning is to seek information.

The prosecutor told her assistant to have a team of investigators **inquire** ***(not enquire)*** about the possibility of election fraud.

The investigators made their **inquiries** ***(not enquiries)*** but discovered nothing.

Instead, Rather

Instead means in place of, in preference to.

Rather means extent or degree, or more willing.

McRay decided to major in public relations **instead of** ***(in place of, not rather than)*** biology.

The county commissioner said he is "**rather** ***[extent or degree]*** tired" of politics and will not seek re-election.

He said he would **rather** ***(more willingly)*** retire than serve another four-year term.

Inter, Intern

Inter means to bury.

Intern usually refers to a person such as a mass media or a medical student serving a period of professional training.

Although mistakes made in using these two words are rare, errors are particularly embarrassing because they usually are found in obituary announcements.

The body will be **interred** ***(not interned)*** in Forest View Cemetery, according to the obituary announcement.

Inter, Intra

Use **inter** to mean between or with each other.

Use **intra** to mean within or inside of.

Intercollegiate football consists of competition involving teams from different colleges and universities.

Intramural football consists of competition involving teams from within the same school.

Interesting, Intriguing

Interesting means to arouse curiosity or to excite attention; the opposite of boring.

Intriguing means to beguile, puzzle, cause to wonder.

Broadcasters hope their live interviews on television will be **interesting** ***(excite attention).***

Detectives consider obscure clues **intriguing** ***(puzzling, a cause to wonder).***

In Which, Where

Be careful not to fall into the careless habit of using **where** when the words **in which** would be more appropriate. Use **where** when you want to point out a direction or a location, and use **in which** when the reference is not to a direction or a location.

The governor read a speech **in which** ***(not where)*** he provided details of his platform.

The professor distributed an outline **in which** ***(not where)*** she listed course requirements and examination dates.

Journalists should be careful about getting themselves into situations **in which** ***(not where)*** they would have to reveal names of confidential sources or go to jail for contempt of court.

It's, Its

Embarrassing errors result from misuse of **it's** and **its,** and such mistakes occur frequently in all news media. Carelessness usually is to blame, but occasionally the cause is ignorance. That's why the error is so embarrassing.

Fortunately, the solution is simple. **It's** is a **contraction** for ***it is,*** and **its** ***(without the apostrophe)*** is a **possessive pronoun**. When confused about which to use, just say **it is** at the point where the word is to be placed in the sentence. Your ear will provide the answer.

"**It's** [*contraction for* **it is**] a small project, but **its** *[possessive pronoun]* worth to the company is immeasurable," the executive vice president said.

Jail, Penitentiary, Prison

A city or a county **jail** is where individuals are incarcerated during a trial or after being found guilty of committing a misdemeanor.

A state or a federal **penitentiary** or **prison** is where individuals are incarcerated after being found guilty of committing felonies.

The journalist was ordered to report to the county **jail** to be incarcerated for contempt of court.

Judge Markita A. Dodson sentenced the man convicted of armed robbery to 15 years in a federal **penitentiary/prison.**

Jury *as a singular,* Jury *as a plural*

The advice for **jury** is the same as that given previously for ***faculty***. Save yourself from awkwardness by using jury only as a collective singular:

The **jury is** ***(singular)*** deliberating.

Of course, you may use **jury** correctly as a plural if the reference is to members acting individually instead of as a unit:

The **jury are** ***(plural)*** walking to their seats.

To most readers and listeners, however, **jury as a plural seems awkward.** Such awkwardness is easily avoided by using **jurors** or **members of the jury** for the plural reference.

Last, Past

Writers and broadcasters sometimes mistakenly use **last** before a period of time (week, month, year) when they really mean **past. Last** should be used to refer to the ***final*** week, month or year, and **past** should be used to refer to the ***previous*** week, month or year.

During the **past** ***(not last)*** year, the president vetoed 22 bills. ***(The writer is referring to the year that just ended, not to the last year the person served as president.)***

"The **past** ***[not last]*** four years were the best of my life," the valedictorian told the graduating class. ***(The graduate is referring to the previous four years, not to the final four years of his life.)***

"Although I watched television coverage of the Olympics every night during the **past** ***[not last]*** week, my work schedule will keep me from seeing the competition next week."

"The **last** ***[not past]*** week of the Olympics is my favorite time to watch the games because that's when most of the final competitions are scheduled."

Later, Latter, Ladder

Later is the opposite of ***earlier.***

Latter is the opposite of ***former*** (or is the last person, place or thing referred to or listed).

Ladder has nothing to do with the other two except that spelling errors sometimes cause it to be misused for ***latter.***

The press conference started two hours **later** than scheduled.

"If I could choose between another term as governor or one as a U.S. senator, I'd take the **latter** ***[the last one listed],*** " he said.

Fire departments rarely have **ladders** ***(not latters)*** that can reach higher than the seventh floor of tall buildings.

Lay, Lie

How often do you hear someone say, "I think I'll **lay** down for a few minutes," or "I **laid** in one position for so long my whole body hurts"? The mistakes are common, and they result from a misunderstanding of the verbs **lie** and **lay.**

Explained simply, **lie** is intransitive and means **to recline** and **lay** is transitive and means ***to place.*** Put another way, a person may **lie** down (**recline**) for a nap, but if the room is cold, he had better ***lay (place)*** another blanket on the bed.

Mayor Mary L. Ritter said she always **lies** ***(not lays)*** on her office couch a few minutes and prepares herself mentally for each press conference.

She said she **lay** ***(not laid)*** there longer than she intended today and was five minutes late for the conference.

The mayor joked that she would have **lain** ***(not laid)*** there all afternoon had she known how tough the reporters' questions were going to be.

These three examples represent the principal parts of the verb **lie (lie, lay, lain),** meaning **to recline.** Compare them with the principal parts of the verb ***lay*** **(lay, laid, laid),** meaning ***to place.***

"Please **lay** ***[place]*** your notes on my desk," the advertising director instructed the copywriter.

"I **laid** ***[placed]*** them there more than an hour ago," the copywriter replied.

When he was far enough away to be certain the advertising director couldn't hear him, the copywriter told another employee, "I have **laid** ***[placed]*** my notes on that desk at the same time each day for three weeks. You'd think he'd catch on by now."

One additional significant point requires some explanation. Remember that once a person **lays** ***(places)*** an object somewhere, that object then **lies** ***(reclines, sits, rests)*** there.

The city architect said the bricks used to construct the new town hall should **lie** in place for a hundred years.

Lead, Led

Lead (when pronounced to rhyme with ***head***) is a ***noun*** or an ***adjective*** meaning a soft, heavy metal.

Lead (when pronounced to rhyme with ***deed***) is a ***verb,*** an ***adjective*** or a ***noun*** meaning to guide, show the way, be in command of.

Led is the past tense of the verb ***lead*** (rhymes with ***deed).***

Problems arise when writers substitute **lead** (rhymes with ***head***) for **led** as the past tense verb.

(Incorrect) She **lead** the congregation in singing. (***Led*** is the correct word to use in the past tense.)

(Correct) The speaker admitted that he had **led** ***(past tense of lead)*** a life of crime before committing himself to God three years ago.

(Correct) The rock is as heavy as **lead (noun meaning *a heavy metal*),** the geologist explained.

(Correct) The director will **lead** ***(present tense verb that means to guide and rhymes with*** **deed*)*** the choir through the special Christmas program of music.

Leave, Let

Use **leave** to mean to depart by choice or by request or command.

Use **let** to mean to permit.

To meet her deadline, the reporter had to **leave** ***(depart from)*** the meeting an hour before it ended.

The coach finally decided to **let** ***(permit)*** female sports reporters into the dressing room after games.

Do not substitute ***leave*** for **let** in such sentences as "**Let** ***[not leave]*** us try a little harder to get the interview," and "**Let** ***[not leave]*** us not forget to respect the privacy of our sources."

There is another use that is outdated and usually is restricted to old movies featuring monarchs and their courts. It refers to permission to depart:

"I will attend to that immediately, **by your leave *[with your permission to depart],*** Your Highness."

Legible, Readable; Illegible, Unreadable

Legible refers to the quality of printing or penmanship. If the quality is good, it is **legible;** if it is bad, it is **illegible.**

Readable refers to subject matter, meaning that it is interesting and easy to read. **Unreadable** means that the subject matter is not interesting or easy to read.

As a group, English teachers enjoy a good reputation for writing **legibly *(good quality).***

Successful feature writers have a proven ability to write **readable *(interesting, easy-to-read)*** material.

No group of professionals has a more notorious reputation for **illegible *(poor quality)*** penmanship than physicians.

Editors frequently reject articles because they are **unreadable *(uninteresting, difficult to understand).***

Lend, Loan

The simplest and easiest way to deal with **lend** and **loan** is to use **lend** as a ***verb*** and **loan** as a ***noun.***

You may **lend *(verb)*** money to someone, but what that person receives from you is a **loan *(noun).***

The Small Business Administration will **lend**/has **lent *(verb)*** money to eligible companies at a low interest rate.

The Water Resources Commission is seeking a $6.5 million **loan *(noun)*** from federal agencies.

Libel, Slander

Libel is a recorded ***(written, printed, pictured, tape-recorded)*** defamation.

Slander is an unrecorded ***(spoken)*** defamation.

The union president sued the newspaper for **libel *(printed defamation)*.**

Slander *(spoken defamation)* is difficult to prove because, unlike libel, there is no record of the allegedly defamatory words.

Linage, Lineage

Linage refers to the number of lines.

Lineage refers to ancestry and line of descendants.

Lighted, Lit

Light*ed* and lit are recognized by *The Associated Press Stylebook* as the past tense of **light.**

The candles were **lighted** ***(past tense).***

The candles were **lit** ***(past tense)***

Loath, Loathe

Loath, an adjective, means unwilling, reluctant.

Loathe, a verb, means to feel disgust or to detest.

The governor is **loath** ***(reluctant)*** to submit himself to regular press conferences.

The editor **loathes** ***(is disgusted by)*** sloppy reporting.

Looking Into, Investigating, Studying, Considering

When journalists write or broadcast that the district attorney is **looking into** the possibility of filing criminal charges, they could express themselves more precisely by substituting **considering, studying, investigating** or some other more appropriate word.

When the district attorney is searching for something in her briefcase, she is **looking into** her briefcase. This is the proper use of **looking into.**

The principal said she would **consider** ***(not look into)*** the student's appeal of a failing grade.

Loose, Lose

Spelling, not meaning, is the problem when choosing between these two words. **Loose** sometimes is mistakenly substituted for **lose.** The opposite, however, rarely happens.

Loose (rhymes with ***moose***) means the opposite of ***tight.***

Lose (rhymes with **shoes**) means the opposite of ***win*** or ***find.***

Armstrong University's undefeated basketball team didn't expect to **lose** ***(not loose)*** in the first round of the tournament.

Majority, Plurality

In an election, a **majority** refers to more than half of the votes.

A **plurality** is distinguished from a majority when three or more candidates compete in an election. **Plurality** refers to the excess number of votes that separates the leading vote-getter from the second-place finisher.

Johnson received 75 percent of the vote, a clear **majority** ***(more than half)*** over his opponent.

Kiser received 40 percent of the vote, a 2,522-vote **plurality** in the five-person race.

Mantel, Mantle

Journalists rarely need to use either of these words, but when they do, spelling can be a problem. The meanings are so different, no one would confuse one for the other.

Use **mantel** to refer to a shelf above a fireplace.

Use **mantle** to refer to a cloak (a loose, sleeveless garment worn over other clothing) or to something that cloaks or covers.

Your notes are on the **mantel** ***(shelf).***

A **mantle** ***(cloak or covering)*** of white covered the ground after the unexpected snowfall last night.

Marshal, Marshall

Marshal is an official (military, police, fire, parade).

Marshall is a person's name.

A field **marshal** ***(official)*** is the highest-ranking officer in the army of many countries.

Marshall University is named in honor of John **Marshall,** chief justice of the United States from 1801 to 1835.

Maxim, *not* Old Maxim

See **Adage, *not* Old Adage,** page 226.

May, Might

Both **may** and **might** can be used to express a possibility or a wish.

Use **may** for the ***present*** tense.

Use **might** for the ***past*** tense.

"You **may** ***[possibility]*** want to delay publishing the story until the information is confirmed by a second source."

"**May** ***[wish]*** all your stories be prize winners."

The source **said** ***(past tense)*** he **might** ***(possibility)*** have provided the information, but he couldn't remember.

The source **says** ***(present tense)*** he **may** ***(possibility)*** be willing to provide the information, but only off the record.

Use **might** instead of **may** to express a decreased possibility.

"You **might** ***[decreased possibility]*** complete the story before the last deadline, but I doubt it," the editor cautioned the reporter.

Maybe, May Be

Maybe, one word, is an ***adverb*** meaning perhaps.

May be, two words, is a ***verb*** meaning perhaps.

Maybe ***(adverb)*** you can become a feature writer after you've worked as a copy editor for a couple of years.

"A position **may be** ***[verb]*** available within six months," the advertising director said.

Media, Medium

Media is plural.

Medium is singular.

The news **media** ***(plural)*** are often accused of invading the private lives of public officials.

"The **medium** ***[singular]*** of television **has** become an indispensable part of American family life," the network president said in his address.

Memento, *not* Momento

Memento is a hint or a reminder of the past, or a souvenir. Some writers misspell the word as m***o***mento because that's the way they pronounce it. There is no m***o***mento, although there is a m***o***mentous, which means of great importance or consequence.

The photographer's office is filled with **mementos** ***(not momentos)*** collected during her 50-year career.

Miner, Minor

A **miner** is a person who excavates coal, gold, silver or some other valuable substance.

Minor refers to something lesser in size or in importance.

Coal **miners** may work underground or on the surface.

The accident was **minor,** causing no injuries and little damage to the three cars.

Moot, Mute

Moot refers to something debatable, doubtful or of little practical value.
Mute means silent, declining to speak or incapable of speech.

The argument over the size of the proposed airport became a **moot** *(of little practical value)* point when legislators defeated the proposal.

Even though reporters were shouting questions at him, the president was **mute** ***(declined to speak)*** as he walked to his plane.

More Than, Less Than; Over, Under; Fewer, Less

Use **more than** and **less than** to refer to a number or an amount.
Use **over** and **under** to refer to positions or places.

The largest band in Saturday's homecoming parade will have **more than** ***(not over)*** 200 members, according to its director.

Less than ***(not under)*** a ton of metal was used in the huge sculpture dedicated this morning in front of the library.

"Do not extend your hands **over** ***[position]*** your head during the tour, for the passageway becomes narrower as we reach the end of the tunnel," the guide warned.

"Your safety belt is tucked **under** ***[position]*** the arm rest of your seat," the guide said.

Use **less** for bulk or quantity (singular nouns) and **fewer** for things that are referred to individually and can be counted (plural nouns).

"We have **less** than a month's supply of newsprint ***[bulk or quantity]*** in stock," the pressroom supervisor reported to the publisher.

"I have **fewer** than a dozen reporters ***[individuals, can be counted]*** to cover a city of 250,000 people," the editor complained to the publisher.

Most *as a singular,* Most *as a plural*

See None as a ***singular***, None as a ***plural***, page 291.

Native, Resident

People are **natives** of the place where they were born.

People are **residents** of the city or town in which they currently reside. Of course, they are both **natives** and **residents** if they live in the city or town of their birth.

The chancellor is a **native** of Atlanta ***(she was born in Atlanta),*** but for the past 22 years she has been a **resident** ***(established a residence there)*** of San Francisco.

Nauseated, Nauseous, Nauseating

Nauseated means ***to feel*** sick or disgusted.

Nauseous and **nauseating** means ***causing*** sickness or disgust.

"I ate so much food at last night's awards dinner that I felt **nauseated** ***[sick]*** all morning."

The candidate's behavior at the political rally was **nauseating** ***(disgusting)***.

The fumes from the paint were **nauseous** ***(caused sickness).***

Do not write or say, however, that you **are nauseous.** That would mean you consider yourself sickening or disgusting.

(Incorrect) "I am **nauseous *[meaning I am sickening or disgusting].***"

(Correct) "I am **nauseated *[feel sick].***"

Naval, Navel

Naval refers to a navy and military ships.

Navel refers to a "bellybutton."

The United States has been a world **naval** ***(navy)*** power since the presidency of Theodore Roosevelt.

When she played the starring role in the television show "I Dream of Jeannie," Barbara Eden was not permitted to wear a costume that exposed her **navel** ***("bellybutton").***

None *as a singular,* None *as a plural*

The indefinite pronoun **none** can be either singular or plural depending on its **antecedent** ***(the noun or the pronoun to which it refers).***

When **none** is used to mean ***not one,*** it is **singular;** when used to mean ***not any,*** it is **plural.** When the potential for confusion is great, don't use **none.** Use ***not one*** **for singular** and ***not any*** **for plural.**

The first step in determining whether to use **none** as a singular or as a plural is to **determine what there is none of** (money? crops? outfielders? citizens? boots?). After locating the antecedent, the writer can decide quickly whether to use a singular or a plural verb.

If the **antecedent** means a ***quantity*** or an ***amount*** (such as liquid, fighting, cement, flour, sand, patriotism), the verb should be **singular** because no one would expect a reader or a listener to consider each particle or element separately.

> **None** of the **flour** ***(the singular noun to which*** **none** ***refers)*** is ***(singular verb)*** worth saving.
>
> **None** of the **cement** ***(the singular noun to which*** **none** ***refers)*** was ***(singular verb)*** of sufficient quality to meet government standards.

If the writer intends **none** to mean ***several*** or ***a number that can be counted*** (such as journalists, leaders, oceans, desks), the verb should be **plural.**

> **None** of the **leaders** ***(the plural noun to which*** **none** ***refers)*** are ***(plural verb)*** available to meet with members of the press.
>
> **None** of the **oceans** ***(the plural noun to which*** **none** ***refers)*** are ***(plural verb)*** safe from pollution.

The rules for **none** also apply to its fellow indefinite pronouns **all, any, some, most** and **such.**

(a) Number, *(the)* Number

Number takes a ***plural verb*** when preceded by the article **a.**
Number takes a ***singular verb*** when preceded by the article **the.**

The article **a** is used when the ***antecedent*** of **number** is considered ***individually,*** and the article **the** is used when the ***antecedent*** of **number** is considered ***collectively.***

> A **number** of **editors** have arrived ***(plural verb)*** for the conference. (The **editors** are being considered **individually.**)
>
> **The number** of **editors** attending is ***(singular verb)*** the largest in the 10-year history of the conference. (The **editors** are being considered as a **group.**)

O, Zero

O is a letter.
Zero is a number.

Sometimes when speakers are providing a telephone or a license number or an address, they will pronounce zero as an **O** (letter) instead of as a **zero** (number). Doing so is rarely confusing, but those who want to be precise will avoid interchanging **O** and **zero.**

(Avoid) The witness said the license number of the suspect's car is "four, seven, **O**, one, three."

(Use) The witness said the license number of the suspect's car is "four, seven, **zero,** one, three."

Officers, *not* New Officers

Members of an organization elect **officers, *not* new officers.**

Officers are presumed to be new unless incumbents retain their offices (in which case they are re-elected).

Kiwanians donated $5,000 to charities, arranged their annual awards dinner and elected **officers *(not new officers)*** at last night's meeting at the Concord Hotel.

On, Onto, On To

Use **on** as a ***preposition*** to mean meeting or touching a surface, or to continue.

Use **onto** as a ***preposition*** meaning to advance toward and upon.

Use **on to** as two words with **on** by itself as an ***adverb*** and **to** as a ***preposition*** or as an ***infinitive.***

The reporter sat **on *(touching the surface)*** the edge of the desk as he interviewed the chief of surgery at Acme Memorial Hospital.

"Get **on *[continue]*** with your cross examination," the judge directed the defense attorney.

The photographer walked **onto *(toward and upon)*** the roof to get a clear view of the parade.

When the advertising executive retired, she said she hoped to go **on *(adverb)* to *(preposition)*** "bigger and better things such as golfing, traveling and taking afternoon naps."

The mayor went **on *(adverb)* to *become (infinitive)*** governor, but she lost her subsequent attempt for a seat in Congress.

Ordinance, Ordnance

An **ord*i*nance** is a law enacted by a municipal body. It is a word used frequently by journalists.

Ordnance refers to military weapons and ammunition. It is a word used infrequently by journalists but whose spelling often is confused with **ord*i*nance.**

The **ord*i*nance** ***(municipal law)*** raising city fire fees passed by two votes.

A group of citizens demanded that City Council members refuse a request from the National Guard to permit storage of **ordnance** ***(weapons, ammunition)*** in a building near an elementary school.

Over, Under

See **More Than, Less Than,** page 290.

Pair, Pare, Pear

Only the middle example is troublesome. A **pair,** of course, is two (a pair of shoes/motorcycles/basketballs), and **pear** is a fruit.

Pare means to trim the outer layers or edges of something.

The city treasurer told council members that they must **pare** ***(trim/reduce in size)*** expenses to avoid a deficit.

Palate, Palette, Pallet

The **palate** is the roof of the mouth.

A **palette** is the board on which an artist places paints.

A **pallet** is a simple bed/mattress originally made of straw.

Partial, Partly

Keeping these words from being exchanged carelessly for each other is difficult, but the goal should be to separate their meanings whenever possible.

Use **partial** to mean favoring one person, place or thing over another ***(and avoid using it to mean*** **part** ***or*** **a portion of).**

Use **partly** to mean incomplete or a portion of.

The president said he is **partial** to ***(favors)*** Sen. Robert A. Brinkman's proposal.

The weather will be **partly** ***(not completely)*** cloudy with a 40 percent chance of rain.

The city editor was **partly** ***(not partially)*** responsible for the error.

The rooms are **partly** ***(not partially)*** furnished.

Although some journalists will insist that **partially** should be used in the following examples ***(because* partly *does not make sense),*** better word choices are available.

The proposal would offer a **partial** solution to the problem, the city manager said. ***(Just write that the proposal would solve part of the problem.)***

The student received a **partial** scholarship to attend Acme University. ***(Just write that the student received half or a third or some dollar amount of a scholarship.)***

Passable, Passible

Spelling, not meaning, is the source of potential confusion between these two words.

Passable means able to be passed, traversed or crossed; barely satisfactory but adequate.

Passible means capable of feeling; sensitive.

Although the rainstorm had caused flooding in many parts of the region, the meteorologist at the local television station reported that all bridges were **passable *(capable of being crossed).***

"My photography professor wasn't impressed with my research paper, but she said she considered it **passable *[barely satisfactory but adequate].***"

"Biblical scholars differ on a great many things, but virtually all agree that Job was **passible *[capable of feeling or suffering],*** " the professor of religion told his class.

Passed, Past

Use **passed** as a verb.

Use **past** as several parts of speech but never as a verb.

He **passed *(verb)*** the section of the test on grammar but failed the part on spelling.

Time **passed *(verb)*** slowly for the reporter waiting impatiently for the interview.

Because he missed an important deadline, the reporter averted his eyes as he walked **past *(preposition)*** the editor.

"There were times in my **past *[noun]*** when I wanted to seek public office, but I'm happy I didn't," the syndicated columnist said.

In the **past *(adjective)*** year, 2,500 students graduated from Acme University.

Peak, Peek, Pique

A **peak** is the highest point/elevation or the maximum degree.

To **peek** is to take a brief look, usually through a small opening.

To **pique** is to excite, to stimulate or to wound pride.

The actor James Dean died tragically at the **peak** ***(highest point/maximum degree)*** of his career.

The press secretary **peeked** through the slightly open door to determine who had arrived for the governor's press conference.

When the governor dodged a simple question, she unintentionally **piqued** ***(stimulated)*** the curiosity of the reporters, who responded with a flurry of follow-up inquiries. (Because **pique** is not a commonly used word, mass communicators may want to avoid it in favor of one of the synonyms listed above.)

Pedal, Peddle, Petal

Pedal means to operate a lever with the foot (bicycle, organ, sewing machine).

Peddle means to travel from town to town selling articles usually small enough to carry.

Petal is a segment or leaflike part of a flower. Of course, it has nothing to do with **pedal** and **peddle** except for occasional spelling problems caused by mispronunciation.

Some trick riders can **pedal** ***(operate)*** a bicycle with their hands and steer with their feet.

In some areas of the country, a person must purchase a license before he or she can **peddle** ***(sell)*** articles on street corners.

Petals ***(leaflike part)*** are often the most colorful part of the flower.

People, Person

Person is used to refer to one individual.

People is used to refer to two or more individuals.

These distinctions follow Associated Press style. Not everyone agrees, but journalists should make exceptions only when permitted by their school media or company policy.

The disagreement concerns the exclusive use of **people** for the plural of **person.** Some school media and professional media organizations use the following reasoning:

When a small number of individuals are involved, the use of **persons** is advocated rather than **people.** Another way of deciding which to use is to determine whether the individuals are being considered separately or as a group. For separate consideration, use **persons;** for a group, use **people.**

Every **person** ***(singular)*** who submits a letter to the editor must provide an address and a telephone number.

Eight **people** ***(plural)*** submitted letters today. (This is an example of a sentence in which some editors and news directors would prefer **persons** because the individuals are being considered separately.)

The American **people** ***(referred to as a group)*** value their freedom of expression.

Persecute, Prosecute

Persecute means to harass, especially on the basis of religion, race, politics and so forth.

Prosecute means to bring legal action against.

Persecution ***(harassment)*** in their native countries remains a primary reason why people seek refuge in the United States.

The defendant was **prosecuted** ***(had legal action brought against him)*** for armed robbery.

Pleaded, *not* Pled

Use **pleaded** exclusively for the past tense of **plea.**

Arrested by security police when he attempted to rob a bank, the suspect **pleaded** ***(not pled)*** guilty.

Poor, Pore, Pour

Poor is an ***adjective*** meaning lacking in financial and material resources.

Pore is a ***verb*** meaning to study or to read with care, or it is a ***noun*** referring to the small openings in the skin.

Pour is a ***verb*** meaning to flow, usually in a continuous stream.

The old man had no winter clothing, for he was too **poor** ***(lacking in financial and material resources)*** to be able to purchase any.

The editor **pored** over ***(studied with care)*** the editorial before approving it for publication.

The dermatologist cautioned members of the junior high school health class that they must wash their skin thoroughly to prevent their **pores** ***(small openings in the skin)*** from becoming clogged and infected.

By tipping the pot gently, even a weary journalist trying to meet the final deadline will be able to **pour** ***(cause to flow)*** the coffee without spilling it.

Precede, Proceed

Precede means to go before.

Proceed means to go on, to continue.

Mrs. Johnson was **preceded** ***(to go before)*** in death by her husband.

The judge said she would not **proceed** ***(continue)*** with the trial until everyone was seated.

Premier, Premiere

Premier means first in rank, leader.

Premier*e* means first performance.

He became **premier** ***(leader)*** at the age of 52.

Her play will have its **premiere** ***(first performance)*** Friday.

Pretense, Pretext

A **pretense** is a false appearance or action intended to deceive; a pretended claim.

A **pretext** is a false or fabricated reason or excuse developed to hide the real reason.

The investigative reporter discovered that the hospital director's claim that he had a medical degree was only a **pretense** (a ***pretended claim*)**.

The foreman of the city garage was fired, but the official reason, tardiness, was only a **pretext** to hide the theft of government property, the mayor said off the record.

Principal, Principle

Principal means first in rank or the amount of a debt excluding the interest. It's used as a **noun** or an **adjective.**

Principle means a fundamental truth. It's always used as a noun.

Frieda L. Parklin is **principal** ***(the top administrator)*** of Flagship High School.

Marlon Brando played the **principal** ***(first in rank)*** role in the movie.

During the first years of repayment of a house loan, only a small amount of money is applied to reducing the **principal** ***(amount of the debt excluding the interest).***

Honesty is one of the main **principles** ***(fundamental truths)*** by which journalists live.

"Never compromise your beliefs when a **principle** ***[fundamental truth]*** is at stake," the minister advised his congregation.

Profit, Prophet

Few journalists confuse these words, but mistakes occur frequently enough among students to make an explanation worthwhile.

Profit is gain, financial or otherwise.

Prophet is a name for a person who has the ability to foretell the future or to interpret divine will.

People who invest in the stock market hope to make a **profit** ***(financial gain).***

Holy books record the works of many **prophets** ***(people who can interpret divine will or foretell the future).***

Profit, Revenue

Profit is gain, financial or otherwise.

Revenue is a source of income or the total income of a business or a branch of government.

Business officials are critical of journalists who confuse **profit** with **revenue,** particularly when **revenue** is reported as **profit. Profit** is what is left of the **revenue** after all expenses have been paid.

Acme Oil **revenue** ***(income)*** increased by 5 percent during the fiscal year, company officials reported. However, they said the company did not realize a **profit** ***(financial gain)*** because of increased operating expenses.

Prophecy, Prophesy

Prophecy is a ***noun*** meaning a prediction.

Prophesy is a ***verb*** meaning to predict.

Many **prophecies** ***(noun)*** recorded in holy books have come true.

Many figures in holy books **prophesied** ***(verb)*** to people who often ridiculed the predictions.

Neither of these words should be used by journalists to indicate that a ***guess*** or a ***calculation*** is being made. ***Predict*** and ***estimate*** are better for that.

> Sen. Walker F. Farnstein **predicts** ***(not prophesies)*** that he will win re-election.

Prostate, Prostrate

Confusing these words can be quite embarrassing.

Prostate refers to the prostate gland, which is part of the male reproductive system.

Prostrate refers to lying face down on the ground or on some other surface or to make helpless.

> **Prostate** ***(referring to the prostate gland)*** cancer is such a threat to adult males that regular examinations are recommended by the American Medical Association.
>
> The traitors **prostrated** themselves ***(lay face down)*** before their country's ruler and begged for mercy.

Proved, Proven

Use **proved** as a ***verb.***

Use **proven** as an ***adjective.***

> The news director's hunches have **proved** ***(verb)*** to be true more often than not.
>
> "When you asked me for a **proven** ***[adjective]*** method for obtaining the number of votes we needed, I was embarrassed to tell you I didn't know," the chairman said.

Pupil, Student

Pupil refers to children in their elementary school years and is used to indicate that they are in the charge of a tutor or an instructor.

Student refers to people in their high school and college years and is used to indicate that they are learners and observers at a higher level than pupils are.

Where does the **pupil** designation end and the **student** reference begin? Some media guidelines put the cutoff at the end of the eighth grade. Others suggest that **student** is an appropriate designation for all grades and ages. That's simple, and it makes sense. Perhaps the only exception worth arguing for concerns a student of the fine arts who (young or old) is studying with a great master of a particular subject. In such an instance, being referred to as a **pupil** is considered an honor.

My 10-year-old cousin, a **student/pupil** ***(either one)*** at Phelps Elementary School, plans to become a broadcast journalist.

My feature story is about a man who returned to high school when he was 53 to become a **student** again.

After college, Mario N. Costello went to Europe to become a **pupil** of a world-renowned composer.

Purebred, Thoroughbred

Purebred refers to an animal that belongs to a long-established line with characteristics undisturbed by mixing with other animals.

Thoroughbred also refers to animals of pure and unmixed stock, but when the **"T"** is capitalized, **Thoroughbred** refers specifically to a breed of race horses whose ancestry can be traced to horses registered in the English Stud Book.

A **purebred** English setter took first place in the dog show.

Thoroughbred horses can sell for millions of dollars.

Quiet, Quite

Use **quiet** as an ***adjective*** or a ***noun*** and use **quietly** as an ***adverb*** to mean with little or no sound.

Use **quite** to mean completely, wholly or to an extreme.

The scene of the riot is now **quiet** ***(adjective modifying the noun scene).***

The **quiet** ***(noun)*** was the most beneficial part of the vacation.

The swimmers moved **quietly** ***(adverb modifying the verb moved)*** through the water.

"She is **quite** ***[to an extreme]*** a reporter," the editor said in describing the Pulitzer Prize winner he had just hired.

Raise, Rear

Parents may **raise** or **rear** children, according to some journalistic guidelines. However, journalists who prefer a more traditional use of the language will tell you that **plants are** ***raised*** and **children are** ***reared.*** Their belief is worthy of respect.

"We must help people in underdeveloped countries learn to **raise** their own ***crops,***" the Peace Corps official said.

"If they are to **rear** their ***children*** in a healthful environment, they must have an ample supply of food," he said.

Raise, Rise

See **Arise, Raise, Rise,** page 240.

Rarely *or* Rarely If Ever, *not* Rarely Ever

Something may **rarely** happen or **rarely if ever** happen, but **rarely ever** is unacceptable. Instead of **rarely ever,** select **rarely** or **never,** whichever is accurate.

"Our copy editors **rarely** make spelling errors."

"Our editors **rarely if ever** overlook a potentially libelous statement."

"Our editors **rarely/never** ***[not rarely ever]*** make unethical decisions." (Whether **rarely** or **never** is used depends on the writer's meaning.)

Ravage, Ravish

Ravage means violent and destructive action resulting in ruin.

Ravish means to rape or to seize and carry off by force. (Although **ravish** can mean ***enrapture,*** it is the negative meaning that writers and broadcasters sometimes misuse. Because of the potential for confusion, writers and broadcasters may want to use a more specific word.)

Twenty-nine counties were **ravaged** ***(experienced destruction)*** by the floods resulting from melting snow.

Members of the crime ring forced their way into the house, stole all items of value and **ravished** ***(raped)*** two women.

Real, Very

Use **real** as an ***adjective.***

Use **very** as an ***adverb.***

"A **real** ***[adjective]*** minister would not steal from his church," the prosecutor told the jury.

The document is **real** ***(adjective),*** according to the specialists who examined it.

By adding **ly, real** can be changed from an ***adjective*** to an ***adverb.***

Remember, however, that some editors insist that **really** should be used only in casual speech and avoided by journalists.

The reporters were **very** ***(adverb)*** tired, but they were pleased with their election-night coverage.

Everyone agrees that the president is a **very** ***(adverb)*** good speaker.

Some editors claim that **very** is unnecessary because it gives no additional meaning to the word or words it modifies. Others argue that it adds significant emphasis. In the absence of a company policy on the use of the word, each writer must make his or her own judgment. Under all circumstances, however, overuse of **very** should be avoided.

Rebut, Refute

See **Disprove, Dispute,** page 262.

Reconsider/Re-examine, *not* Revisit

Reconsider means to take up again with the possibility of making changes.

Re-examine means to study again.

Revisit means to go again for a brief stay.

The advertising director said he will **reconsider** ***(take up again and possibly make changes)*** his decision to fire his assistant.

The pathologist decided to have the murdered man's body exhumed and **re-examine** ***(again study)*** it.

The magazine editor said she plans after retiring to **revisit** ***(to go again for a brief stay)*** all the places where she lived when she was a child.

Avoid using **revisit** in the following context:

The university president said she is willing to **reconsider** ***(not revisit)*** her decision to eliminate foreign language requirements.

Recur, Reoccur

How much simpler life would be if an event that **occurs** and then repeats itself would just ***reoccur.*** Unfortunately, most authorities recognize no such word. The word for such a repetition is **recur (recurred, recurring, recurrence).**

To complicate things further, a few experts insist that both **recur** and **reoccur** may be used correctly, depending on the writer's meaning. If the meaning is that an event repeats itself just once, **reoccur** is proper. If the event repeats itself on a continuing basis, **recur** should be used. However, **recur** also may be used correctly for an event that repeats itself just once.

Not one of these guidelines is of much comfort to journalists trying to meet deadlines. They need quick, simple directions. Consider these two:

1. Forget **reoccur** and use **recur** exclusively. That's the most common solution and the one most experts insist is correct.
2. Forget both **recur** and **reoccur** and substitute ***repeat, happen again, return, reappear, renew*** or some other appropriate word unrestricted by such narrowly drawn distinctions.

Refuse, Decline

When a source chooses not to answer a reporter's question, does the source **refuse, decline** or do something else?

Does the police chief **refuse** to speculate on the cause of a murder, or does he **decline,** or does he just offer **no comment**?

These shades of difference are important, and journalists must take care to select the word(s) that most accurately describes the source's attitude. (See **Admitted, Said,** page 226).

> The presidential candidate **refused** to answer reporters' questions about his alleged use of illegal drugs. He said the subject was none of the reporters' business.

> The presidential candidate **declined** to provide details about how he would bring the budget deficit under control if he is elected. He said he does not have enough precise information yet to make an intelligent statement.

Regain, Retain

Regain means to get back or to recover.

Retain means to keep or to continue to hold.

Numerous school administrators have been annoyed or angered over the years by student journalists who report that a department, a school, or a college has **regained** accreditation it never lost. The accurate word is **retained. Regained** would be appropriate only if accreditation had been lost in the previous accreditation period.

> The Department of Sociology **regained** ***(got back)*** its accreditation after losing it four years earlier.

> The School of Journalism **retained** ***(kept)*** its accreditation for the 21st consecutive year.

Regardless, *not* Irregardless

Irregardless is not considered standard English and is likely to be edited out of your copy, **regardless** of how many times you hear or see it used.

The students said they plan to go white-water rafting, **regardless** ***(not irregardless)*** of the dangers.

Regretful, Regrettable

Regretful means for a person to feel sorrow/remorse for something he/she said or did.

Regrettable refers to what caused a person to be regretful.

The professor **regretted/felt regretful for** embarrassing the student in front of his classmates.

The students agreed that the professor's bad judgment was **regrettable.**

Reign, Rein

Reign refers to the period of rule by a hereditary head of state.

Rein/reins can refer to the leather straps used to control an animal wearing a bit and bridle. Mass communicators use the word more frequently to refer to political, social, or economic pressure applied to restrain, guide or control errant behavior.

The American Revolution came during the **reign** ***(period of rule)*** of England's George III.

Many executions occurred in the French Revolution, especially during the **Reign** of Terror ***(1793–94).***

The guide told the inexperienced riders to pull gently on the **reins** ***[leather straps]*** if the horse started running too fast.

The president told his closest advisers, "We'll have to **rein in** ***[restrain, control]*** the press secretary if he keeps telling the news media more than we want them to know."

Reluctant, Reticent

Reluctant means unwilling or opposed to.

Reticent means uncommunicative or unwilling to speak.

McOwen was **reluctant** ***(unwilling or opposed)*** to take the assignment as a foreign correspondent.

Even the most talkative politicians become **reticent** ***(unwilling to speak***) when they don't like the reporters' questions.

Respectfully, Respectively

Respectfully means in a dutiful or deferential manner ***(honor, esteem, consideration).***

Respectively means relating or pertaining to two or more persons, places or things in the order in which they are listed.

The ambassador **respectfully** ***(with honor)*** laid a wreath on the tomb of the unknown soldier.

Basketball teams from the University of Kentucky and the University of North Carolina won the Southeastern Conference and the Atlantic Coast Conference championships, **respectively** ***(meaning that Kentucky won the Southeastern and North Carolina, the Atlantic).***

Using **respectively** can sometimes be so complicated it should be avoided. Just report that the University of Kentucky won the Southeastern Conference championship and the University of North Carolina won the Atlantic Coast Conference title.

Role, Roll

A **role** is the part that an actor plays.

Roll means to move along by repeatedly turning over, or roundish bread.

Seldom, Seldom If Ever, *not* Seldom Ever

See **Rarely, Rarely If Ever, *not* Rarely Ever,** page 302. The same rule applies.

Should Have, *not* Should Of

See **Could Have, Should Have, Would Have, *not* Could Of, Should Of, Would Of,** page 257.

Sit, Set

Sit means to assume a seated position.

Set means to place.

A reporter can **sit** ***(in a seated position)*** through a press conference.

She **sat** through a three-hour press conference last week.

During her five years of covering the mayor's office, she has **sat** through many lengthy conferences.

Unlike **sit, set** forms all of its principal parts without changing its spelling.

The reporter **set** ***(placed)*** her portable video display terminal on the same desk where she **set** ***(placed)*** it Monday and **has set** ***(placed)*** it every other day throughout the trial.

Remember that once a person **sets** ***(places)*** an object somewhere, that object then **sits** ***(remains in place)*** there.

A reporter can **set** ***(place)*** a portable video display terminal on her knees, but she probably will not be comfortable after it **sits** ***(remains in place)*** there for more than a few minutes.

Sole, Soul

Sole refers to the only one of a kind, the bottom of the foot or shoe, or a type of fish.

Soul refers to a person's spirit, as separate from the body, the essential part of something; a human being.

Some *as a singular,* Some *as a plural*

See **None** ***as a singular,*** **None** ***as a plural,*** page 291.

Sometime, Some Time

Sometime, one word, means at some unspecified time.

Some time, two words, means an unspecified **quantity** of time.

The Pulitzer Prize winner said she hopes to progress from writing features to writing novels **sometime** ***(an unspecified time)*** before she retires.

However, she said she will have to spend **some time** ***(an unspecified quantity of time)*** preparing herself financially before she can try her luck as a creative writer.

Spaded, Spayed

Ground is **spaded** ***(shoveled)*** but a female animal is ***spayed, not "spayeded" (operated on to prevent pregnancy).***

Spilled, *not* Spilt

Use **spilled** exclusively as the past tense of **spill.**

Stanch, Staunch

Stanch means to stop the flow of blood from a wound, to check or to extinguish.

Staunch means to be steadfast in principle, loyalty.

The prime minister said he would attempt to **stanch** the leaking of secret information to the news media.

Sen. Robert N. Ingles is a **staunch** supporter of his party's platform.

Stationary, Stationery

Station*a*ry means standing still or to be fixed in place.

Station*e*ry is writing paper.

Indoor exercise bicycles are **stationary** ***(they remain in one place).***

Employees are cautioned not to write personal letters on company **stationery** ***(writing paper).***

Supposed to, *not* Suppose to

Although **suppose** means to consider or to believe to be true (**Suppose** the boss walked through that door and caught you sleeping on the job), **supposed,** followed by **to,** means to expect or to require (You are **supposed to** be working, not sleeping on the job).

Always add a **d** to **suppose** when the word is followed by an infinitive (to work, to run, to talk, to give).

Sure To, *not* Sure And

See **Try To, not Try And,** page 310.

Telecast, Televise

Telecast is a ***noun.***

Televise is a ***verb.***

The **telecast** ***(noun)*** will begin at 8 p.m.

A public broadcasting station will **televise** ***(verb)*** the debate.

That, Which

For a detailed explanation of the essential relative pronoun **that** and the nonessential relative pronoun **which,** refer to page 0 and also read about antecedents of relative pronouns on pages 9 and 78–79.

Their, There, They're

Their is a plural possessive pronoun.

There is used to refer to a place, a point in time, or it may be used as an exclamation.

They're is a contraction for **they are.**

Members of the Legislature will be assigned **their** ***(plural possessive pronoun used to take the place of the noun members)*** seats next month.

"Your desk is over **there** ***[place],*** " the manager told the new account executive.

"Your story should begin **there** ***[a place, or a point in time],*** " the editor said.

"**There!** ***[an exclamation]*** I knew you could do it," the public relations director said.

"**They're** ***[they are]*** my best writers," the editor said.

Titled, *not* Entitled

Use **titled,** not **entitled** (having the right to do or to claim something) when referring to the name of a book or an article.

In 1975, he wrote an award-winning book **titled** ***(not entitled)*** *Anatomy of an Underdog.*

Because he is the publisher's nephew, he is **entitled** ***(has a right)*** to special treatment.

To, Too, Two

Of these three words with identical pronunciations but different meanings, only **too** presents much of a problem. Writers sometimes omit the second **o,** either through carelessness or misunderstanding.

To is a **preposition** if followed by a noun or a pronoun object.

Council members are going **to** ***(preposition)*** a **convention** ***(object)*** this weekend.

To is an ***infinitive*** if followed by a verb.

Sean W. O'Hara plans **to enter** ***(infinitive)*** the competition.

Too is an ***adverb*** meaning ***in addition*** or ***extremely.***

The mayor will go, **too** ***(in addition).***

The storm was **too** ***(extremely)*** severe for the small boats to withstand.

Two means a pair of, a couple of, or one plus one.

Two ***(a couple of)*** assistant vice presidents will be added to the staff next month, the president of the advertising firm announced.

Tortuous, Torturous

Tortuous means winding, twisting, full of curves and bends.

Torturous refers to extreme suffering and pain.

European road races are run on **tortuous** courses ***(full of curves and bends).***

The United Nations condemns all **torturous** methods ***(causing pain and suffering)*** of extracting information from prisoners of war.

Both words also may be used figuratively.

The reporter's **tortuous *(twisting, winding)*** writing style resulted in a **torturous *(painful)*** experience for anyone who had to edit his articles.

Mass communicators may want to use one of the synonyms listed above in place of **tortuous,** which commonly is confused with some form of the word **torture.**

Toward, *not* Towards

Use **toward** exclusively.

She is working **toward *(not towards)*** a degree in philosophy.

Tradition, *not* Old Tradition

See **Adage, *not* Old Adage,** page 226.

Troop, Troupe

Troupe is used to refer to a company of actors.

Troop is used to refer to most other types of groups (soldiers, police, scouts and other organized bodies).

Try To, *not* Try And

A tennis player will **try *to*** win, not **try *and*** win.

To write or broadcast that the player will **try *and*** win is to presume or to predict that he or she will win.

The same reasoning applies to **be sure to/be sure and.**

"We're a 30-point underdog, but we're going to **try *to [not try and]*** win," the coach said.

"Even if we are expected to lose, we hope our fans will be **sure *to [not be sure and]*** support us with their presence at the game."

Unaware, Unawares

Unaware means not aware or cognizant.

Unawares means unexpected, without warning.

The daydreaming reporter was **unaware** ***(not cognizant of the fact that)*** the editor was calling his name.

The rain caught the spectators **unawares** ***(without warning).***

Under Way, *not* Underway

In almost all journalistic usages, **under way** is two words.

Undoubtedly, *not* Undoubtably

There is no such word as **undoubt*ably.*** People who use this spelling probably do so because they mispronounce **undoubt*edly.***

"He **undoubtedly** ***[not undoubtably]*** meant 3 p.m. because it's highly unlikely we'd be meeting at 3 a.m.," the secretary said.

Unidentified, Unknown

Unidentified means someone or something has not been named or verified as being a specific, particular person or thing.

Unknown refers to someone or something beyond a person's knowledge or understanding.

The **unidentified** ***(not verified)*** suspect is being pursued by law enforcement officers in three states.

Students worry about the **unknown** ***(things beyond their knowledge or understanding),*** especially before they take final examinations.

"We know what was stolen," the detective said. "What is **unknown** is the ***identity*** of the thief."

Avoid reporting that someone being pursued by police is **unknown** ***(the unknown robber).*** That person surely is known by a number of people. What the police do not know is the person's identity. Report that the person has not been identified.

Used to, *not* Use to (when the meaning is previously or accustomed)

Use to means to put to some purpose. (**Use** that computer **to** continue your work while your machine is being repaired).

Used to means previously, accustomed to, formerly (Dr. Pinkston **used to** ***[formerly/previously]*** be a professor of journalism before he became editor of the Acme Gazette).

Vain, Vane, Vein

Vain refers to excessive self-admiration.

Vane refers to a device designed to show the direction of the wind.

Vein refers to blood vessels or a seam of coal or gold.

"Do some politicians dye their hair because they are **vain** ***[subject to excessive self-admiration]*** or to make themselves appear younger to voters?" the columnist asked.

Weather **vanes** ***(devices that show the direction of the wind)*** are common sights on barn roofs.

One frightening challenge student nurses face is inserting a needle successfully into a patient's **vein** ***(blood vessel)*** on the first effort.

(a) Variety, *(the)* Variety

Variety takes a ***plural verb*** when preceded by the article **a** and a ***singular verb*** when preceded by the article **the.** The article **a** is used when the ***antecedent*** of **variety** is considered ***individually,*** and the article **the** is used when the ***antecedent*** is considered ***collectively.***

A **variety** of ***courses*** **are** available to experienced journalists who want to continue their education. **(The antecedent is *courses* and the courses are being considered *individually;* therefore, the plural verb *are* is used.)**

The **variety** of ***courses*** **was** designed to attract as many students as possible. **(The antecedent is *courses* and the courses are being considered *collectively;* therefore, the singular verb *was* is used.)**

Verses, Versus

A **verse** is a piece of poetry or a division of a chapter in the Bible.

Versus means against, a contest between two athletes or two teams, a court case pitting one party against another.

Waive, Waiver, Waver

Waive ***(verb)*** and **waiver** ***(noun)*** mean to voluntarily give up or to abandon a right, privilege or claim.

Waver means to sway, to be uncertain or indecisive.

When reporting about classes or other requirements, student journalists sometimes write or broadcast that a class was **waved, waivered or wavered.** They mean to say that a class was **waived** or that an administrator issued a **waiver** excusing a student from the requirement.

The dean accepted McGeorge Eddy's four years of military service and **waived** ***(not waved or waivered)*** the required classes in physical education.

The dean refused to issue a **waiver** to Eddy's brother because the young man had served only six months of active duty.

Eddy's brother challenged the dean's decision, but the administrator did not **waver** from his ruling.

Want, Wish

Only one potential conflict exists in deciding whether to use **want** or **wish.** When reporters write or broadcast that some organization or club is available to people who **wish** to join, they probably are overestimating the desire the potential recruits have for membership. Unless these people are gazing at a star, they undoubtedly are **wanting,** not **wishing.**

"Adults who **want** ***[not wish]*** to join may apply in person before April 15," the club president said.

Who, Whom

See pages 21–22.

Who's, Whose

Who's is a contraction for ***who is.***

Whose is a possessive pronoun.

When confused about which to use, just say **who is** at the point where the word is to be placed in the sentence. Your ear will provide the answer. (Also see **It's, Its,** page 282.)

Who's ***(who is)*** going to determine **whose** ***(possessive pronoun)*** system will be used in the newsroom?

Won, *as used with* Elected *and* Selected

To be **elected,** a person usually has ***to compete.***

People can be **selected** for a position or an honor without competing or even being aware they are under consideration. They don't **"win"** the honor or the position because they ***did not compete*** for it.

Win or **won** may be used to refer to the outcome of a competition but not to the outcome of a **selection** in which people did not compete.

She **won** ***(successfully competed in)*** the election.

He was **selected** ***(without competing)*** for the Lions Club's "Outstanding Young Man of the Year" award for providing free medical treatment to underprivileged children.

Would Have, *not* Would Of

See **Could Have, Should Have, Would Have, *not* Could Of, Should Of, Would Of,** page 257.

Your, You're

Your is a possessive pronoun.

You're is a contraction for ***you are.***

When in doubt about which to use, just say **you are** at the point where the word is to be placed in the sentence. Your ear will provide the answer. (Also see **It's, Its,** page 282, and **Who's, Whose,** page 313.)

"**Your** ***[possessive pronoun]*** press secretary said she will tell us when **you're** ***[you are]*** ready to begin the conference," the president's aide explained.

REFERENCE 2 WORDS FREQUENTLY MISSPELLED

The following words are presented in alphabetical order for quick reference and with the most troublesome letters set in bold type for quick study. The words were selected because they are commonly used by mass communicators and are frequently misspelled. Some words such as advi**ser** and cance**l**ed are presented in the spelling journalists use rather than a form (advis**or,** cance**ll**ed) followed by others.

a**bb**reviate
a**bd**icate
a**bd**uct
ab**eya**nce
abri**dgm**ent
a**bro**gate
ab**sc**ess
absen**c**e
a**cc**elerate
a**cc**elerat**o**r
a**cc**ept**a**nce
a**ccess**
a**ccessi**ble
a**cc**identa**lly**
a**cc**laim
a**ccomm**odate
a**cc**ompan**ie**d
a**cc**omplish
a**cc**um**u**late
a**cc**ust**o**med
a**che**
ach**ie**ve
a**ck**nowle**d**ge
a**cq**uaint
a**cquiesc**e
a**c**quit, a**cquitt**ed
a**cross**
a**dj**acent
admi**ra**ble
admi**ssi**ble
adol**escen**t
adverti**se**ment
advi**c**e
advi**sa**ble
advi**ser**
a**eri**al
aerobic
a**ff**ida**vit**
a**ffilia**te
a**gg**ravate
a**ggr**e**ss**ive
a**ggressor**
agre**e**able
a**isle**
alco**hol**
a**lien**ate
a**lle**gation
all**ege**
a**ll**eg**ia**nce
a**ll**ev**ia**te
alle**ys**
a**ll**ot, a**ll**o**tt**ed
alman**ac**
al**trui**stic
alumin**um**
amat**eur**
ambass**ador**
ambul**a**nce
am**nesia**
ana**logy**
ana**lyze**
an**ec**dote
a**nnihi**late
a**nn**ual
ano**nymity**
ano**nymous**
an**tithe**sis
an**xi**ous
apo**logize**

a**pp**aratus
a**pp**ear**a**nce
a**ppell**ate
a**ppe**tite
Ar**c**tic
Arg**u**ing
arg**um**ent
a**rraign**ment
arti**cle**
as**c**end
as**c**end**a**nt
as**c**ent
asp**irin**
a**ss**a**ss**in
ass**au**lt
a**ss**ent
a**ss**e**ss**
aster**isk**
athe**i**st
a**th**lete
a**t**mos**phere**
attorn**eys**
author**ize**
autop**sy**
aut**umn**
aux**ilia**ry
ba**cc**al**aure**ate
ba**c**hel**o**r
ba**llis**tic
ba**lloon**
bank**ruptcy**
Ba**p**tist
barbe**cue**
barg**ain**
ba**rri**cade
basic**ally**
ba**tt**al**ion**
ba**zaar**
beco**m**ing
begg**ar**
behavior
bel**ie**v**a**ble
bel**ie**ve
bene**f**i**t**ed
bisc**ui**t
bi**zarr**e
blas**ph**emy
boo**kk**eeper
bouillon
boulevard
boyco**tt**
brac**elet**
bril**liant**
bro**chu**re
bull**e**tin
buoyant
burgl**ar**
bus**iness**
bu**s**y
caf**e**teria
ca**ffe**ine
calend**ar**
ca**mouflage**
camp**aign**
cance**l**ed
can**did**ate
ca**rica**ture
catastrop**he**
cat**e**gory
caucus
cell**ar**
ceme**t**ery
cen**sus**
cente**nnial**
chang**ea**ble
character**istic**
chas**tise**
ch**ie**f
chi**mn**ey
choc**o**late
c**h**ord
Christ**ia**n
ch**ro**nology
cig**arette**
ci**nna**mon
citi**z**en
clim**b**
coin**ci**de
col**le**g**ia**te
co**lo**nel
colu**mn**
co**mm**end**a**ble
co**mmit**ment
co**mmittee**
comp**ara**ble
compe**l**
con**cede**
conc**eivable**
conc**ei**t
conc**ei**ve
con**ci**se
congra**t**ulations
Co**nn**e**ct**icut
con**quer**
cons**cience**
cons**cientious**
cons**cious**
consen**sus**
consist**e**nt
cont**a**gious
contem**pt**
contin**uous**
contra**dict**
conven**ie**nce
conven**ie**nt
coo**ll**y
coron**e**r

co**rr**espond**e**nce
co**rrobo**rate
coun**selo**r
co**u**rag**eous**
co**ur**te**o**us
cred**i**bility
cred**i**ble
criti**cize**
cru**c**ial
cupfu**ls**
dai**ly**
dec**ei**ve
deduct**i**ble
defend**a**nt
defen**s**e
defens**i**ble
defe**rr**ed
def**i**n**i**te, def**i**n**i**t**e**ly
Del**a**ware
del**e**gate
depend**e**nt
des**c**end**a**nt
des**ira**ble
d**e**sp**air**
d**e**sper**a**te
dete**rre**nt
detr**i**men**tal**
develo**p**
di**ff**er**e**n**c**e
d**i**le**mm**a
d**i**m**i**nish
di**s**appoint
dis**ass**emble
dis**astr**ous
di**sc**ern
dis**c**ipline
di**sc**rim**i**nate
dis**ea**se
disg**uise**
dispens**able**
di**ss**atisfied
di**ss**en**s**ion
disting**uish**
d**i**vine
don**or**
dorm**i**tory
e**c**sta**sy**
effic**ie**nt
eigh**t**een
el**i**g**i**ble
emba**rr**ass
e**mi**n**e**nt
employ**ee**
encoura**ge**ment
end**ea**v**o**r
enorm**ou**s
enthu**sias**m
entir**ely**
entr**a**nce
env**iron**ment
equi**pp**ed
equ**iva**lent
e**rr**on**eo**us
espec**ially**
essen**tial**
evident**ly**
exa**gg**erate
excell**e**nce
exception**ally**
ex**cerpt**
exci**ta**ble
excu**sable**
exer**cise**
ex**hau**st
ex**hib**it
exh**ila**rate
exist**e**nce
exorbit**a**nt
expen**s**e
expl**ici**t
exten**s**ion
extin**ct**
extor**t**ion
extrem**ely**
fam**ili**a**r**
fami**liariz**e
fanta**s**y
fa**sc**inate
f**easi**ble
Feb**r**uary
f**eu**d
fic**titiou**s
fi**dg**et
fi**e**rce
fi**e**ry
fi**sc**al
for**ci**bly
for**e**head
for**eig**n
for**e**see
forf**ei**t
form**er**ly
f**raudu**lent
ful**fill**
fundamen**tal**
f**uro**r
g**au**ge
gen**ius**
gover**n**ment
gramm**ar**
gr**amm**atic**all**y
gr**ie**v**a**nce
g**ua**rant**ee**
g**ua**rant**y**
g**ua**rd
gu**b**ernator**ia**l
guid**a**nce

ha**lle**lu**jah**
Ha**ll**oween
ha**rass**
heigh**t**
h**einou**s
hemo**rrh**age
hero**es**
h**i**ndr**a**nce
hitc**hh**ike
hom**ic**ide
hop**e**less
ho**p**ing
ho**pp**ing
hum**oro**us
hung**rily**
h**ygie**ne
h**y**pocr**is**y
h**y**pocrite
h**y**pothesis
i**c**i**c**le
iden**tity**
idio**syn**crasy
ignor**ant**
i**ll**eg**al**
i**ll**ic**it**
imminent
imp**ea**ch
impl**e**ment
improm**ptu**
im**pugn**
in**acc**urate
inadmiss**i**ble
in**augu**rate
incalcul**a**ble
incident**ally**
incomp**e**t**e**nt
inco**rr**ig**i**ble
incred**ible**
independ**e**nce
indic**t**ment
indispens**a**ble
inevit**a**ble
infa**lli**ble
infect**iou**s
infla**mma**ble
infla**mma**tory
influent**ial**
ingen**iou**s
in**itia**tion
init**ia**tive
innoc**e**nc**e**
innocent
innoc**uou**s
i**n**oculate
i**n**put
insist**e**nce
int**e**grate
inte**ll**ectu**al**
inte**ll**igen**ce**
inter**cede**
int**er**esting
inte**r**f**ere**
inter**pre**t
inte**rrupt**
irrel**e**v**a**nt
irresist**i**ble
irrespons**i**ble
irrit**able**
jeal**ou**s
jud**gm**ent
jud**ici**ary
ke**ros**ene
kidna**pp**ing
kinderg**a**r**t**en
knowl**edg**e
lab**ora**tory
la**dd**er
la**p**se
la**tt**er
le**giti**mate
l**ei**sure
len**gth**
l**eni**ent
l**iai**son
li**c**ense
lieuten**a**nt
light**n**ing
li**ka**ble
liv**eli**hood
lon**e**liness
Louis**iana**
mag**azi**ne
maint**e**n**a**nce
malf**easance**
malic**iou**s
manag**ea**ble
man**eu**ver
mari**jua**na
ma**rri**age
Massa**chu**se**tt**s
math**e**matics
medi**ocre**
mer**e**ly
meta**pho**r
mil**ea**ge
mini**a**ture
mi**n**i**m**um
mis**c**e**ll**an**eous**
mis**chie**v**ou**s
mi**ss**pell
mi**s**use
mo**rale**
mosquit**oes**
munici**pal**
m**u**rm**u**r
mu**s**cle
myster**iou**s

n**ai**ve
narco**tic**
ne**c**e**ss**ary
negl**i**g**e**nce
n**eigh**b**o**r
n**euro**tic
n**eu**tral
nick**el**
n**ie**ce
nigh**tt**ime
nin**e**teen
nin**e**ty
ni**nt**h
notic**ea**ble
n**uisa**nce
null**ify**
obed**ience**
obs**c**ene
obsol**ete**
obst**acle**
o**cc**a**s**ion
o**cc**u**rr**ed
o**ff**en**s**e
o**mitt**ed
op**inio**n
opossum
o**pp**or**tu**nity
opt**i**mistic
or**ch**es**t**ra
origin**al**
outra**geou**s
ove**rr**un
pageant
pam**ph**let
para**ll**el
para**ly**ze
parl**ia**mentary
particul**ar**
par**t**ner
pas**t**ime
peac**ea**ble
pen**icilli**n
pen**i**tent**iary**
perc**ei**ve
pere**nnia**l
perm**a**n**e**nt
permi**ssi**ble
p**er**secute
per**seve**rance
persist**e**nt
perspiration
pers**ua**de
pi**c**ni**c**
pi**c**ni**ck**ed
pi**e**ce
pla**cebo**
pla**giarize**
pla**gue**
pla**nn**ed
pl**ea**s**a**nt
pneumonia
po**ss**e**ss**
potat**o**
potatoes
prec**ede**
pre**c**ed**e**nt
pred**ecessor**
pre**fer**ence
pre**j**udi**c**e
prem**ier**
prem**iere**
p**rerequi**site
pres**e**nce
prest**ige**
prev**a**lent
princi**pal**
princi**ple**
pri**vi**le**ge**
pro**ce**dure
pro**fess**or
pro**fit**
prom**i**n**e**nt
pro**nunc**ia**t**ion
prop**a**ganda
prophe**cy**
prop**het**
p**ro**secute
prot**ei**n
Protest**a**nt
P**sych**ology
pum**pk**in
p**ur**sue
quan**tity**
qua**rr**el
question**n**aire
q**uor**um
ra**ck**et
ra**cqu**et
re**cede**
re**cipi**ent
rec**eipt**
rec**ei**ve
re**ci**pe
re**cipi**ent
re**cipro**cal
re**cogniz**e
re**c**o**mm**end
rect**ify**
refe**rr**ed
regre**tt**able
reh**ear**sal
r**eim**burse
rel**eva**nt
rel**ie**ve
rel**igio**us
remembr**a**nce
rep**e**tition

repe**titiou**s
repl**ied**
repugn**a**nt
reser**voir**
resis**tant**
resis**ti**ble
respectfu**lly**
respectiv**ely**
rest**au**rant
reta**lia**te
rhythm
ridi**culou**s
roo**mm**ate
sacri**fi**ce
sal**a**ble
sar**casm**
s**cene**ry
s**ch**edule
s**c**i**sso**rs
sec**ede**
sec**reta**ry
s**ei**ze
s**eiz**ure
sens**i**ble
serg**ea**nt
sever**e**ly
shep**he**rd
she**riff**
sh**ie**ld
shi**n**ing
s**ie**ge
sil**houette**
simi**lar**
sim**u**ltan**eou**s
sincer**e**ly
si**za**ble
soph**o**more
s**ou**ven**ir**
sov**ereig**n
spons**or**
station**ary**
station**ery**
sto**pp**ing
stre**t**ch
stric**t**
submers**ible**
su**bpoe**na
su**c**ceed
suit**a**ble
super**in**ten**d**ent
supervis**or**
sur**e**ly
s**ur**prise
suscep**tible**
suspi**c**ion
suspi**cious**
s**ylla**ble
s**y**mpathy
s**y**non**y**m**ou**s
s**y**nopsis
tang**ible**
t**ariff**
ten**ant**s
tenden**cy**
te**net**s
Te**nn**e**ssee**
theat**er**
tho**rough**
th**ough**
thr**ough**
toler**a**nce
tomat**o**
tomat**oe**s
tort**oise**
tra**g**edy
transfe**rr**ed
tr**uly**
tw**elfth**
uncontro**lla**ble
us**a**ble
us**i**ng
va**cill**ate
vac**uu**m
val**ua**ble
veg**e**table
vehic**le**
vend**or**
veng**ea**nce
verba**tim**
versa**tile**
vers**es**
vers**us**
vet**era**n
vet**erin**arian
veto**es**
v**ili**fy
vi**lla**ge
vill**ai**n
vis**i**ble
w**arra**nt
W**edne**sday
we**i**rd
whe**rev**er
whe**th**er
whisk**ey**
whis**tle**
w**ie**ld
w**ie**ner
wi**ll**ful
Wis**c**on**s**in
wi**thh**eld
worshi**p**ed
wri**t**ing
wri**tt**en
y**ie**ld
zer**os**

REFERENCE 3 IRREGULAR VERBS

Take a look occasionally at the following list of the principal parts of irregular verbs. You probably know most of them. Concentrate on those that still give you trouble.

Irregular Verbs (Principal Parts)

Present	Past	Past Participle
arise	arose	have/has/had arisen
awake	awoke	have/has/had awaken
be (is, am, are)	was/were	have/has/had been
bear	bore	have/has/had borne
beat	beat	have/has/had beaten
become	became	have/has/had become
behold	beheld	have/has/had beheld
begin	began	have/has/had begun
bend	bent	have/has/had bent
beseech	besought	have/has/had besought
bespeak	bespoke	have/has/had bespoken
bet	bet	have/has/had bet
bid (offer)	bid	have/has/had bid
bid (command)	bade	have/has/had bidden
bite	bit	have/has/had bitten
bleed	bled	have/has/had bled
blow	blew	have/has/had blown
break	broke	have/has/had broken
bring	brought	have/has/had brought
broadcast	broadcast	have/has/had broadcast
build	built	have/has/had built
burst	burst	have/has/had burst
buy	bought	have/has/had bought
cast	cast	have/has/had cast
catch	caught	have/has/had caught
choose	chose	have/has/had chosen
cling	clung	have/has/had clung

Present	Past	Past Participle
come	came	have/has/had come
comply	complied	have/has/had complied
cost	cost	have/has/had cost
creep	crept	have/has/had crept
cry	cried	have/has/had cried
cut	cut	have/has/had cut
deal	dealt	have/has/had dealt
dig	dug	have/has/had dug
do	did	have/has/had done
draw	drew	have/has/had drawn
drink	drank	have/has/had drunk
drive	drove	have/has/had driven
eat	ate	have/has/had eaten
fall	fell	have/has/had fallen
feed	fed	have/has/had fed
feel	felt	have/has/had felt
fight	fought	have/has/had fought
find	found	have/has/had found
flee	fled	have/has/had fled
fling	flung	have/has/had flung
fly	flew	have/has/had flown
forbid	forbade	have/has/had forbidden
forget	forgot	have/has/had forgotten
forgive	forgave	have/has/had forgiven
forsake	forsook	have/has/had forsaken
freeze	froze	have/has/had frozen
get	got	have/has/had got/gotten
give	gave	have/has/had given
go	went	have/has/had gone
grind	ground	have/has/had ground
grow	grew	have/has/had grown
hang (suspend)	hung	have/has/had hung
(execute)	hanged	have/has/had hanged
have	had	have/has/had had
hear	heard	have/has/had heard
hide	hid	have/has/had hidden
hit	hit	have/has/had hit
hold	held	have/has/had held
hurt	hurt	have/has/had hurt
keep	kept	have/has/had kept
kneel	kneeled/knelt	have/has/had kneeled/knelt
know	knew	have/has/had known
lay (to place)	laid	have/has/had laid
lead	led	have/has/had led

Present	Past	Past Participle
leave	left	have/has/had left
lend	lent	have/has/had lent
let	let	have/has/had let
lie (to recline)	lay	have/has/had lain
lose	lost	have/has/had lost
make	made	have/has/ had made
mean	meant	have/has/had meant
meet	met	have/has/had met
mistake	mistook	have/has/had mistaken
pay	paid	have/has/had paid
put	put	have/has/had put
quit	quit	have/has/had quit
read	read	have/has/had read
rid	rid	have/has/had rid
ride	rode	have/has/had ridden
reply	replied	have/has/had replied
ring	rang	have/has/had rung
rise	rose	have/has/had risen
run	ran	have/has/had run
say	said	have/has/had said
see	saw	have/has/had seen
seek	sought	have/has/had sought
sell	sold	have/has/had sold
send	sent	have/has/had sent
set	set	have/has/had set
sew	sewed/sewn	have/has/had sewed/sewn
shake	shook	have/has/had shaken
shine (light)	shone	have/has/had shone
shoe	shod	have/has/had shod
shoot	shot	have/has/had shot
shrink	shrank/shrunk	have/has/had shrunk/shrunken
sing	sang	have/has/had sung
sink	sank/sunk	have/has/had sunk
sit	sat	have/has/had sat
slay	slew	have/has/had slain
sleep	slept	have/has/had slept
slide	slid	have/has/had slid
sling	slung	have/has/had slung
sow	sowed/sown	have/has/had sowed/sown
speak	spoke	have/has/had spoken
spend	spent	have/has/had spent
spin	spun	have/has/had spun
spit	spat	have/has/had spat

Present	Past	Past Participle
spring	sprang/sprung	have/has/had sprung
stand	stood	have/has/had stood
steal	stole	have/has/had stolen
stick	stuck	have/has/had stuck
sting	stung	have/has/had stung
stink	stank/stunk	have/has/had stunk
stride	strode	have/has/had stridden
strike	struck	have/has/had struck
string	strung	have/has/had strung
strive	strove	have/has/had striven
swear	swore	have/has/had sworn
sweep	swept	have/has/had swept
swim	swam	have/has/had swum
swing	swung	have/has/had swung
take	took	have/has/had taken
teach	taught	have/has/had taught
tear	tore	have/has/had torn
tell	told	have/has/had told
think	thought	have/has/had thought
throw	threw	have/has/had thrown
tread	trod	have/has/had trodden
try	tried	have/has/had tried
understand	understood	have/has/had understood
wake	waked/woke	have/has/had waked/woken
wear	wore	have/has/had worn
weave	wove	have/has/had woven
win	won	have/has/had won
wind	wound	have/has/had wound
wring	wrung	have/has/had wrung
write	wrote	have/has/had written

REFERENCE 4 WORDINESS AND TRITE EXPRESSIONS

Space and time are urgently important considerations for print and broadcast mass communicators. That explains why teachers and professionals place such emphasis on eliminating wordiness. The space and time saved by writing and speaking concisely allows for additional material to be printed and broadcast.

The following list of "wordy" and "edited" words and phrases provides an opportunity for immediate improvement in both our professional and private lives. Perhaps more than any other writers and speakers, journalists try to reduce their use of wordiness and trite expressions.

Wordy	**Edited**
absolutely certain/sure	certain/sure
actual fact	fact
advance notice/planning/warning	notice/planning/warning
a field of 10 candidates	10 candidates
all of a sudden	suddenly
along the lines of	like
anticipate in advance	anticipate
any and all	use *any* or *all,* but not both
appointed to the position of	appointed/named
arrived at the conclusion	concluded
as a general rule	generally/as a rule
as a matter of fact	in fact
as of now	now
asked the question	asked
assemble together	assemble
at an earlier point in time	earlier/then
at one fell swoop	simultaneously
at that point in time	then
at the present time	now
at the same time as	simultaneously
at this point in time	now
a total of 33	33
autopsy to determine the cause of death	autopsy

Wordy	**Edited**
aware of the fact that	knows
based on the fact that	because
basic and fundamental	use *basic* or *fundamental,* but not both
big in size	big
bind together	bind
biography of his life	biography
blend together	blend
bond together	bond
both of the applicants/candidates	both applicants/candidates
bouquet of flowers	bouquet
break half in two	break in half/break in two
brief minute	minute
brutal beating	beating
by the name of	named
by the same token	likewise/also
came to an agreement	agreed
cancel out	cancel
city of Dallas/Atlanta/Detroit	Dallas/Atlanta/Detroit
classified into groups	classified
close down/up	close
close proximity	proximity
close scrutiny	scrutiny
combined together	combined
completely destroyed/eliminated/full	destroyed/eliminated/full
connect together	connect
consensus of opinion	consensus
considering the fact that	considering
continue on	continue
convicted felon	felon
cooperate together	cooperate
current trend	trend
dangerous weapon	weapon
descend down	descend
divide up	divide
double-check twice	double-check
dropped down	dropped
drowned/electrocuted to death	drowned/electrocuted
Dr. Raweena Jamison, Ph.D.	use *Dr.* or *Ph.D.,* but not both
due to the fact that	because
during the course of	during
each and every	use *each* or *every,* but not both
early pioneer	pioneer
Easter Sunday	Easter
either/neither one	either/neither
end result	result

Wordy	Edited
entwined together	entwined
experienced veteran	veteran
extend an invitation	invite
eye witness	witness
fall down	fall
falsely fabricate	fabricate
false pretense	pretense
fellowship together	fellowship
50th golden wedding anniversary	use *50th* or *golden,* but not both
final outcome	outcome
first and foremost	use *first* or *foremost,* but not both
first annual	first
first/last of all	first/last
five straight wins in a row	use *straight* or *in a row,* but not both
follow after	follow
for free	free
for the purpose of	to
free gift	gift
free of charge	free
free up	free
front headlight	headlight
full and complete	use *full* or *complete,* but not both
funeral services	funeral
fused together	fused
future dreams/hopes/plans	dreams/hopes/plans
gather together	gather
grateful thanks	thanks
handsome in appearance	handsome
has 15 points in the game	has 15 points
hope and trust	use *hope* or *trust,* but not both
hopes and desires	use *hopes* or *desires,* but not both
huddle together	huddle
hurry up	hurry
if and when	use *if* or *when,* but not both
in a timely manner	promptly
in light of the fact that	because
in order to	to
in spite of the fact that	despite
in 10 different states/countries	in 10 states/countries
in the absence of	without
in the event that	if
in the near future	soon
is/are in the process of	is/are

Wordy	**Edited**
Jewish rabbi	rabbi
Jewish synagogue	synagogue
join in	join
joined together	joined
kneel down	kneel
knit together	knit
last but not least	use *last* or avoid using altogether
linger on	linger
link together	link
local residents	residents
lodged in jail	jailed
made good his/her escape	escaped
make a decision	decide
matinee performance	matinee
merge together	merge
mesh together	mesh
might possibly	use *might* or *possibly,* but not both
mix together	mix
mulch together	mulch
most unique	unique
narrow down	narrow
necessary requirements	requirements
never at any time	never
new baby	baby
new innovation	innovation
new officers were elected	officers are new unless re-elected
off of	off
often times	often
old adage/cliché/habit/ maxim/proverb/tradition	don't use *old*
on account of	because
on any given day/night	on any day/night
on Wednesday/on March 11	don't use *on*
on the other hand	conversely
over with	over
past/previous experience	experience
past history	history
people who are registered may	people registered may
perfectly clear/flat/level/round/ square/straight	clear/flat/level/round/square/straight
personal benefits	benefits
pizza pie	pizza
plan ahead	plan
postpone until later	postpone

Wordy	Edited
present incumbent	incumbent
rear taillight	taillight
recur again	recur
refer back	refer
reinstate again	reinstate
repeat again	repeat
revert back	revert
Rio Grande river	Rio Grande
rise up	rise
root cause	cause
sad tragedy	tragedy
seeing as how	because
serious crisis	crisis
75-year-old senior citizen	75-year-old citizen
sit down	sit
16-year-old youth	use *16-year-old* or *youth*, but not both
so on and so forth, etc.	don't use
spliced together	spliced
split apart	split
stand up	stand
staple together	staple
start up	start
state of Ohio/Utah/Maine	Ohio/Utah/Maine
still remain	remain
successful achievements	achievements
sum total	use *sum* or *total*, but not both
take into consideration	consider
tangled together	tangled
temporary reprieve	reprieve
10 p.m. tonight	use *10 p.m.* or *10 tonight,* but not both
the current temperature	the temperature
the issue in question	the issue
the reason is because	the reason is
the time has arrived/come	now
there's time out on the court/field	there's time out
those interested may apply/attend/join	don't use *interested;* it's obvious
tied together	tied
topple over	topple
true and accurate	use *true* or *accurate,* but not both
true fact	fact
tuna fish	tuna

Wordy	Edited
12 noon/12 midnight	noon/midnight
two alternatives	two choices
ultimate outcome	outcome
united together	united
unpaid debt	debt
until such time as	until
various and sundry	use *various* or *sundry,* but not both; sometimes neither is necessary
various differences/reasons	differences/reasons
weld together	weld
well-known singer	if true, well-known is not needed
whether or not	whether (unless *not* is needed for clarity)
will be attempting/meeting/speaking	will attempt/meet/speak
will conduct an investigation	will investigate
will hold a meeting	will meet
will meet again in the future	will meet again
with the exception of	except
write down	write

Trite Expressions

Most people are unaware of how many trite expressions they use in their everyday speaking and writing. Mass communications students and professionals, however, are made aware of them quickly and repeatedly by teachers and editors who strike them from submitted copy. Some writers and broadcasters become so self-conscious about trite expressions that they simply eliminate all of them.

Although trite expressions deserve to be stricken from our writing and our broadcasting in most circumstances, eliminating them is probably not the best solution. Instead, we should be on guard to use them only when we can do so effectively.

Remember that what made trite expressions trite was their overuse. Some, such as "red hot" and "cool as a cucumber," may be considered bad writing and speaking from their first use onward. However, others, such as "reign of terror" or "snatched victory from the jaws of defeat," were repeated because they were so good.

Sometimes a writer is smart enough to create an effective variation from a trite expression. When a politician lost a race in which he had a significant lead, one writer observed that the politician "snatched **defeat** from the jaws of victory." It's so clever that any of us would have been proud to have thought of it.

The point is to use trite expressions only when you can do so effectively. In most circumstances, your writing will be better if you eliminate them.

add insult to injury
agree to disagree
aired their differences
all things considered
all work and no play
angry mob
as a matter of fact
at a loss for words
at first blush
auspicious event
beat a dead horse
beat a hasty retreat
beautiful but dumb
benefit of the doubt
between a rock and a hard place
bite the bullet
bitter end
blanket of snow
blessing in disguise
boggles the mind
bone of contention
bored to death/tears
bottom line
brave as a lion
broad daylight
burning question
by hook or crook
can of worms
can't see the forest for the trees
chain reaction
charmed life
chip off the old block
city fathers/mothers
clear as a bell
cold as ice
considered opinion
cool as a cucumber
costs an arm and a leg
country mile
cross he/she must bear
crying need
crystal clear
cutting edge
daring daylight robbery
date with destiny
days are numbered
dead as a doornail
deadly earnest
depths of despair
diamond in the rough
drunk as a skunk
early bird catches the worm
easier said than done
eloquent silence
eminently successful
epic struggle
every cloud has a silver lining
exercise in futility
far cry
fat chance
fate worse than death
fell through the cracks
finishing touch
food for thought
fools rush in
for all intents and purposes
foregone conclusion
foreseeable future
gala occasion
generous to a fault
get nowhere fast
give the green light to
goes without saying
good as gold
grave concern
green as grass
green with envy
grind to a halt
hard as a rock
head over heels
heavens to Betsy
high as a kite
hit the nail on the head
hope for the future
hopping mad
hop to it
hornswoggled
horsing around
hostile environment
hot potato

hungry as wolves
ignorance is bliss
in a New York minute
in no uncertain terms
in the nick of time
in this day and age
innocent bystander
iron out
keeping his/her options open
labor of love
last/final analysis
last but not least
legend in his/her own mind
legend in his/her own time
living on borrowed time
lock, stock, and barrel (hook, line, and sinker)
mad as a hornet
make a killing
make hay while the sun shines
matter of life and death
mission of mercy
moment of truth
more than meets the eye
no sooner said than done
not at first glance
on the face of it
own worst enemy
pleased as punch
point with pride
pretty as a picture
pushing the envelope
put all your eggs in one basket
quick as a wink
rain coming down in sheets
red hot
red-letter day
reign of terror
riot of color
second to none
select few
sharp as a tack
since time immemorial
sings like a bird
sky high
slick as a whistle
slow as molasses
snatch victory from the jaws of defeat
straight as an arrow
superhuman effort
sweeping changes
take the bull by the horns
taking them one at a time
tender mercies
that's what it's all about
the whole nine yards
thorn in our side
throw caution to the winds
tight as a drum
tower of strength
untimely end
view with alarm
where there's smoke, there's fire
whirlwind tour
wise as an owl

REFERENCE 5 WHEN TO USE A HYPHEN, ONE WORD, OR TWO WORDS

Students and professionals alike are annoyed or frustrated by the complicated rules governing the use of hyphens (see Chapter 26 beginning on page 199). Under deadline pressure, there is no time for comprehensive review. Therefore, the following list in alphabetical form is provided with permission from *The Associated Press Stylebook* for a quick check before a deadline.

able-bodied
aboveboard
absent-minded
ad-lib **(noun, verb and adjective)**
A-frame
aftereffect
afterthought
air base
air-condition/air-conditioned **(adjective and verb, *but avoid using as a verb*)**
aircraft
airfare
airline(s)
airmail
airtight
airways
all-around
all-clear
all-out
all right
all-star
alltime **(noun)**; all-time **(adjective)**
also ran **(noun)**
antibiotic

anticlimax
antidote
antifreeze
anti-labor
antiseptic
anti-social
antithesis
antitrust
anti-war
archrival
artifact
artworks
ashtray
automaker, autoworkers
awe-struck
awhile **(adverb);** a while **(noun)**
baby boomer
baby-sit/sitting/sat
baby sitter
backup **(noun and adjective);** back up **(verb)**
backyard **(adjective);** back yard **(noun)**
ball carrier
ballclub/park/player/room
barroom
best seller **(noun)**
bigwig
bilingual
bimonthly
bipartisan
blackout
blastoff **(adjective and noun);** blast off **(verb)**
blue-blooded **(adjective)**; blue blood **(noun)**
bona fide
boo-boo
brand-new **(adjective)**
break-in **(adjective and noun)**; break in **(verb)**
breakup **(adjective and noun)**; break up **(verb)**
brother-in-law (same for father, mother, daughter, son, sister)
brownout

buildup **(adjective and noun)**; build up **(verb)**
bull's eye
businesslike
bylaw
bypass
byproduct
call-up **(adjective and noun)**; call up **(verb)**
carefree
car pool
carry-over **(adjective and noun)**; carry over **(verb)**
cave-in **(adjective and noun)**; cave in **(verb)**
cease-fire **(noun and adjective);** cease fire **(verb)**
chain saw
changeable
changeover
change-up **(adjective and noun)**; change up **(verb)**
checkup **(noun)**; check up **(verb)**
churchgoer
citywide
cleanup **(adjective and noun)**; clean up **(verb)**
clear-cut **(adjective)**
cloak-and-dagger
close-up **(adjective and noun)**
coastline
coattails
co-author/chairman/chairwoman/host/owner/pilot/star/worker
coed
coequal
coexist
colorblind
cooperate
copy editor
copyright
countercharge
counterproposal
countryside
courthouse
court-martial, courts-martial
courtroom

cover-up **(adjective and noun)**; cover up **(verb)**
crackup **(adjective and noun)**; crack up **(verb)**
crisscross
cross-examine, cross-examination
crossfire
crossover **(adjective and noun)**
cure-all
cutback **(adjective and noun)**; cut back **(verb)**
cutoff **(adjective and noun)**; cut off **(verb)**
dark horse
data base
daylight-saving time
daylong
daytime
dead center
dead-end **(adjective)**; dead end **(noun)**
dean's list
deathbed **(adjective and noun)**
deep-sea **(adjective)**
deep-water **(adjective)**; deep water **(noun)**
die-hard **(adjective and noun)**
double-click
double-faced
dressing room
drive-in **(noun)**
dropout **(noun)**; drop out **(verb)**
dust storm
easygoing
editor in chief
e-mail
empty-handed
en route
everyday **(adjective)**; every day **(adverb)**
eyestrain
fact-finding **(adjective)**
fallout **(noun)**; fall out **(verb)**
far-flung **(adjective)**
far-off **(adjective)**
far-ranging **(adjective)**

farsighted
firearms
flagpole
flare-up **(noun)**; flare up **(verb)**
flip-flop
floodwaters
folk singer
folk song
follow-up **(adjective and noun)**; follow up **(verb)**
frame-up **(noun)**; frame up **(verb)**
free-for-all **(adjective and noun)**
free-lance **(verb and adjective);** free-lancer **(noun)**
freewheeling
front-line **(adjective)**; front line **(noun)**
front-page **(adjective)**; front page **(noun)**
front-runner
full-length **(adjective)**
full-scale **(adjective)**
fund-raising **(adjective)**; fund raising **(noun)**; fund-raiser **(noun)**
getaway **(noun)**
get-together **(noun)**
go-between **(noun)**
goodwill **(adjective)**; good will **(noun)**
grant-in-aid, grants-in-aid
groundswell
grown-up **(adjective and noun)**
half-baked
halfhearted
half-mast
handmade
hand-picked
hangover
hanky-panky
headlong; head-on **(adjective and adverb)**
helter-skelter
hideaway
hide-out **(noun);** hide out **(verb)**
high-tech
hit-and-run **(adjective and noun)**; hit and run **(verb)**

ho-hum
holdup **(adjective and noun)**; hold up **(verb)**
homemade
hometown
horsepower
hush-hush
ice storm
in-depth
industrywide
input
jukebox
keynote
knickknack
knockout **(adjective and noun)**; knock out **(verb)**
know-how
kowtow
lawsuit
left/right-handed **(adjective)**; left/right hand/hander **(noun)**
left-wing **(adjective)**; left wing, left-winger **(noun)**
lifelike
life-size
lifestyle
lifetime
liftoff **(adjective and noun)**; lift off **(verb)**
like-minded
longtime **(adjective);** long time **(adverb)**
makeup **(adjective and noun)**; make up **(verb)**
merry-go-round
mix-up **(adjective and noun)**; mix up **(verb)**
mock-up **(noun)**
moneymaker
monthlong
mop-up **(adjective and noun)**; mop up **(verb)**
narrow-minded
nationwide
nightclub
nighttime
nitpicking
nitty-gritty

oceangoing
odd-looking
odd-numbered
oddsmaker
off-color
offhand
officeholder
off-season
offshore
one-sided
outdated
outpatient **(adjective and noun)**
output
outscore
outtalk
overrate
override
peacekeeping
peacetime
pigeonhole
pileup **(adjective and noun)**; pile up **(verb)**
playoff **(adjective and noun)**; play off **(verb)**
point-blank
policy-making **(adjective and noun)**; policy-maker **(noun)**
pullback **(noun)**; pull back **(verb)**
pullout **(noun)**; pull out **(verb)**
push-button **(adjective and noun)**
push-up **(adjective and noun)**; push up **(verb)**
putout **(noun)**; put out **(verb)**
quick-witted
re-elect (and other words after **re-** if they begin with **e**)
right-wing **(adjective)**; right wing, right-winger **(noun)**
rip-off **(adjective and noun)**; rip off **(verb)**
roll-call **(adjective)**; roll call **(noun)**
roundup **(adjective and noun)**; round up **(verb)**
runner-up, runners-up
running mate
rush-hour **(adjective)**; rush hour **(noun)**
secondhand **(adjective and adverb)**; second hand **(noun)**

second-rate

seesaw

sellout **(noun)**; sell out **(verb)**

send-off **(noun)**; send off **(verb)**

setup **(adjective and noun)**; set up **(verb)**

shake-up **(adjective and noun)**; shake up **(verb)**

shape-up **(adjective and noun)**; shape up **(verb)**

short-lived

showcase

showoff **(noun)**; show off **(verb)**

showroom

shut-in

shut-off **(noun);** shut off **(verb)**

shutout **(noun);** shut out **(verb)**

single-handed, single-handedly

sit-down **(adjective and noun)**; sit down **(verb)**

sit-in **(adjective and noun)**; sit in **(verb)**

smashup **(adjective and noun)**; smash up **(verb)**

speedup **(adjective and noun)**; speed up **(verb)**

springtime

stand-in, standoff, standout **(adjective and noun)**; stand in, stand off, stand out **(verb)**

stopgap

storyteller

strong-arm **(adjective and verb)**

summertime

takeoff, takeout, takeover, takeup **(adjective and noun)**; take off, take out, take over, take up **(verb)**

tape recording **(noun)**; tape-record **(verb)**

telltale

throwaway **(adjective and noun)**

thunderstorm

tidbit

tie-in, tie-up **(adjective and noun)**; tie in, tie up **(verb)**

tiptop

titleholder

touch-tone

trade-in **(adjective and noun);** trade in **(verb)**

trade-off **(adjective and noun)**; trade off **(verb)**

tryout **(noun)**; try out **(verb)**
tuneup **(adjective and noun)**; tune up **(verb)**
upside-down **(adjective)**; upside down **(adverb)**
U-turn **(adjective and noun)**
vote-getter
walk-up **(adjective and noun)**; walk up **(verb)**
wartime
washed-up **(adjective)**
wastebasket
weekend
week-kneed
weeklong
well-to-do
well-wishers
white-collar **(adjective)**
whitewash
wholehearted
wildlife
window dressing **(noun)**; window-dress **(verb)**
windswept
windup **(adjective and noun)**; wind up **(verb)**
wintertime
word-of-mouth **(adjective and noun)**
workday
work force
working-class **(adjective)**; working class **(noun)**
workplace
workweek
worldwide
write-in **(adjective and noun)**; write in **(verb)**
wrongdoing
year-end **(adjective)**
yearlong
zigzag

INDEX